WITHDRAWN

WORLD COMMUNISM

The Disintegration of a Secular Faith

WORLD COMMUNISM

The Disintegration of a Secular Faith

RICHARD LOWENTHAL

OXFORD UNIVERSITY PRESS
LONDON OXFORD NEW YORK

Library of Congress Catalogue Card Number: 64-20265
First published by Oxford University Press, New York, 1964
First published as an Oxford University Press paperback, 1966
A version of this book was published in Germany, under the title
Chruschtschow und der Weltkommunismus,
by Verlag W. Kohlhammer GmbH., Stuttgart, in 1963
This reprint, 1967
Printed in the United States of America

PREFACE TO THE AMERICAN EDITION

When I first decided to turn a number of my papers dealing with inter-Communist conflicts into a consecutive account of the disintegration of world communism, I was prompted by the conviction that this process had become irreversible—that, in the words of the concluding essay, we are today entitled to look back on the various phases of the Communist world movement as on a finished period of history. Since the German edition of this book went to press in the spring of 1963, nothing has happened to shake that conviction. On the contrary, the Sino-Soviet conflict reached a new climax with the twin events that took place in Moscow in July 1963—the failure of the meeting between delegations of the Central Committees of the Soviet and Chinese Communist parties, and the success of the negotiations on a nuclear test ban between Russia, the United States, and Britain; and the flood of ideological documents and historical disclosures since released has shown the roots of the conflict to be even deeper and the consequences even more far-reaching than I assumed.

In the body of the present edition, account has been taken of these new or newly disclosed facts only in the notes, apart from the addition of a few lines in the epilogue. Otherwise the English text differs from the German only by the inclusion in

Chapter 5 of two brief sections referring to the American discussion on the "originality" of Mao Tse-tung, and by those liberties of phrasing that must be permitted to an author acting as his own translator. Inasmuch as our increased knowledge of the facts may give rise to new reflections on the interpretation of the conflicts described, the present preface seems the place to indicate them briefly.

The first such point concerns the importance of Khrushchev's destruction of the Stalin myth for the development of the Sino-Soviet conflict. The aggressive defense of Stalin's memory by the Chinese Communists, which began after the Twenty-second Congress of the CPSU, has developed into a general attack on Khrushchev's domestic policies and his new "revisionist" party program with the 25-point proposal for the "general line" of the Communist world movement, which the Chinese published in June 1963, on the eve of their bilateral talks with the Soviet leaders; and in their subsequent commentaries on the "Open Letter" with which the Soviet Central Committee replied to that document, the Chinese have tried to prove that Khrushchev's "secret speech" at the Twentieth Congress of the CPSU in February 1956 was the original cause of the conflict, because its "wholesale negation of Stalin" had "opened the floodgates" to a general revision of the Marxist-Leninist doctrines defended by the late leader.

In this form, the Chinese version of the origin of the conflict does not correspond to the known historical facts. While it is perfectly credible that the Chinese leaders were shocked and worried by the crude form of Khrushchev's action—by the brutality with which he disclosed Stalin's crimes without regard for the continuity of doctrinal authority, and also by the fact that he had not consulted them in advance—the record shows that they welcomed much of the substance of his criticism, including the strictures on Stalin's "Great Power chauvinism" as shown in his dealings with Yugoslavia; and the Soviets in turn appear to have taken Chinese advice into account in their much more cautious and "balanced" public statement on the "personality cult" of June 30, 1956. Subsequently, Chinese advice and criticism clearly influenced Soviet policy toward both Poland and Hungary during and after the October crisis of 1956; in backing Gomulka's desire for increased autonomy but urging the utmost severity against the Hungarian revolution, the Chinese worked for preserving the unity of a reformed Soviet bloc under Russian leadership, and they worked largely with and through Khrushchev. During the entire critical year of 1957, the Chinese seem to have strictly refrained from backing Khrushchev's "Stalinist" opponents at home (who were then still powerful), while working actively for the restoration of Soviet authority in the bloc; and this loyal co-operation culminated on one side in the secret October agreement on military-technological aid (of which the Chinese now claim that it entitled them to expect assistance in the development of nuclear weapons), and on the other in Mao Tse-tung's insistence on the "leading role" of the Soviet Union and the CPSU during the November conference of Communist Party leaders in Moscow. Thus if there were differences during that period, there was also steady consultation and adjustment on the basis of mutual confidence, surpassing anything that had existed in Stalin's time and far removed from the later atmosphere of conflict.

Yet if Khrushchev's dethronement of the Stalin idol was not the starting-point of the conflict, it certainly, by weakening Soviet authority, became a source of a new sense of self-confidence and world-wide ideological responsibility among the Chinese Communist leaders. Though Mao had won power only by emancipating himself from Stalin's instructions in Chinese affairs, he had always accepted him as a great teacher of Marxism-Leninism and as the unquestioned ideological guide of the Communist world movement; and both the crudity of Khrushchev's de-Stalinization and the subsequent waverings of Soviet policy in Eastern Europe must have convinced the Chinese leader that the heir to Stalin's power lacked the capacity for a similar role. The idol had fallen, but its place remained empty and no Russian seemed able to fill it; while the very fact that Khrushchev had listened to Mao's advice in the hour of peril must have confirmed the latter in his growing conviction that it was up to him to supply the needed ideological leadership. If in Moscow he stressed the need for Soviet primacy because of the facts of power, he nevertheless took the initiative on a variety of international issues in the confident belief that his own ideological superiority would prevail.

In retrospect, it seems clear that this new confidence of the Chinese leaders has been one of the crucial factors in the development of the Sino-Soviet conflict. While I have stated my reasons for believing that the direct cause of the latter has been a clash of national interests—the growing Chinese disappointment at the lack of Soviet willingness to aid Chinese development and take risks on China's behalf to the extent desired—the repeated failure of all attempts at compromise was due only to the Chinese decision to transfer the conflict to the ideological plane; and Peking's persistence in this decision, in spite of the obvious risks of a split, is explicable only in terms of this conviction of Mao's ideological superiority. Since 1956–57, the Chinese had come to feel that their one-sided material dependence on their Soviet ally could henceforth be compensated by Soviet ideological dependence on Chinese authority, and it was this belief that made them think they were playing a trump card in opening the ideological attack. But Khrushchev, who had been willing enough to listen to confidential and friendly criticism while he was struggling to consolidate his rule over Eastern Europe, was bound to reply with a sharp counterattack to a public attempt to put pressure on him when he was in firm control; and the Chinese took this refusal to acknowledge their claim to ideological superiority not as proof that they had overplayed their hand, but as evidence that the new ruler of the Soviet Union had hardened in his determination to follow the road of revisionism and treason to the bitter end, and that it was now the duty of every good Communist to work for his overthrow.

It was at this point that Chinese attacks ceased to be comprehensible as a mere ideological expression of national interests and became imbued with an ideological zeal that seemed no longer to care how much it damaged those interests by jeopardizing all hope of further Soviet aid: from the time of the Twenty-second Congress of the CPSU at the latest, the Chinese were embarked on a crusade against Stalin's unworthy successor, aiming no longer primarily at obtaining specific changes of Soviet foreign policy, but at winning world-wide recognition for themselves as the true guardians of the Marxist-Leninist tradition.

Here, then, is the deepest connection between the two most dramatic phases of the process of disintegration described in this book—the East European crisis of 1956 and the Sino-Soviet break: both start from the destruction of the Stalin myth because that action created a vacancy of authority in the Soviet bloc and the world Communist movement. The East European October was the direct effect of that action on countries where the Communist leadership was now divided between Stalin's henchmen and his surviving victims. The Chinese challenge was the delayed repercussion of the proven incapacity of the Soviet leaders to fill the void—to regain international authority beyond the confines of their imperial power. Of the three major blows that the Communist faith has suffered in the course of the Khrushchevian decade, the second and third—the Hungarian revolution and the Chinese schism—are in that sense inconceivable without the first—the destruction of the Stalin myth, which in its doom involved the myth of Soviet infallibility.

Yet the absence of international authority created by Khrushchev's de-Stalinization, and the opportunity it has opened for the Chinese claim to represent the orthodox tradition of Marxism-Leninism, are not the only reasons for the growing role that Chinese attacks on Khrushchev's "revisionist" domestic program and Soviet countercharges of "Stalinist dogmatism" against Mao have come to play since the Twenty-second Congress of the CPSU. Beyond the rivalry for world-wide leadership, the debate on "Stalinism" versus "revisionism" reflects the different needs of Communist parties ruling societies in different stages of economic and social development.

The central domestic problem facing Stalin's Russian heirs, and the most important reason for Khrushchev's decision to destroy the Stalin myth, has been the need to adapt the rule of the CPSU to the conditions of a growing industrial society. Khrushchev understood at an early stage that Soviet society could not develop further without a drastic change in the methods of governing it, a major reduction in the role of police coercion, and a major increase in the role of material incentives; and he knew that the party bureaucrats trained by Stalin could not be induced to change their methods unless the legend of Stalin's infallibility was destroyed first. The very fact that Khrushchev wanted to accomplish the change while maintaining the primacy of an ideological party forced him to take the risk of an ideological break.

Again, the claim in Khrushchev's 1961 program that the Soviet Union was no longer a "dictatorship of the proletariat" but a "state of the whole people" was intended to emphasize the change of political climate brought about by the disappearance of mass terrorism: the important point was not that state and party were no longer proletarian—which everybody knew they had long ceased to be in Stalin's time—but that the regime no longer wished to describe itself as a dictatorship. The ideological revision reflects the belief of the Soviet leaders that, at the present stage of development, single-party rule can best be justified by disguising rather than emphasizing its dictatorial character: within certain limits, a climate of relaxation now seems to serve the stability of the regime better than the extreme of totalitarian tension.

By contrast, the entire development of China since June 1957 has been dominated by Mao's conviction that his regime could only be maintained if ideological militancy was kept up in a climate of permanent internal and external tension—a conviction forced on him by the flood of both popular and intellectual criticism that came to the surface during the temporary relaxation of the "Hundred Flowers Campaign." It was not only the shock of Hungary, but this internal shock that made Mao insist on branding "revisionism" as the main danger during the Moscow conference of the same year; and we know now that at this conference, where he sought not a quarrel but the closest possible collaboration with the Soviet leaders, the Chinese delegation expressed serious doctrinaire qualms about the concept of the "peaceful" or "parliamentary road to socialism" which Khrushchev had introduced in his report to the Twentieth Congress—even though the new formula intended nothing more reformist than a "legal" seizure of power of the type exemplified by the Prague coup of 1948. Underlying these qualms was the Chinese fear of any theory that, by seemingly blurring the picture of an irreconcilable world-wide struggle, might interfere with their determination to maintain the atmosphere of a besieged fortress at home; and during the following years, that determination has clearly been an important contributing factor both in shaping the domestic policies of the "Great Leap Forward" and in causing the Chinese leaders to engage in various international conflicts.

To men with this outlook, the Khrushchevian "abandonment" of the dictatorship of the proletariat must have appeared not only as a tactical opportunity for appealing to Communist traditionalists in the Soviet Union, the Soviet bloc, and the Communist world movement against such "revisionism," but as a really dangerous encouragement of opponents of their own harsh regime inside China; hence their insistence that the dictatorship must be maintained for the entire period until the building of communism has been completed, because new bourgeois elements may arise again and again and must be fought ruthlessly to prevent a capitalist restoration. In the Chinese "Ninth Commentary" on the Soviet "Open Letter," which reads like a political testament of Mao Tse-tung, this insistence comes close to Stalin's 1937 thesis that the class struggle must become sharper with the progress of socialist construction—a thesis correctly denounced in Khrushchev's "secret speech" as the ideological justification for the blood purges: the Chinese now argue that this struggle against the hydra-headed danger of capitalist restoration may last "from five to ten generations" or "one or several centuries," and may enter particularly acute phases at any time during this period. The domestic motivation of this argument becomes evident in the document's concluding appeal to the Chinese party to train in time loyal successors to the first generation of revolutionaries, lest revisionist careerists of Khrushchev's ilk gain power and co-operate with the neo-capitalist elements in turning society away from the true socialist path.

If the different concepts that the Soviet and Chinese Communist leaders hold of the best methods for maintaining power in their respective conditions have thus greatly enlarged the field of the ideological dispute, it is equally true that the involvement of those concepts in the dispute has made them less liable to short-term change. On one side, Khrushchev's new party program has created additional obstacles to any return to "Stalinist" methods of rule; on the other, Mao's testament seeks to bind his successors to reject forever the policy of differential wages and privileges for foremen, technicians, and bureaucrats which has played a vital role in Soviet (and particularly in Stalinist) construction. The Sino-Soviet conflict thus tends to perpetuate the differences in the social climate of the two Communist powers.

To the conflicting needs of the Soviet and Chinese Communist regimes to emphasize respectively the growth of personal security and comfort or the preservation of a state of permanent tension at home, there corresponds an equally divergent emphasis on the socialist potential of the advanced industrial workers or the revolutionary potential of the underdeveloped nations abroad.

The Chinese Communists have long seen their own revolution as the natural model for the colonial and ex-colonial peoples of Asia, Africa, and Latin America. Since 1959–60, one of the basic Chinese charges against Khrushchev's diplomacy of "peaceful co-existence" has been that it seeks to put the brake on anti-imperialist, revolutionary movements in the interest of limiting Soviet risks; conversely, Chinese strategy has aimed at frustrating Soviet diplomacy by pushing such movements regardless of risks.

Yet underlying all such strategic considerations there has been an increasing Chinese realization that it is only the masses of these underdeveloped nations who can still be described as having "nothing to lose but their chains," and that they alone still constitute a reservoir for armed revolutionary struggle. Early in 1963, this view was first expressed by the Chinese in the formula that the countries of Asia, Africa, and Latin America now constitute "the main focus of imperialist contradictions," and that the struggle of their peoples would be "decisive" also for the ultimate victory of the proletariat of the advanced industrial countries; and this formula has been repeated in the 25-point proposal for a "general line" of June 1963. The Russians have not hesitated to reply to these statements by charges of "racialism," accompanied by dire warnings that any attempt to "isolate" the struggle of the colonial and ex-colonial peoples from the advanced "socialist" countries and from the advanced proletarian movements of the industrial West could only lead them into certain defeat.

Now it is certainly true that Lenin, in seeking to forge the alliance between the Western industrial proletariat and the colonial revolutionary movements, regarded the former as the vanguard and the latter as a kind of massive auxiliary force of the world revolution. But it is equally true that in the four decades since Lenin died, the Communist proletarians have failed to win power in any advanced industrial country, while Communist revolutions have been victorious in various parts of the underdeveloped world. In tending to transfer the revolutionary mission from the "internal proletariat" of the West to its "external proletariat" (in the terms coined by A. J. Toynbee), the Chinese Communists are thus in conflict with Marx and even with Lenin, but in accord with historical reality.

Nor are their Russian opponents any closer to Leninist orthodoxy; for while clinging to the belief in the decisive role of the industrial proletariat which Lenin took over from Marx, they have been forced by experience to modify Lenin's vision of the revolutionary uprising of the workers in favor of the attempt to trick the workers into supporting a Communist seizure of power by means of the "parliamentary road." The truth is that, in the light of all recent history, it is no longer possible to maintain Lenin's belief in the urgency of revolution and in the leading role of the working class of the advanced countries at the same time, and that Peking and Moscow have plunged for the opposite horns of this dilemma. The schism in the Communist world movement thus forces the disintegration of the Leninist synthesis into the consciousness of the Communist leaders: while the Chinese are increasingly discarding the Marxist elements in Leninism, the Soviets are criticizing their neglect of objective economic conditions with Marxist arguments that often read like a paraphrase of those once used by the Russian Mensheviks against Lenin.

On the Soviet side, this development has gained increased momentum following the failure of Khrushchev's prolonged efforts to achieve the collapse of the Western alliance by nuclear blackmail while avoiding the risk of world war, and his subsequent turn toward a phase of relative *détente* in foreign policy coupled with a concentration on efforts to raise the domestic standard of living. In seeking to justify this turn in the face of the persistent ideological attacks from Peking, Khrushchev is now quoting Lenin to prove the primacy of economic construction after the seizure of power, and Suslov has even described the "building of communism" at home as the foremost *international* duty of the Soviet Communists. Moreover, while under Stalin the building of "socialism in one country" was pursued by means of a permanent revolution from above,

Khrushchev is increasingly identifying the achievement of "communism in one empire" with straightforward progress in economic performance and the standard of living, hence with the decline of social tensions; and while this evidently corresponds better to the needs of present-day Soviet society than the Chinese recipe, the Chinese may be right in doubting whether it corresponds to the long-term needs of maintaining the party dictatorship. It is easy to see that such a dictatorship is necessary for maintaining a policy of permanent conflict abroad and permanent revolution at home; it is less plausible in the long run that a similar regime should be required to promote peaceful economic progress—even though it is now called the leadership of the party in a "state of all the people."

What all this amounts to is that it is becoming increasingly difficult to maintain the hold of the Communist ideology over both the Soviet elites and the Soviet masses at the present stage; and this means that it becomes correspondingly more difficult to ensure the continuation of the primacy of the party after each new crisis of succession. The basic cause of this difficulty is, of course, the growth of a modern industrial Soviet society, whose social climate is characterized both by new material needs and by a more widespread capacity for critical thought. But while this new climate has contributed to deepening the divergence between the policies and doctrines of the Soviet and Chinese Communists, it is also true that the logic of the conflict with Peking has forced the Soviet leaders to move farther and faster toward a revision of the Leninist tradition than they would otherwise have done. The disintegration of the Communist faith that first became visible in the emergence of different national versions has begun to affect developments within the original citadel itself.

Berlin R.L.
Summer 1964

FROM THE PREFACE TO THE GERMAN EDITION

When Lenin's Bolshevik Party seized power in Russia in November 1917, it saw itself as the champion of a basically new social order that would triumph all over the world with historical necessity: their victory, so the Bolsheviks believed, was the first stage of world revolution.

Since then a completely new social order has indeed been created in Russia under the rule of that party; and the poor and backward country that was defeated in the First World War has been transformed into the Soviet Union of today—a modern industrial nation that has victoriously survived the horrors of World War II, conquered an empire in Eastern Europe, and developed into a nuclear world power that knows no equal outside the United States. Yet during all these changes spanning almost half a century, the ruling Communist Party of the Soviet Union has maintained—in peace as in war, in times of consolidation and pause no less than in times of violent expansion, under Khrushchev as under Lenin and Stalin—its commitment to the goal of world-wide revolution and the total antagonism toward the non-Communist world implied by it; and this antagonism, which in 1917 only dominated the minds of the Soviet leaders and their Communist followers, has become the actual axis of world politics ever since the Soviet Union grew into a world power.

The size of the Bolshevik achievement in power politics, coupled with a continuity of conscious goals unheard of in the history of revolutions and with the intensity of the threat represented by a world power that sees its own role in those messianic terms, has led not a few among the opponents of Bolshevism to accept an unhistorical concept of Soviet expansion proceeding "according to plan," and to overlook uncritically the inner contradictions of this whole development. Some look for the secret of Bolshevik success in the systematic unity of a doctrine that seems to foresee all possible situations and to provide a guide to action for each of them; others regard the doctrine as a mere cloak for the will to power of a "world-conspiracy," whose wirepullers are ready to set aside their proclaimed creed without any scruple whenever this seems expedient for achieving their political power objectives of the moment. Both these interpretations of Soviet policy—purely in terms of applied doctrine or purely in terms of power politics—see it as free from contradictions; hence the exponents of both are necessarily surprised by the actual about-turns and crises of that policy.

Yet the truth is that the history of the Soviet Union and the Communist world movement has in no way evolved according to plan; nor are the successes that rightly impress us in the least identical with those that the Bolshevik leaders were led to expect by their doctrine. Their belief in the Marxist-Leninist scheme of thought has been perfectly genuine, and they could not preserve the cohesion of their party and their regime without it; but it has repeatedly involved them in illusions which they subsequently had to correct in order to maintain their power. Thus the doctrine itself has had to be reformulated again and again, the continuity of the goals notwithstanding, and this process of adjustment has often led through painful crises. The transformation of a backward, primarily agrarian Russia into the present Soviet society with its bureaucratically planned industry and its—still backward—collective farms is a truly remarkable achievement, but something utterly different from that creation of a classless society based on the free association of producers and active mass participation in the administration that was the vision of its founders; and the discrepancy between Lenin's concept of world revolution and the actual development of Soviet world politics is no less radical.

Marxism-Leninism, like any ideology promising a harmonious final solution of all human conflicts, aims at fulfilling incompatible aspirations; and this incompatibility, hidden in immanent ideological exegesis, is uncovered step by step once ideology is confronted with reality. World revolution meant to Lenin that the proletarians of industrial Europe would be able to follow on their own the Russian model and set up Communist dictatorships in their countries; but this did not happen. It meant to Stalin that the Soviet system would extend its sway only by the direct expansion of the power of the Russian empire; but Tito and Mao conquered power by their own efforts. It meant to Khrushchev, who had to face the effective independence of China and Yugoslavia, the harmonious parallel advance of independent Communist revolutions; but the differences of national interest among Communist states led to irreconcilable disagreements on the interpretation of the doctrine. By the course of events, the history of the Communist world movement has become a critique of its ideology.

During the past decade, in the reign of N. S. Khrushchev, this critique of the ideology by "life itself" has led to the progressive disintegration of the dogmatic unity of the Communist world movement. I have attempted to retrace the main lines of this process and to bring out its inherent, "dialectical" necessity—as an unfolding of the implicit contradictions of the ideology. Each individual chapter was originally written as an analysis of current events. In combining them into a consecutive account, I have eliminated repetitions whenever this could be done without damage to the argument, and have also filled a few gaps and changed all time references to make them fit into the perspective of 1963; but facts that were not known at the time of the original writing have generally been mentioned only in the notes and occasionally in brackets. Even so I am afraid that it has not been possible to take proper account of all our rapidly increasing knowledge of the history of inter-Communist conflicts.

The author is only too conscious of the inevitable defects of any collection of studies that have in this way developed along with their subject. Nobody should expect to find here the sort of comprehensive information and systematic treatment that are offered, for instance, by Zbigniew Brzezinski's book *The Soviet Bloc* or by Donald Zagoria's *The Sino-Soviet Conflict.* My specific contribution, however, lies in the attempt to look at the disintegration of world communism as a whole; and it seems to me that the retracing of the successive stages of this process may prove a useful aproach to its understanding.

Berlin R.L.
Spring 1963

ACKNOWLEDGMENTS

The original versions of Chapters 1, 2, 6, and 8 and of the Epilogue appeared in *Problems of Communism*, Washington, D.C. (Nos. 6/1955, 4/1956, 1/1959, 1/1962, and 2/1963). Chapter 3 was first published in the London *Yearbook of World Affairs* for 1958, Chapter 4 in *Encounter*, London (October 1958). Chapter 5 is based on a series of German broadcasts written for the *Bayerische Rundfunk* in May 1959. Chapter 7 appeared first in the *China Quarterly*, No. 5, London, and was republished in book form in *The Sino-Soviet Dispute*, documented and analyzed by G. F. Hudson, R. Lowenthal, and Roderick McFarquhar, by that review in England and by Frederick Praeger in the United States. I am grateful to all the editors and publishers concerned for permitting the reprinting of this material, with greater or lesser changes, in the present book.

The idea of combining these papers in a coherent account of the disintegration of world communism was stimulated by the necessities of teaching at the Otto-Suhr-Institut and the Osteuropa-Institut of the Freie Universität, Berlin, and by the interest of my German publishers, W. Kohlhammer in Stuttgart. Dr. Hannelore Horn and Mr. Thomas Weingartner, both of the Otto-Suhr-Institut, rendered invaluable help in preparing the notes for both the German and English editions. The work of following developments in the Soviet bloc and the Communist world movement, in sometimes recondite source material and for some years before I had the resources of a university institute at my disposal, was enormously facilitated by the generous assistance of the research department of Radio Free Europe in Munich, first under William E. Griffith and the late Herbert Ritvo, more recently under Richard V. Burks and his team of specialists.

The account of Yugoslav relations with Russia during the crucial phase of 1956–58 presented in Chapter 4 differs from the rest of the book in that much of its material was based not on generally available documents, but on individual communications received from well-informed Yugoslavs; I have therefore preserved its original character as a personal report. A final word of gratitude goes to my Yugoslav friends—not only for this information, but for the broader insights into the problems of East European communism that I owe to many earlier visits to their country.

CONTENTS

WORLD COMMUNISM
The Disintegration of a Secular Faith

The materialist conception of history is not a cab to be taken at will; and it does not stop for the leaders of revolutions.

MAX WEBER IN *Politik als Beruf*

1

1955: TITO'S REHABILITATION

Of all the moves made by the post-Stalin Soviet governments in their effort to achieve an international *détente,* none has aroused as much discussion as the visit of a high-level Soviet delegation to Belgrade from May 27 to June 2, 1955. The reason for this special attention was the unique origin of the long-standing conflict between the Soviet bloc and Yugoslavia – the fact that it had arisen from a party quarrel among Communists. Until shortly before the Belgrade meeting, Moscow's moves toward a *rapprochement* with Yugoslavia – which over a two-year period led to the resumption of diplomatic relations, to the settlement of frontier conflicts between Yugoslavia and her satellite neighbors, and to a slow revival of trade – could be viewed simply as part of the Russians' over-all endeavor to relax international tension. But the announcement that the Soviet delegation going to Belgrade would be headed by N. S. Khrushchev, First Secretary of the Soviet Communist Party, coupled with Khrushchev's unusual speech upon arrival, thrust the basic issue of party relations into the limelight – and it has dominated the Soviet-Yugoslav picture ever since.

There is no difficulty in understanding why the Malenkov and Bulganin governments should have regarded it as desirable to end the state of military tension on the frontiers of Yugoslavia and the economic boycott of that country by the Soviet bloc; they wished to demonstrate that none of the bloc's small neighbors had any reason to fear its military might. Nor is it difficult to understand why Yugoslavia would have welcomed these diplomatic overtures as a chance to reduce the strain on her economy and to increase her freedom of economic and political maneuver in relation to both East and West. The truly intriguing questions are: first, why Khrushchev should have chosen to combine the normalization of Soviet-Yugoslav diplomatic relations with a certificate that the Yugoslav heretics had remained a Marxist-Leninist party, plus an appeal to them to resume collaboration on a party basis; second, what factors determined the reluctant and ambiguous Yugoslav response to that appeal; and, third, what repercussions were bound to occur in Yugoslavia, in the Soviet satellite states, and in the USSR itself.

THE 1948 CONFLICT

The Stalin-Tito conflict, like the Stalin-Trotsky conflict at an earlier stage, has been the Communist expression of a dilemma familiar in Western history since the wars of religion: the need for sovereign national states to choose in their foreign policy between the demands of ideological solidarity and of national interest. While in the West the decision has tended to go increasingly in favor of national interest, the Soviet leadership has had to face the issue in a different framework. Whether the Soviet leaders regarded themselves as prophets of a revolution in control of a powerful empire, or as rulers of an empire armed with a revolutionary doctrine, they could as little abandon ideology as they could the state interest: their position was more similar to that of the Caliphate in its conquering period than to that of a secular Western state.

Stalin's solution of the dilemma – as brutally simple, and as unique as his solutions for all the contradictions of the state bequeathed by Lenin to his disciples – consisted in making the primacy of Soviet state interest an essential part of the ideology itself: that was the essence of the doctrine of "socialism in one country," later elaborated in the formulas of the "fatherland of all toilers" and of the "leading role of the Soviet Union" in the world-wide struggle of the proletariat. The advance of communism throughout the world was declared wholly dependent on the growth of the might of the Soviet Union. Aided by the fact that for twenty-five years the Communists spectacularly failed to repeat in any other country the Bolshevik victory of 1917, this was understood more and more clearly to mean that Communists could, and should, henceforth take power only under the protection of Soviet bayonets – that Communist revolution would no longer take place on the 1917 model, but only as a consequence of the expansion of Soviet power, as a *revolution from above.*

The victory of the Yugoslav Communist partisans under Tito, won in most of the country before the arrival of Soviet troops and with a revolutionary policy adopted and retained against Soviet advice, was the first serious blow to Stalin's "leading role" doctrine. Tito's strategy, moreover, had been influenced to a large extent by an alternative model, also originally developed against Soviet advice — that of the partisan armies of Mao Tse-tung.[1] It was inevitable that the Yugoslav Communists, having made their own revolution, should feel entitled to pursue their own policies as independent partners rather than as subordinates of the Russian Communists. Not content with defending his national independence, however, Tito by 1948 was beginning to appear as a rival of Moscow's authority by attempting to lead all the Balkan Communists and to influence all the "people's democracies" of Eastern Europe.[2] That menace became obvious at the very moment when Mao, again disregarding Stalin's advice, was launching his final campaign to turn the whole of China into a Communist empire.

In the Cominform resolution of June 1948 which expelled Tito and the Yugoslav Communist Party, the essential charge was disloyalty to the Soviet Union; to any Stalinist, this meant that Tito had broken with Marxism-Leninism. Other charges were put forward, some of them mere propagandist inventions, others reflecting genuine if subordinate differences; but the whole Communist world movement understood that the real issue was "nationalism" — the right for a national Communist party to seize and develop power in its own way — versus "internationalism," a synonym for the "leading role of the Soviet Union." This was confirmed when in all the satellite states the doctrine that each country might pursue "its own road to socialism" — at least *after* the conquest of power — was solemnly condemned and its former spokesmen purged as "Titoists." At the same time the Cominform (transferred from Belgrade to Bucharest) was reconverted into an instrument of centralized Soviet control.

Yet at the very moment when the doctrine of the "leading role of the Soviet Union" was reaffirmed amidst an orgy of arrests and executions, it became obviously untenable. Mao's victory in 1949, coupled with Tito's continuance in power despite Soviet-bloc pressures, clearly belied the claim that the fate of communism everywhere depended wholly on the power of the Soviet Union. While Stalin was alive, his authority was sufficiently strong for him to continue to deny the obvious; when he died, his heirs were bound to make a new attempt to come to terms with the facts of Communist life.

THE EVOLUTION OF TITOISM

The first attempt to work out an alternative doctrine for the relations between independent Communist powers was made by Tito and the Yugoslav Communists between 1948 and 1950. Repudiating the concept of the "leading role of the Soviet Union," they called for fraternal solidarity between independent equals. Socialist states ruled by Communist parties should be natural allies and should learn from each other, but should deal with each other on a basis of equality; they should also be free to devise, in adaptation to local conditions, their own methods of advancing toward the common goal defined by Leninist theory.[3]

This "proto-Titoist" doctrine (which now appears as the germ of the later "polycentric" concept) expressed in ideological form the Yugoslav leaders' desire to regain their place as autonomous members within a reformed Soviet bloc. Yet gradually, as Stalin and his satellites continued to denounce them and to purge their friends as "renegades," "traitors," "fascists," and "agents of imperialism," Tito and his supporters were forced to recognize that this avenue was barred, and so began to seek international support outside the Communist fold while proclaiming their independence of both camps. In practice, this led to an opening of the country to contacts with the non-Communist world, as well as to a number of internal reforms which aimed at winning broader popular support for the regime while still preserving the principles of one-party control, nationalization of industry, and economic planning. In theory, it led the Yugoslav Communists to assert that the Soviet Union's "un-Socialist" urge to dominate alien peoples must be due to reactionary developments and features in Soviet society itself — particularly the growth of a new privileged bureaucratic caste — and that therefore the Soviet system could not be a model for Yugoslavia's Socialist development.

There followed a transitional phase during which the Yugoslav leaders, in proselytizing sectarianism, seemed to claim that they had discovered the only true road to socialism. The impact of internal reform and broadening international experience, however, finally led them to a break with the fundamental Leninist dogma that Communist revolution and party dictatorship are the only means of overcoming the "contradictions of capitalism" anywhere: by 1954, they had arrived at the view that the path of social progress may differ *in principle* as well as in detail, according to the history and the stage of economic development of a country; that "reformist" socialism may be as effective in one condition as Soviet-type communism in another; and that Yugoslavia's own solution is just one among many.

KHRUSHCHEV'S SEARCH FOR NEW FORMS

Yet while the Yugoslav Communists had long since discarded their original thesis of the fraternal solidarity of all Communists against the non-Communist world, as well as their desire to return to a reformed Soviet bloc, the Soviet Communist leaders began after Stalin's death to move steadily toward this "proto-Titoist" solution of their international dilemma. The original driving force in this process, we may presume, was the need to readjust their relations with their powerful Chinese allies, not with the "renegade" rulers of little Yugoslavia.

Immediately after Stalin's death, the Soviet press began to stress the slogans of traditional Leninist internationalism and to soft pedal the "leading role of the Soviet Union." The professional diplomats heading the Soviet missions both in China and in the East European satellite states were replaced one by one by senior party officials, while the downgrading of the secret police and its subordination to party control inside the Soviet Union led to a withdrawal from the satellites of a number of Soviet police representatives and agents. It is probable that the decisive stage in this search for an adjustment of inter-Communist relations was reached with the visit of a Soviet government delegation, headed by N. S. Khrushchev as First Secretary of the Soviet Communist Party, to Peking in October 1954, when Stalin's unequal treaty of alliance of 1950 was renegotiated and relations between the two powers placed on an equal basis. From that date onward, the Soviet press began to speak of "the peace camp led by the Soviet Union *and* People's China."

To the outsider it was obvious that the doctrine of fraternal solidarity between independent and equal Communist governments, as first proclaimed by Tito in 1948 and now adopted by Khrushchev in 1954–55, offered no real solution to the choice between ideological solidarity and national interest. In any co-operation between sovereign states, solidarity will prevail so long as the divergent pull of interest is not too strong; it will break down if there is a serious conflict of national interests. The Stalinist solution worked so long as there were no independent Communist states; the Khrushchev solution was to last only so long as compromises could be worked out without too much difficulty.

TWO CONCEPTS OF THE RAPPROCHEMENT

The attempt to apply the new Khrushchev formula — or outdated Tito formula — to relations between the Soviet Union and Yugoslavia began in October 1954, directly after Khrushchev's return from Peking. Up to then, the "normalization" of Soviet-Yugoslav relations had proceeded on strictly non-ideological lines, as part of the general diplomacy of *détente* between the Soviet bloc and all its enemies. It had led to an exchange of ambassadors, preliminary trade agreements, a near-cessation of frontier incidents, and to unexpected Soviet support for the Yugoslav-Italian settlement on Trieste, which was concluded with Western mediation at the beginning of October; it had also caused Tito, who shortly before had joined the Balkan alliance with Greece and Turkey and shown interest in a possible European Defense Pact, to declare that he would have nothing to do with NATO because of its anti-Communist character. But there had been no word yet from either side about a common ideological basis for the Soviet Union and Yugoslavia.

The first sign of such ideological courtship appeared on October 20 when *Pravda*, on the anniversary of the meeting of Soviet troops and Yugoslav partisans during the liberation of Belgrade, gave emphatic praise, for the first time in six years, to the independent wartime achievement of the partisans "under the leadership of Marshal Tito." On November 6, eve of the anniversary of the Bolshevik revolution, Maxim Saburov of the Presidium of the Soviet Communist Party suggested, after recalling the common struggle of both countries, that their conflict had benefited only "their common enemies." The theme was further elaborated on November 28, the Yugoslav National Day, when Malenkov – then still Prime Minister – Molotov, and Khrushchev appeared at the reception of the Yugoslav Embassy and demonstratively drank to the health of "Comrade Tito and the Yugoslav Communist Party." From that day, it was evident that the Soviet leaders were trying to win back the Yugoslav leaders to the Soviet bloc on the basis of Communist solidarity, by offering them the kind of independent position they had once asked for and which China, favored by far greater strength, had achieved in the meantime.

Between the Soviet decision to try this approach and the announcement of the Khrushchev-Bulganin visit in May lay several months of secret negotiations. From information that I gathered in Belgrade in December 1954 and during the Soviet visit, it appears that the Soviet government first proposed that President Tito should come to Moscow; that from the start they indicated their wish to discuss the ideological differences between the respective Communist parties as well as the problems pending between the two governments; and that both proposals had already reached Belgrade by November when a secret Central Committee meeting was held before Tito's departure for India and Burma. To the proposal of high-level talks, the Yugoslavs replied that in principle it was up to the Soviets to come to Belgrade first, and that an apology for the insults and injuries inflicted on Yugoslavia since 1948 was a prerequisite condition; on the question of fraternal relations between the Communist parties, high Yugoslav party spokesmen after the November session of their Central Committee still held that, owing to the different development of the Soviet and Yugoslav social systems, they wished to retain full freedom of criticism and could agree only to "co-exist" with the Soviet Union in the same way as with other states with different social systems.

Evidently a struggle in the Soviet "collective leadership" preceded the decision to come to Belgrade, for on February 9, 1955, V. M. Molotov made a speech in which there were cautiously critical references to Yugoslavia; President Tito made a sharp rebuttal on March 7, and this rebuttal was subsequently published by *Pravda*.[4] By the time the communiqué announcing the "summit meeting" was published on May 14, the Soviet government must have accepted Tito's diplomatic terms, including the apology; [5] but the announcement that N. S. Khrushchev would lead the Soviet delegation indicated that the Yugoslavs had not insisted on their desire completely to exclude discussion of party issues.

The Soviet approach to the discussion was outlined in *Pravda* on May 18. After reassuring the Yugoslavs that the new relationship with the Soviet Union "in no way implies . . . a deterioration of Yugoslavia's relations with other countries," it nevertheless went on to sketch out the basis for an ideological bloc:

> Of course, it cannot be denied that there are substantial differences in the understanding of a number of important questions of social development. But the fact that public ownership of the basic means of production predominates

> in Yugoslavia; that the principal classes in Yugoslavia are the working class and the working peasantry who have militant revolutionary and patriotic traditions; that there is an age-old, profound community of ideas and culture between the peoples of the U.S.S.R. and Yugoslavia; that the working people of both countries have common vital interests . . . all this shows that there is a firm basis for wide and all-round co-operation between the Soviet and Yugoslav peoples.

The Yugoslav top leaders, however, were determined not to return to an ideological bloc themselves, but rather to use the Soviet overtures for increasing their freedom of maneuver *between* the blocs. Tito underlined this orientation dramatically by traveling to India and Burma at the very moment the decisive exchanges with the USSR were opening, a symbolic gesture that indicated that his ambition was no longer to become a minor European Mao but rather a European Nehru. Just before, Vice President Edvard Kardelj had visited a number of West European Social Democratic leaders, and had taken the occasion of a lecture in Oslo in October to develop systematically the view that Social Democratic reform and Communist revolution were equally good roads to social progress in different historical and economic conditions, and that any dogmatic exclusiveness was harmful for the cause of socialism. The full text of this lecture was published in *Borba,* the daily of the Yugoslav Communist League, on January 1, 1955, and republished later as a pamphlet.[6] Kardelj himself embarked on a speaking tour to educate his party in preparation for the forthcoming discussion with the Russians; the cadres should understand that, as there was progress in the West as well as in the East, in democratic forms as well as in Communist ones, there would be no advantage, from a Socialist point of view, in rejoining the Soviet bloc. That there would be no advantage in doing so from a national point of view, the Yugoslav people knew anyhow.

THE BELGRADE MISSION: SUCCESS AND FAILURE

From the moment of his arrival on Yugoslav soil, Khrushchev tried to force the pace; he must have been driven by an urgent desire to score a spectacular party success, as well as misled by a faulty estimate of the firmness of the position prepared by his hosts. In his very first words on arrival, he surprised them, both by the extent of his apology and by the crudeness of his appeal for a resumption of party ties. From Tito's viewpoint it would have been sufficient if the Russians had described the 1948 break as an inevitable parting of the ways, based on genuine differences of opinion, and had apologized for having needlessly embittered these differences by insulting accusations and attempts to apply economic and military pressure: that was indeed the line later taken by the Western Communist parties (and from 1958 by Khrushchev also). But it was not what Khrushchev then said: he bluntly attributed the entire guilt for the breach to "Beria, Abakumov, and so forth," and explicitly confirmed that the Yugoslavs had remained a Marxist-Leninist party – implying that there had been no serious differences of principle.

On this fiction Khrushchev based his appeal for party relations, plainly addressed over Tito's head to a presumed pro-Soviet rank and file:

> As representatives of the Communist Party of the Soviet Union, the party created by the great Lenin, we consider

> it desirable to have mutual confidence established between our parties. The strongest ties are created among the peoples of those countries where the leading forces are parties which base their activities on the teachings of Marxism-Leninism. . . . We would not be doing our duty to our peoples and to the working people of the whole world if we did not do everything possible to establish mutual understanding between the Communist Party of the Soviet Union and the Yugoslav Communist League, on the basis of the teachings of Marxism-Leninism.[7]

The first public reply was given the next day (May 28) in an editorial in *Borba,* which expressed approval for everything Khrushchev had said about the need to reduce international tension and to improve Soviet-Yugoslav "inter-state relations," but pointedly omitted both the strange apology and the appeal for party contacts, and concluded with a condemnation of "the partition of the world into ideological blocs," which was "not the path that leads to peace." Throughout the stay of the Soviet visitors, the Yugoslav press continued to elaborate on the danger of ideological blocs, and to underline the distinction between "co-existence in the sense of some temporary truce between hostile blocs, created by an ideological division" — that is, the Soviet concept — and the Yugoslav idea of "active co-existence," — that is, "the active co-operation of all countries regardless of differences in their internal systems." [8] In the end, the Yugoslavs failed to get the Soviet delegation to subscribe to their view of ideological blocs, and had to content themselves with an equivocal condemnation of "military blocs" in the joint declaration — equivocal because, as the Yugoslavs well knew, the coherence of the Soviet bloc did not depend on formal military alliances. But on the very day of the signing of the declaration the Yugoslav press once again repeated their own more far-reaching formula that all ideological blocs were a danger to peace:

> It is apparent that the concept of the division of the world into two ideological blocs starts from the inevitability of the ultimate conflict between those two blocs. Therefore, those who start from such a point of view do not accept the possibility of a full and permanent world peace, but only the possibility of postponing the ultimate conflict. . . . Those who consistently work for the preservation of world peace must approach this task with the deep conviction that peace can be preserved not only temporarily but permanently. They must be convinced that a world armed conflict, no matter when it comes, would present a general catastrophe of mankind. . . .[9]

Clearly, this article was attacking the basic Soviet doctrine of the "two camps" in world politics, and also Molotov's latest dictum that a third world war would not destroy mankind, only capitalism.

On the question of Yugoslavia's diplomatic alignment, the Belgrade declaration thus marked a public reaffirmation of her "uncommitted" position — a barrier to closer military ties with the West, but a refusal also to accept one-sided political ties with the East. The same refusal was expressed in a more complicated, but no less decisive, way in the compromise reached, apparently after long and hard discussion, on the question of party relations: on one side, "the two governments have agreed to . . . facilitate co-operation among the social organizations of the two countries through the establishing of contacts, the exchange of socialist experiences, and a free exchange of opinions"; on the other, they recognize that "questions of internal organization, of different social systems, and of different forms of socialist development are solely the concern of individual countries." [10]

Together, these formulas implied that the barriers created in the preceding years both against Soviet influence in Yugoslavia and against Yugoslav influence in the satellite countries should fall; that mutual criticism would be limited by a kind of ideological non-aggression pact, each side granting to the other the right to be "Socialist" in its own way; and that contacts between "social organizations," including Communist parties, should not be based on a common Leninist orthodoxy and would not exclude the continuation of similar or closer ties between the Yugoslav Communists and the Western and Asian Social Democrats, because the Yugoslavs interpreted the right of each country to its own form of Socialist development as covering not only their own and the Soviet case, but also the parliamentary democracies. It was on this point that Khrushchev's attempt to win back Yugoslavia on the basis of fraternal solidarity between independent Communist parties had most conspicuously failed.

THE TUG OF WAR CONTINUES

There is one obvious objection to the above interpretation of the Belgrade meeting: If the Yugoslav leaders were really determined not to return to the Soviet bloc – not even on terms of relative independence and greatly increased prestige – why did they agree to receive the Khrushchev delegation at all? Why were they not content with the fruits of slow and steady normalization, instead of taking the risk of stirring up a difficult discussion in their own party, of arousing the distrust of their people, whose great majority had become profoundly anti-Soviet, and of being misunderstood in the West? They must have known for what stakes Khrushchev was playing; they must have known that, once they had invited him, they could hardly avoid signing a compromise formula that would be ambiguous at the very least.

There are three answers to this question. The first is that there were also risks in refusing such a high-level contact. The Yugoslav leaders were well aware of the determination of the Kremlin to pursue its diplomacy of *détente,* and of the changing international atmosphere. They could not afford a situation in which they might be presented to other countries as an obstacle to peace, or in which the Great Powers, at their impending summit conference, might reach agreement at their expense.

Second, the Yugoslavs were in grave international payments difficulties, but they had huge outstanding demands against the Soviet Union and the satellites, dating from the damage done to them by broken delivery contracts in 1948–49. A Soviet apology for former boycott measures would amount to recognition of the basis for those claims, and the high-level meeting desired by the Soviets was the one way to obtain that apology. Subsequently, the Russians did in fact agree to pay very considerable damages and to grant new credits; negotiations for similar concessions from Yugoslavia's satellite neighbors were more protracted.

Third and last, just as Khrushchev seems to have believed he could draw the Yugoslav leaders closer to the USSR than they themselves wanted to come, so the Yugoslav leaders believed that the breaking down of barriers might start a process beyond the control of the present leaders in the satellite countries, and might even accelerate the process of change inside the Soviet Union. Under cover of the ideological non-aggression pact both sides thus started an ideological tug of war for highly ambitious stakes.

The Soviet argument in this tug of war (exemplified by editorials in *Pravda* of July 16, 1955, and *Kommunist*, No. 11, 1955) stressed Soviet willingness to recognize "separate paths to socialism," but held that Yugoslavia could only resist imperialist pressure for the restoration of capitalism if she adjusted her policies so as to strengthen ties with the Soviet Union and the "people's democracies"; further steps should now be taken toward "the establishment of contact . . . between the CPSU and the League of Communists of Yugoslavia on the basis of the principles of Marxism-Leninism." [11] The Russians thus admitted that the purpose of Khrushchev's Belgrade visit had not been fully achieved at the time, but claimed that the foundations had been laid.

The Yugoslav reply was put forward on the theoretical level in an article by Veljko Vlahovic, of the Yugoslav Communist Central Committee, on "The forms of Co-operation between Socialist Forces," [12] and on the level of practical politics in a speech by Tito at Karlovac on July 27.[13] The Vlahovic article marshaled Yugoslav objections to the Soviet idea of "a rapprochement on the basis of Marxist-Leninist principles" – that is, to a one-sided ideological alignment with the Soviet bloc – and opposed to it the long-term perspective of an all-inclusive International, to which both Communists and democratic Socialists would one day belong.

To the idea of an alignment based on Marxist-Leninist principles, Vlahovic raised three objections: first, Marxist-

Leninist doctrine did not take adequate account of developments in recent decades, such as the liberation of former colonial countries, the emergence of progressive forms of state capitalism, and so forth, and thus any doctrinaire alignment would be an obstacle to an open-minded analysis of these developments; second, progress toward socialism was not confined to movements following a Leninist revolutionary strategy or to any one bloc of states; third, the interests of labor therefore required the co-operation of movements following different strategies in different countries on a basis of mutual tolerance, on the model of the First rather than the Third International, and such broad co-operation was incompatible with the attempts of the representatives of any one doctrine to exercise a "hegemony."

The Vlahovic article thus constituted an open attack on the doctrinal authority of Moscow and the organizational authority of the Cominform. In part, that attack served the defensive purpose of preserving the special position of the Yugoslav Communists in their friendly but independent contact with both Soviet Communists and Western Social Democrats. But in part, it also aimed offensively to loosen the Soviet hold over the East European satellites, inasmuch as that hold was exercised through party ties and based on doctrinal arguments. If one of the basic differences in the interpretation of the Belgrade declaration was that Moscow conceded the right to a "different road to socialism" only to independent Communists, while Belgrade admitted it also for "reformists," the other main difference was that Khrushchev would grant even such independence in the development of Communist power only to those who had already effectively taken it, like China and Yugoslavia, while Tito now began to urge it for the satellites.

This latter point was strongly underlined in Tito's Karlovac speech in which he attacked "certain leaders in neighboring countries." His attack clearly had a dual political objective: to discredit the leaders who had conducted the former anti-Titoist campaign by forcing an open revision of the show-trials of the period, and also to induce the satellite states to develop, through direct contact with Yugoslavia, a new relationship which would be more than merely a kind of appendix to the new relationship begun by the Soviet Union. Strategically, both demands were aimed at ending the satellite status of the Communist states of East and Southeast Europe; this was also the purpose of his demand for a dissolution of the Cominform.

There is evidence that the Yugoslav leaders at that time regarded such a "Titoist" development as feasible and even probable in some of the satellites; for example, they called attention not only to the release of a number of former "national Communists" but to such phenomena as the successful refusal of the Hungarian Communist ex-Premier Imre Nagy to recant after he had been deposed, and to the continued popularity of figures like Nagy, or Gomulka in Poland, inside their Communist parties. There is just as much evidence, however, that the Soviet leaders were not then ready to grant such independence to their satellites; for one thing, preparations for the coordination of the new five-year plans which were to start throughout the Soviet bloc with the beginning of 1956 showed clearly that the Soviet leaders now intended to introduce a detailed division of labor within their empire on a scale that seemed incompatible with effective national autonomy.[14]

Tito's trumpet calls, however, produced a great deal of inner-party discussion in Eastern Europe; and since the application of police measures inside the satellite Communist parties was now shunned, such discussion proved difficult for Moscow's controllers to stifle. Thus Khrushchev's experiment had not only failed to induce Belgrade to accept the kind of fraternal Communist ties offered to it, but it had reproduced in a new form the old struggle between the USSR and Yugoslavia for the East European "sphere of influence," which was one of the main factors of the original breach.

In effect, Khrushchev's attempt to create "brotherly" relations between Communist states in a belated application of Lenin's original doctrine was to prove only the first phase in the breakdown of the forcible synthesis that had been imposed by Stalin on the contradictions of his empire.

2

1956: THREE ROADS TO "SOCIALISM"

The Twentieth Congress of the Soviet Communist Party saw the first attempt since Lenin's time to systematize the experience of communism as an international movement.[1] Never before had the Soviet leaders cast a theoretical eye on the Communist victories in China and Yugoslavia as well as on their own successes in Eastern Europe, viewing them as historical events from which new lessons could be learned by Communists everywhere. Never before had they explicitly told the Communist parties all over the world that there were other models to be followed than the Soviet.

In Western discussion of the Congress, the importance of this new departure has tended to be overshadowed by the sensational reassessment of Stalin's role in Communist history and by the major changes in Soviet domestic politics connected with it. Yet the renewal of serious interest in the problems of "world revolution" was itself one of the major aspects of the breach with the Stalin tradition – an aspect that in the minds of Mr. Khrushchev and his team clearly formed a necessary complement to the diplomacy of "peaceful co-existence" and to the attempt to consolidate the CPSU's domestic position by a series of major reforms.

The one element in the reformulation of revolutionary theory that at once aroused some discussion among non-Communists was the Soviet leaders' recognition that a "peaceful" or "parliamentary" road to "socialism" is possible under certain conditions. This was widely interpreted as an attempt to trick Western democratic Socialists and Asian nationalists into alliances of the "Popular Front" type. But while this interpretation is correct as far as it goes, most commentators seem to have missed the really new element in the theory. For the "Popular Fronts" of the 1930's were explicitly confined to the purpose of "defending democracy within the capitalist framework," by creating governments friendly to the Soviet Union; [2] this limitation was still implicit in Stalin's attempt to revive the "Popular Front" strategy in his 1952 speech to the Nineteenth Party Congress.[3] Today, however, the "parliamentary road" is advocated as a means to achieve "socialism," that is, full Communist power.

It is true that Soviet spokesmen at the Twentieth Congress cited examples of past successful application of the strategy for this end. But they could find them only among countries where Soviet military pressure had played the decisive role in achieving this sort of "socialism" (as in Czechoslovakia and the Baltic states)[4] — the only condition in which Stalin had ever sanctioned the seizure of power. By contrast, at the Twentieth Congress the proximity and assistance of Soviet power were no longer mentioned as a condition for the future success of the "peaceful road"; in principle, therefore, attempts by the Communists to seize full control by this method were henceforth permissible anywhere on the globe.

Because the revival of Soviet interest in world revolution was widely overlooked, the importance of the dissolution of the Cominform was as widely underestimated. Observers rightly recognized that this demolition of an outworn façade need not weaken the secret liaison machinery linking the Russian Communists with Communist parties in other countries. But they scarcely commented on the reception given this demonstrative gesture by such gifted and ambitious leaders as Palmiro Togliatti in Italy, who saw in it the green light for independent experiment in seeking the right road to power.[5] It was also overlooked that one of the effects of the move was to enable Soviet diplomacy to disclaim responsibility for such experiments more effectively. After all, the years between the dissolution of the Comintern in 1943 and the formation of the Cominform in 1947 saw the greatest expansion of Communist power since the Russian Revolution; the period of the Cominform, for all its sharpening of conflict between East and West, saw in fact the freezing of the borderline of Communist rule in Europe.

THE MODEL OF THE "RED OCTOBER"

When Messrs. Khrushchev, Mikoyan, Suslov, and Shepilov reviewed the conditions of Communist victory at the Twentieth Congress, they took a decisive step to free communism from a doctrinaire prejudice which had dogged its steps since the early days of the Comintern. For up to then, the only theoretically recognized model of the Communist seizure of power had been Lenin's October Revolution — a model that had never been successfully imitated in a period of almost forty years.

Lenin and his contemporaries sincerely believed that their conquest of power had in its social essence been a working-class revolution against the bourgeois state, and they tended to regard its most striking political features — the taking of local power by Soviets and the uprising of armed workers in the capital — as the necessary forms for that social content. The Soviets were organs for direct mass activity, analogous to the Paris Commune admired by Karl Marx. In the Bolshevik view only these organs could paralyze the bourgeois state machine and destroy it at its roots, while only an armed uprising could overthrow the bourgeois-democratic central government and seize power. The example of the German revolution of 1918, though unsuccessful, confirmed this belief. For in Germany, too, workers' and soldiers' councils were formed (partly under the influence of Russian events), and in the following years a series of armed clashes took place between the Communist minority among the workers and counter-revolutionary military formations serving the "bourgeois republic." The Bolshevik leaders chose to view this development as proof of the typical character of their own experience.

Today it is clear that Lenin was totally mistaken both about the social and historical character of his own revolution and about the importance of its political forms. The revolution arose not from the oppression of the workers in a capitalist society, but from the retarded development of such a society; the historical role of the revolution was not to end exploitation but to modernize an underdeveloped country by dictatorial methods. The Soviets were not typical organs of working-class rule, but unique — and very temporary — forms of mass organization in a country where, owing to Tsarist oppression, the tradition of stable democratic organizations was lacking. This is why they never achieved comparable importance in Germany and never were formed in other advanced countries. (It is also why revolutionary workers' and soldiers' councils did spontaneously arise in the Hungarian people's revolt against a totalitarian Communist regime in October 1956.) The uprising in the Russian capital, finally, was victorious only because of the absence of a tradition of "bourgeois democracy"; in no country with established parliamentary institutions did the workers show the expected tendency to rise "against the state."

The really decisive political feature of the October Revolution was neither the role of the Soviets nor that of the workers' uprising in Petrograd, but the seizure of power by the centralized Bolshevik Party; it was this that made Lenin's victory the first of the totalitarian revolutions of the twentieth century. By contrast, the Soviets and the workers' uprising merely arose from the fact that this revolution was grafted onto the earlier, uncompleted democratic revolution against Tsarism, the last of the great democratic revolutions of European history. Yet, Lenin, who for all his insistence on the role of the party remained unaware of the true implications of the instrument of power he had forged, still saw himself as the heir of the democratic-revolutionary tradition of the West; hence his belief that the role of the Soviets, or of Soviet-like organs, and the workers' uprising would be repeated in the industrially advanced "bourgeois democracies."

In that belief, the Communist parties of the West marched for fifteen years from defeat to defeat. In countries with large organized labor movements, slogans like "Bildet Arbeiterraete!" or "Les Soviets partout!" proved absurd even in times of revolutionary crisis; and even where millions of workers voted Communist, as in Germany during the great depression of 1929–32 or in France in the 1930's, they did not show the slightest inclination to rise against the "bourgeois-democratic state."

Toward the end of the postwar crisis, Karl Radek became the first Bolshevik leader to perceive the error; on the basis of the experience in Germany, he persuaded the Comintern in 1922 to adopt a demand for "workers' governments" (or "workers' and peasants' governments") as a "transitional slogan"[6]—in other words to call on the workers to press for parliamentary governments of the "united front," which were then to be urged on to extra-constitutional measures, until the resistance of the old ruling classes and their bureaucracies would convince the workers of the need to establish proletarian dictatorships. In a sense, Radek may thus be regarded as the originator of the present concept of the "parliamentary road to socialism"; but after the defeat of the German Communists in 1923, his ideas were condemned as "opportunist" and the old doctrine restored in its full rigidity.[7]

STALIN AND THE "PEACEFUL ROAD"

Yet under Stalin the restoration of the old doctrine did not imply a return to the old illusions about a working-class revolution in the West; on the contrary, it was a form of writing off the prospects of such a revolution, of turning the Comintern into a mere auxiliary of the Soviet state while proceeding with the "building of socialism in one country." But as Stalin, empirically following the logic of power, became gradually conscious of the true implications of the type of party that Lenin had led to victory, he was bound to see also the possibilities for foreign Communist parties in a new light. At home, he proceeded to resolve the contradiction between the democratic-revolutionary heritage in Lenin's ideas and the realistic needs of a totalitarian state by liquidating the former and consistently developing the latter; abroad, he began to explore the possibilities of using dependent totalitarian parties as instruments not of popular revolution but of the infiltration of foreign governments, with the aim of influencing their international policy in the interest of the Soviet Union. The first large-scale experiment of this type was the policy imposed on the Chinese Communists from 1924 to 1927, which led to their affiliation with the Kuomintang, their filling of many key posts in its political machine during the northward offensive, and finally to an attempt by the CPC leadership to put the brake on the peasant revolution in a vain effort to avoid conflict with Chiang Kai-shek.[8] The fact that this policy ultimately failed must not be allowed to obscure its historical importance in pioneering a completely new type of Communist activity.

That experiment in China had been facilitated, however, by the accepted Leninist doctrine that in the national revolution of such a backward, "semi-colonial" country the immediate aim of the Communists could not be the "dictatorship of the proletariat" but only an alliance with all "progressive" classes; the strategy of infiltration was justified as the political form of that alliance.[9] It took the victory and consolidation of Nazism in Germany to make Stalin agree to a modified application of this strategy in democratic, industrial countries.

Mussolini had been the first to see that the technique of the centralized party and the one-party state could be applied for gaining and preserving power without accepting the Bolshevik ideology or program. He also recognized that such a party was by its very nature independent of any particular "class basis" – that it could afford to rely on different social strata in turn. Applying these observations, he demonstrated how such a party could exploit the institutions of a parliamentary democracy in order to seize power "legally." This lesson was not understood in Russia at the time, but it was carefully applied by Hitler. By the summer of 1934, when Hitler had proved by the Roehm purge of June 30 that he was not the stooge of the Reichswehr which Stalin had believed him to be, the latter began to take him seriously [10] both as a danger to the USSR and as a model for new and significant political techniques. The time had come for Bolshevism to return to the Fascists the compliment of imitation.

In the meantime, the Communist parties in the West, while losing much of their early strength, had gone through many Kremlin-imposed changes of leadership. Admiration for the power and ruthlessness of Stalinist Russia, rather than belief in a repetition of Lenin's revolution, had become the decisive article of faith. Stalin now decided to use the parties to try and bring about "anti-Fascist" governmental coalitions; for the first time in their history, they were to attempt seriously to influence parliamentary politics within the bourgeois state by using all the unscrupulous maneuverability of a totalitarian party to this end. But as in China ten years earlier, the aim was not to seize power and carry out a social revolution, but to influence foreign policy in alliance with all "progressive" classes. This time, the reason given for limiting the objective was not the backwardness of the countries concerned but the need, with Hitler on the doorstep, to avoid civil war, and the danger to the Soviet Union if the Western countries without strong Communist parties — particularly Britain and the United States — should be scared into Hitler's camp by the specter of Communist revolution.

Here was the essence of the "Popular Front" strategy: it was the first great experiment in using totalitarian Communist parties to gain influence within the state machine of Western democracies by parliamentary means. Since the objectives were limited to foreign policy, Communist parties were ordered to modify their social and economic programs to keep them within the "capitalist framework." [11] The strategy was thus an attempt to combine the lessons of the Chinese experiment and of Hitler's victory in a spirit completely foreign to the Leninist tradition. Again, it failed in the end. But in France it resulted in large permanent gains by the Communist Party; and in Spain it led temporarily to almost complete Communist control of the remnant of the Republican state machine, after the civil war and "non-intervention" had made the government dependent on Soviet supplies and advisers. From this experience, Stalin learned how successful the new technique of "legal" seizure of the state machine might be, if combined with dependence on the Soviet Union.

FROM "POPULAR FRONT" TO "PEOPLE'S DEMOCRACY"

The new strategy was abandoned between the time of the Munich agreement and the German attack on the USSR — that is, during the period of Soviet-German negotiations and of the Stalin-Hitler pact. But after Hitler's invasion of Russia, the same policy was readopted under the slogan of "National Liberation Fronts" in occupied Europe and of "National Unity" in other allied countries. The Soviet directive to all Communists during this phase was to build up their organizations and to occupy key posts, but to be extremely moderate in their programs so as not to frighten the Western powers. In the process of liberation, Communists everywhere were instructed to join coalition governments on the broadest possible basis, not even rejecting at first the leadership of turncoat generals in ex-Axis countries. But it quickly became obvious that Stalin intended to make completely different use of these coalitions, according to whether the countries concerned were in his own military sphere or in that of the Western powers.

In Soviet-occupied Eastern Europe, the Communists were for the first time encouraged to follow the "parliamentary road to socialism" to the bitter end – that is, to treat the coalition partners as Mussolini and Hitler had treated theirs once they had control of the physical means of power and the machinery of official propaganda. The individual Communist parties were given considerable latitude in the timing and tactics they adopted to eliminate, split, or swallow rival parties, to enforce single-list elections, and to carry out economic "revolutions from above." But everywhere the result of "people's democracy" was the same within a few years – the imposition of absolute Communist Party rule as an extension of direct Soviet control.

In Western Europe, on the other hand, the Communists were warned strictly against any measures that might bring them into conflict with the Western allies for as long as Allied troops remained in their respective countries. (There were also repeated warnings of this kind in the borderline case of Yugoslavia, but they were disobeyed by the Yugoslav Communist leaders.) After that, the

Russian attitude seems to have been ambiguous for some time; the indications are that Stalin never wished any Communists to make a bid for total power, either by parliamentary or violent means, in countries where they could not be physically backed by Soviet forces and kept afterwards dependent on the "leading role of the Soviet Union," but that he was prevailed upon to tolerate a certain amount of experiment. It is a fact, at any rate, that a number of Western Communist leaders in 1946 made statements interpreting the coalition governments of this time as stages in a "people's democratic" development, which might peacefully lead to "socialism" by the "parliamentary road," and the Italian Communists, at least, showed considerable confidence that they might come to power as independently on this road as Tito had done on the road of civil war.[12] Those ideas could not have been put forward without at least the tentative approval of Stalin, but he never committed himself to them in public.[13] It was only after the end of the Communist participation in West European governments, the formation of the Cominform, and finally the conflict with Tito, that these hopes faded and the Western Communists returned – after some ill-prepared attempts at revolutionary mass action – to sterile and rigid opposition.

Since the Twentieth CPSU Congress and the dissolution of the Cominform, the West European Communists have been resurrecting these statements of 1946, and again it is the Italians who do so with the greatest self-confidence and apparent conviction.[14] Khrushchev's "Leninist revival" has resulted in the first explicit theoretical recognition of the strategy of the "parliamentary road" which had been developed, gropingly and gradually over more than twenty years, by Stalin; but it has also freed that strategy from its Stalinist limitation to either foreign policy objectives or to states under Soviet military control. In contrast to Lenin, the present leaders know as clearly as did Stalin that they are dealing not with working-class risings against the bourgeois state, but with totalitarian techniques for legally seizing the state machine; in contrast to Stalin, they believe in the "world revolution" – that is, in the possibility and desirability of Communist victories outside the immediate Soviet sphere.

THE PATH OF THE PARTISANS

The possibility of such victories must have been impressed even on a reluctant Stalin by two Communist movements that followed an altogether different road from either Lenin's or his own – the Chinese and the Yugoslav. Mao Tse-tung apparently had from the beginning been opposed to one aspect of Stalin's Chinese policy of the 1920's – the attempt to brake the peasant revolution in the interest of preserving the Communist-Kuomintang alliance.[15] After the defeat of this policy, some of the military specialists of the Chinese Communist Party, including Chou-En-lai, undertook a number of unsuccessful attempts to imitate the Leninist tactics of the armed workers' uprising, even though conditions were plainly unfavorable. Meanwhile Mao, then still far from the leadership of the party, took to partisan warfare in a mountainous region.

It seems evident that Mao at first acted not from a conscious strategic concept of the Chinese road to power but from an instinct of political self-preservation, guided by the immemorial tradition of Chinese peasant risings. Only gradually, as this partisan warfare was moderately successful while all else failed, did Mao's strategic concept develop. Some Western students of communism have seen his originality in the bold decision to rely on guerilla tactics in the countryside and to avoid decisive battles for the control of big towns even though this meant building up an army and even a party organization in which the peasants formed the great majority, contrary to Communist doctrine. Yet the difference between Mao's partisan warfare and the traditional peasant rising was no less vital; it consisted in his gradual creation of a mobile force, officered partly by intellectual and working-class cadres, but consisting mainly of uprooted peasants, who could be used outside their region of origin.[16] The famous "long march" to the Northwest, like the equally heroic marches of Tito's partisans during the war, was the visible symbol of the complete emancipation of the new army from its original social basis; despite the peasant origin of most of its members, it was no more a class force of peasants than a class force of workers, but a truly totalitarian creation.

The success of Mao's policy depended in part on the creation of new local government organs — which acted also as organs of agrarian revolution — in whatever area was held at any time by the partisan forces. The "Soviets" arose in China, as did later analogous organs in Yugoslavia, not as spontaneous forms of mass organization but as auxiliary institutions of the military rule imposed by the party. Another element of success was the transfer of experienced Communist cadres from the cities to the "Soviet areas." The party leadership long obstructed this, however, since it would have implied recognition that the uprising in the countryside had, contrary to traditional doctrine, become the party's main task; only after Mao had struggled for years against the "working-class" prejudices of successive Moscow-imposed leaderships were the latter forced by persecution themselves to join the "Soviet areas." [17] After the Twentieth Party Congress in Moscow, Mao at last openly attributed such "sectarian" resistance to the errors of Stalin.[18]

In Yugoslavia, Tito based his partisan activity from the start on a study of the Chinese experience, transferring the Central Committee and the largest possible number of urban cadres to the mountains and using the latter as soon as possible to form "proletarian brigades" in order to achieve mobility.[19] Years later, Svetozar Vukmanovic-Tempo, the Yugoslav leader who had been in charge of liaison with Communist partisans in neighboring countries, saw one of the principal causes of the defeat of the Greek Communists in their repeated hesitation to take similar steps.[20]

While Mao's partisan strategy succeeded in preserving the Communist force for years as a potential contender for power and an actual factor of anarchy, it would not have led to victory without the Japanese war and occupation; the latter acted as a decisive solvent of all state authority and at the same time gave the Communists an opportunity to add the appeal of nationalism to their program. The German occupation played an even more important role in Yugoslavia, for without it no partisan war would have started. Similarly, Japanese occupation and anti-colonial revolt offered the Vietnamese Communists their opportunity. By contrast, Communist attempts to apply "Chinese tactics" of guerilla uprisings in independent Asian countries after 1948 have been as uniformly unsuccessful as the attempts to apply "Russian tactics" in Europe after World War I.

During both the Sino-Japanese war and World War II the importance of "National Front" tactics was fully recognized by Stalin, and he urged on all Communist partisan forces a corresponding moderation of their program – in the Chinese case more or less successfully,[21] in the Yugoslav case with very limited and temporary success only. But the final struggle for power was initiated in both cases against his advice;[22] and it is doubtful whether the later guerilla actions elsewhere were ever intended by Moscow to be more than harassing operations. When in 1949 the victorious Chinese Communists proclaimed to the world movement that their revolution should become the model for all colonial and semi-colonial countries, their claim received from the Russians the same kind of guarded and tentative approval as the idea of the "peaceful road" for Western Europe had received in 1946; the speech by Liu Shao-ch'i that formulated the claim was reprinted in the Cominform weekly and in *Pravda*,[23] but no Soviet leader and no resolution of the CPSU endorsed it explicitly, and no discussion of the consequences of such approval took place in public; hence the Russians remained free to repudiate the claim whenever they pleased. It was only at the Twentieth Congress that partisan warfare of the Chinese and Yugoslav type was explicitly recognized by Moscow as one of the "roads to power" that parties might use as a model in similar circumstances.

ALL ROADS LEAD TO POWER

The Soviet leaders made no attempt at the Twentieth Congress to map out in detail the several "roads to power" they now profess to sanction for foreign Communists, or even to lay down a complete list of them — except in the purely formal sense that any future conquest of power could be described as either "legal" or "violent." This confinement to broad generalities was deliberate; in fact, leading Soviet spokesmen emphasized that it would be absurd to expect a revolution to take only one or a few prescribed forms in all countries and conditions. In short, the new line was aimed precisely at emancipating world communism from any hampering doctrines about the form of revolution; the Soviet leaders had at last come forth with the stark recognition that it is the achievement of power alone which matters.

Such power is still described in Leninist terms as "the dictatorship of the proletariat under the leadership of its Communist vanguard." But the sanction both of the Fascist-Stalinist technique of the "legal" *coup d'état* and of the Maoist-Titoist strategy of partisan warfare suggests full awareness on the part of the Soviet leaders that the alleged proletarian class content of the dictatorship is a fiction, and that its totalitarian form as a dictatorship of the Communist Party is the only relevant reality. Ironically enough, they seem finally to have achieved this theoretical insight into the essence of their own system at an historical moment when the growth of new social forces with the achievement of industrialization makes the continued preservation of party dictatorship increasingly difficult even in the Soviet Union itself.

3

1956–57: THE FIRST IDEOLOGICAL CRISIS

Khrushchev's forceful repudiation of Stalin's methods both for governing the Soviet Union and for controlling other Communist states was intended to inaugurate an ideological rebirth of Soviet and international communism; instead, it produced a severe political and ideological crisis in Russia's East European empire and in the Communist world movement at large. The world conference of Communist parties held in Moscow in November 1957, on the occasion of the fortieth anniversary of the Bolshevik seizure of power, marked the end of this "crisis of de-Stalinization." The declaration of principles, adopted at that conference by all ruling Communist parties except the Yugoslav, showed that Khrushchev had succeeded in restoring the unity of the Soviet bloc and of the international movement on a new basis. But it also offered eloquent testimony that its authors continued to be haunted by the unfamiliar specter of fundamental ideological heresy arising from within the movement itself.

Since the crisis first came into the open in 1955, it had revealed three principal aspects. First, there was the crisis of Soviet authority – the refusal of many leading Communists and some entire parties further to recognize the Soviet Union as the sole model and its leaders as necessary guides for their own decisions; this is the phenomenon loosely known as "national communism." Second, there was the open expression of doubt by a number of hitherto leading Communists about some of the fundamental principles of Leninism, such as the need for a monolithic, centralized party and a single-party state controlled by it; such "revisionism" had not appeared on any serious scale for more than thirty years. Third, there was an outright loss of faith in the truthfulness of the Communist leaders and the value of Communist ideology as a whole by large numbers of ordinary party members and sympathizers, most striking among intellectuals but not confined to them; this loss of ideological attraction was marked both in satellite Europe and throughout the Western world, and occurred even in the Soviet Union, though hardly any signs of it had yet appeared among the underdeveloped states of Asia.

The principal political milestones of the crisis are well known. It began with the first major disavowal of Stalin's doctrines and policies at the end of May 1955, when N. S. Khrushchev as First Secretary of the Soviet Communist Party and N. Bulganin as Minister President of the USSR went to Belgrade, publicly admitted that the Soviet government had been wrong to try to force its views on Communist Yugoslavia and to treat Marshal Tito as a "Fascist" and an "agent of imperialism" when he refused to comply, and proclaimed that the Yugoslav Communists had remained a "Marxist-Leninist" party with which fraternal relations should be resumed by all good Communists. It gathered momentum with the disclosure of

Stalin's methods of inner-party terrorism and the damage done by them to the Soviet state in Khrushchev's "secret speech" to the Twentieth Congress of the CPSU in February 1956, followed in April by the dissolution of the Cominform. It reached its dramatic climax in the revolutionary events in Eastern Europe in October 1956: the defiant proclamation of independence in their internal affairs by the Polish Communist leaders, accomplished in the teeth of protests and threats by the Soviet rulers; and the initially successful rising of the people of Hungary against the Soviet-imposed Communist dictatorship, which led to the formation of a coalition government of democratic parties and to the proclamation of Hungarian neutrality before it was drowned in blood by armed Soviet intervention. Finally, the development of the crisis included the independent ideological initiatives undertaken by the Chinese Communists, the stubborn resistance of writers in Russia and other Communist states against the party's ideological control, as well as the outburst of open polemics between "orthodox" and "heretical" Communist parties in the winter of 1956–57.

Thus the immediate cause of the ideological crisis had clearly been the disavowal of Stalin's policies and the disclosure of his crimes by his successors and former accomplices; without the shattering effect on Soviet authority of the Belgrade journey and the "secret speech," the October revolutions in Poland and Hungary would have been inconceivable. But this in itself requires an interpretation of Stalin's significance for Communist ideology. If he had just been the indispensable symbol of authority needed to maintain the unity of a world-wide centralized movement, the iconoclasm of Khrushchev would appear to have been an act of wanton folly. In fact, however, Stalin's name stood for a peculiar ideological synthesis — a brutal but consistent solution of some of the basic contradictions inherent in the Leninist myth. The idol *had* to be broken because the synthesis was no longer workable; the ideological crisis continues because those basic contradictions have re-emerged into full view.

STALIN'S IDEOLOGICAL ACHIEVEMENTS

The first of these contradictions concerns the character of the Bolshevik revolution and of the Communist Party. Lenin saw his own victory as the culmination of one of the great democratic revolutions of Europe, and his party as the "Jacobins" of the working class. Yet by his insistence on centralized control he had in fact created a totalitarian party which could change its "social basis" at will and become purely an instrument of power; his victory was thus the beginning of the first of the totalitarian revolutions of our century — the first stage in the creation of the first single-party dictatorship. Throughout Lenin's life, the fiction of the "basically" democratic working-class party and of the "dictatorship of the proletariat" — a fiction in which he himself somehow managed to retain his belief — kept coming into conflict with the reality of the totalitarian party dictatorship over all classes, the workers included. Stalin's solution consisted in eliminating step by step the remaining concessions to the democratic and proletarian fiction by turning the governing party into a party of bureaucrats, while maintaining that the rule of any Communist party was *by definition* the "dictatorship of the proletariat" — whether it actually enjoyed working-class support or not.

The second contradiction concerns the duration of the dictatorial regime. The "dictatorship of the proletariat" had originally been justified as necessary for the transitional period until the economic power of the former ruling classes had finally been broken; after that, state power, conceived as an instrument of oppression, would gradually "wither away." But the Bolshevik Party had no intention of renouncing its monopoly of power after the final destruction of the capitalist and landowning classes, nor even after the "liquidation of the kulaks as a class" by forced collectivization. Stalin's solution consisted in laying down the doctrine that the more the "construction of socialism" advanced, the more the class struggle was bound to sharpen; this absurdity (proclaimed in the spring of 1937, at the height of the great blood purge) [1] served as a justification for maintaining the dictatorship by turning its terroristic power periodically against ever new groups, thus keeping Soviet society in a state of permanent revolution from above.

The third contradiction arose between the state interests of the Soviet Union and the interests of "world revolution" as represented by the Communist parties outside it. How far should the Soviet state shape its foreign policies to aid the cause of world revolution, and how far was it entitled to sacrifice the latter to its own consolidation? Stalin's solution, formulated first in the slogan of "socialism in one country," later in that of "fatherland of all toilers," consisted in declaring as a matter of doctrine that the state interests of the Soviet Union constituted the supreme interest of international communism, to which every loyal Communist must willingly sacrifice every other consideration. It followed that the victory of communism in any other country was not only highly improbable, but indeed undesirable unless it depended on Soviet aid and thus coincided with an extension of Soviet state power, and that any new Communist states that did come into existence had to be subordinated to the "leading" Soviet Union just as completely as all Communist parties.

It was this last doctrine that led to the conflict with Tito's Yugoslavia and threatened to lead to a far more vital conflict with Mao Tse-tung's China – the only other country where Communists had taken power primarily by their own efforts; it was this, then, that Stalin's heirs first recognized as untenable. A journey to Peking by Khrushchev, Bulganin, and Mikoyan in the autumn of 1954 preceded their journey to Belgrade, and one of the central theses of the Twentieth Congress was the recognition of the growth of a "Socialist world system," that is, a plurality of sovereign Communist states.

But by the time of that Congress the second of the Stalinist doctrines mentioned – the justification of ever new purges by "the sharpening of the class struggle" – seemed equally impossible to maintain. Having greatly weakened the secret police in an effort to revive the party organization, Stalin's heirs found themselves under growing pressure to offer to the leading administrative, technico-economic, and military strata of the Soviet Union guarantees against any return to Stalin's blood purges; finally they were driven both to disavow the doctrine and to admit through the mouth of Khrushchev its horrible results.[2] With the discarding of the doctrinal covers, the terrorist actions ordered by Stalin against potential opponents at home and against potential "Titoists" in Eastern Europe stood revealed in their naked ugliness as the crimes of a tyrannic regime; and the sudden collapse of the late dictator's authority tended to involve in its fall both the international authority of the Soviet Union and the personal authority of his former collaborators and present heirs.

"DE-STALINIZATION" AND THE CRISIS OF AUTHORITY

In renouncing the claim to total subordination of all Communist parties and governments to centralistic Soviet discipline and recognizing their formal "equality," Khrushchev had not intended to abandon Soviet political leadership, but to give it a more solid foundation: international unity, including Yugoslavia, was to be placed on the basis of fraternal solidarity, and the Soviet Union would more than regain in moral and political authority what it lost in detailed centralized machine control. Similarly, in disavowing Stalin's methods of internal control, he did not intend to weaken the justification for the Bolshevik dictatorship but to reassure the leading strata of Soviet society that these methods had been mere accidental distortions, and that the party dictatorship was now returning to its sound basic principles. Yet in fact, the simultaneous admission of Stalin's "Great Power chauvinism" and of his disregard for "Socialist legality" aroused among Communists everywhere profound doubt about the "leading role of the Soviet Union," and searching questions about the inherent dangers of its system of government.

The leadership of the Communist parties was split by the shock. The French Communists, like most of the established satellite leaders and some of Khrushchev's critics within the Soviet Communist Party, tended to defend Stalin against his latest detractors, to uphold the infallibility of the Soviet Union against its own new leaders, and to deny the fitness of the Yugoslav heretics to be received back into the fold. Others, with the Italians and Poles in the van, eagerly welcomed the new departure as a chance to increase their own autonomy, but in doing so went much beyond Khrushchev's intentions.[3] In satellite Eastern Europe the issue quickly developed into a bitter struggle for power between the former executors of Stalin's policies – including his anti-Titoist purges – and their surviving and now rehabilitated victims, who, backed by Yugoslavia, called for the wholesale replacement of the old leaders and the adoption of new policies.

The reforms demanded by the critics began with a slowdown of industrialization, a better price structure, the end of the forced delivery system for peasants, and permission for them to leave the collective farms. These demands could be supported not only by the example of Yugoslavia but by that of the "new look" reforms introduced in Hungary on Soviet prompting in 1953–54, immediately after Stalin's death. But now they were put forward not as part of a Soviet change of "line," but in the name of the right of each nation to follow "its own road to socialism" and of the need for the local Communists to regain popular support – in short, as the platform of an "anti-Stalinist" faction determined to put the demands of their own people ahead of those of the Kremlin.[4] The new "national communism" thus clearly contained the germ of that "rightist deviation" – democracy.

Moreover, in most cases these demands for practical economic reforms were combined with other ideas which had been developed by the Yugoslav Communists in the years of their struggle against Stalin, but which remained unacceptable to Khrushchev because of their far-reaching ideological implications. One of these was the proposal to transfer the management of the factories to elected workers' councils; while the practical importance of this proposal was limited, it had for years been used by Yugoslav theorists to contrast their "Socialist workers' self-government" with the "bureaucratic state capitalism" of Stalinist Russia. Another "revisionist" doctrine developed during Yugoslavia's years of isolation was that progress toward socialism was no monopoly of the Communist bloc but might also be achieved by "reformist" methods in the advanced industrial countries of the West; hence a Socialist country might serve its cause better by keeping on good terms with both blocs than by joining the Russians in a military alliance.[5] This interpretation of "different roads to socialism" went far beyond the one accepted at the Twentieth Congress by the Soviet leaders, who merely admitted different roads to Communist power; but it proved highly attractive to critical satellite Communists like Imre Nagy in Hungary.[6]

The ferment in Eastern Europe also brought a third element to the surface: a moral revulsion among the Communist intelligentsia against lies and inhumanity. Communist writers and poets, in particular, realizing that their talents had been misused for years to justify crimes and mislead their people, passionately hoped to redeem themselves by telling the truth and by boldly defending humanistic values. Where conflicts among the leaders gave them a chance to express themselves, as in the outburst of free speech in the Polish press and in the discussions of the Petoefi Club in Budapest, they contributed decisively to the climate in which the events of October 1956 became possible.[7]

As the nature of the forces unleashed by Khrushchev's action became obvious, the Soviet leaders sought to apply the brakes and to confine personal and policy changes in satellite Europe to the inevitable minimum: [8] from the summer of 1956 they began to back the former Stalinist leaders against all critics in return for perfunctory gestures of self-criticism. Only in Poland and Hungary were they no longer able to prevent the new forces from breaking through.

POLAND AND HUNGARY

The Polish Communist leaders were in a special position, because the condemnation of Stalin's prewar purges entailed the rehabilitation both of their own party, which had been dissolved by the Comintern in 1938 as "penetrated by police spies," and of its prewar leaders then executed in Russia; [9] many surviving senior Polish Communists had been deported to Soviet labor camps at the time and released only after the war. It was thus inevitable that the party should eagerly welcome the results of the Twentieth Congress of the Soviet Communist Party. Moreover, the party's "Stalinist" leader, Boleslav Bierut, had died at the time of the Congress, while all the victims of the 1949 purge of "Titoists" had been allowed to survive in prison, and their leader, Wladyslaw Gomulka, had never confessed to any crime and now enjoyed great prestige as a symbol of national independence. When faced with the Poznan riots at the end of June 1956, the majority of the party leadership thus took the bold decision to treat them not as a machination of the "imperialists," as the Russians wanted, but as an expression of justifiable popular discontent; [10] and a few months later, after a Polish party delegation had attended the Eighth Congress of the Chinese Communist Party in September and had obtained assurance of Chinese backing,[11] they followed this up by offering to Gomulka, who had been granted amnesty in April and readmitted to the party in August, the return to the post of First Secretary. In the atmosphere that had by then developed, Gomulka was able to insist on far-reaching changes in the composition of the Politburo, including the removal of the commander in chief, Soviet Marshal Rokossovsky, as a condition for resuming leadership; the revolutionary change took place in October despite Soviet protests and threats.[12]

The new Polish leadership succeeded in renegotiating the alliance with the Soviet Union,[13] obtaining effective sovereignty in internal affairs on the understanding that it would maintain the party dictatorship and continue to support Soviet foreign policy. It used its new powers not only to satisfy the demands of the peasants and to introduce experimental workers' councils but to restore Catholic religious instruction in State schools by agreement with the Church, to extend the powers of the Sejm – the Polish "parliament" – for supervising the administration, and to allow non-Communist Sejm members to form groups and make their own proposals. While maintaining its monopoly of political power, the Polish Communist Party thus permitted both a considerable degree of free discussion and the formation of pressure groups enjoying a measure of independence, and showed its willingness to take account of such pressures within the limits of its economic possibilities.

By contrast, the Hungarian "Stalinist" leaders, Rakosi and Geroe, having shared responsibility for the execution of Rajk and his "Titoist" associates in 1949, had the strongest possible motives for resisting any change. But they suffered from the disadvantage that they had once before had to criticize their own "mistakes" under Soviet pressure in the early days of the post-Stalin "new look," and that the chief exponent of this popular alternative policy, Imre Nagy, though overthrown by them early in 1955, had remained alive and free. Moreover, the Yugoslav's efforts to influence developments in the satellites had been deliberately concentrated on Hungary, where they regarded Rakosi as a symbol of the Cominform past and Nagy as a potential ally in working for a neutral belt extending from Yugoslavia to Austria.[14] The result was a bitter inner-party struggle leading to increasing paralysis of the regime.

In July 1956 the Russians, alarmed by the growth of open opposition within and without the party in Hungary, forced Rakosi to resign in favor of Geroe, who had supported his policy all along; in late August or early September they sent out a circular to all Communist parties warning that the Yugoslavs, though now considered as friends, showed ideological weaknesses of a Social Democratic type and should not be taken as a model.[15] In September, Khrushchev obtained Tito's support for Geroe at the price of a public disavowal of Rakosi's policy, the solemn reburial of Rajk, and the readmission of Nagy to the party.[16] But when these terms were carried out early in October, and were followed immediately by the Polish events, the effect was to destroy what remained of the Hungarian leadership's authority, so that an unrepentant speech by Geroe on his return from Belgrade was enough to start the Budapest students' riots which became a revolution.

The course of events[17] quickly showed that the Hungarian Communist Party had ceased to exist as a coherent force. The Geroe leadership was conscious of having no following left outside the security police: they first called in Soviet troops, then tried to hide behind Nagy, and finally left the party to be reorganized under a new name and leadership. But the Nagy group realized that it, too, could no longer hope to save a "reformed" party dictatorship of the Gomulka type: when it took control, both the workers and the armed forces had formed revolutionary councils in opposition to the old government, and would have refused to recognize any new one that had a purely Communist basis. They could no longer be won by a change of policy and persons, only by a change of regime: hence the "reformed" Communists had only the choice between a return to parliamentary democracy – that is, a Social Democratic policy – or a return to reliance on Soviet force – that is, a Stalinist policy. Nagy, in forming a coalition government of democratic forces and declaring Hungary neutral, chose the former; Kadar, who had supported him until November 1, in the end chose the latter. "Communism" was reimposed on the workers of Hungary by Soviet tanks.

OUTSIDE THE SOVIET ORBIT

Up to the Polish and Hungarian events of October 1956 the ideological crisis of communism outside the Soviet orbit had not, on the whole, taken dramatic forms. Many active Communists and fellow travelers in the West had indeed been shaken by the admission that the official version of Stalin's prewar and postwar purges in general, and of the conflict with Yugoslavia in particular, had been a pack of lies, and that many of the charges made by their opponents had been substantially true. But while the demolition of the Stalin myth must have severely damaged the roots of their faith, conscious criticism remained still largely confined to the demand for guarantees against being duped in the future, in the form of increased autonomy of the individual parties and more effective "party democracy" within them.

The demand for greater autonomy was classically expressed by the Italian Communist leader, Palmiro Togliatti, in his formula of a "polycentric" Communist movement.[18] Theoretically, this implied a rejection of Soviet world leadership, and therefore the heresy of "national communism." But the Soviet leaders, who were at first so sensitive when the same tendency was shown by Gomulka in Poland, did not react to Togliatti's heretical formula at the time. They did, however, at once attack another statement of Togliatti's: his thesis that it was necessary for Marxists to look for the weaknesses in Soviet society that had made Stalin's abuses possible[19] — clearly an echo of Yugoslav and earlier Trotskyite criticisms of the "bureaucratic degeneration" in Soviet society. The statement of the Central Committee of the Soviet Communist Party of June 30, 1956[20] — the first officially published statement of the revaluation of Stalin's role, and at the same time the first attempt to limit the damage and to react to such danger signs as the Poznan riots and the discussions in the Petoefi Club — strongly denied any such "degeneration" and claimed that, despite Stalin's "mistakes" and "departures from the Leninist norms of party life," the "general line" of the party had always been correct, and Soviet society as a whole had therefore party was compatible with steady progress toward "communism. But this implied the cynical belief that the complete destruction of democratic life within the ruling party was compatible with steady progress toward "communism" – a thinly veiled admission of the fact that freedom of discussion and criticism even within the party, let alone beyond it, was of merely decorative importance for the Soviet concept of Socialist development, under Stalin's successors as under himself. While Togliatti meekly accepted the rebuke,[21] it clearly could not calm those Communists in the West who had become concerned about inner-party democracy

The most far-reaching criticism at this time, however, came from Pietro Nenni, onetime récipient of the Stalin Peace Prize and leader of the Italian Socialist Party, which was tied to the Communists by a long-term pact of "Unity of Action." At first reluctant to accept the piecemeal demolition of his former idol, Nenni turned round after the undenied publication of Khrushchev's "secret speech" and drew the conclusion that the concept of the "proletarian dictatorship" itself had to be "rethought" in the light of these disclosures. They proved, in his view, that this dictatorship, however necessary in Russian conditions to achieve the original aims of the 1917 Revolution, had later hardened, first, into the dictatorship of the Bolshevik Party over the proletariat, and, finally, into the personal rule of Stalin; it followed that single-party rule was dangerous in itself, and could not be accepted as a necessary road to socialism in countries with democratic traditions.[22]

In the summer of 1956, Nenni's complaints still seemed typical of the "fellow traveling" element in the West rather than of an attitude consciously espoused by important groups of party members. But the October rising in Hungary and the subsequent Soviet intervention spread these fundamental doubts both to wider circles and to parts of the inner core of the movement. Critically "sensitized" by the previous shock, the Communist and near-

Communist intelligentsia in the West were no longer ready blindly to believe the official Soviet version of a "Fascist coup" in Hungary, particularly in the face of the contrary evidence from Polish, Yugoslav, and individual Western Communists who had been on the spot.[23]

FROM "NATIONAL COMMUNISM" TO "REVISIONISM"

Yet, if the workers of Hungary had really risen in order to overthrow the rule of the Communist Party, then the claim that the party dictatorship was identical with the rule of the working class was manifestly absurd; and so was the identification of the interests of Soviet power with those of the international working-class movement, if the fact had to be faced that Soviet troops had crushed a genuine workers' rising for reasons of power politics. But the first pseudo-identity – that between the party dictatorship and the rule of the working class – is, as we have seen, the fundamental dogma of Communist ideology, the one that even Khrushchev at the height of his iconoclastic period never dreamed of touching; whoever doubts it departs from orthodox Marxism-Leninism and becomes a "revisionist." For the second pseudo-identity, between Soviet power politics and international working-class interests, Khrushchev himself had admitted implicitly, by his criticism of Stalin and his concessions to Tito, that it could be temporarily disturbed by Soviet "mistakes" – but he had hoped to restore confidence in the ability of the new leaders to avoid such mistakes. By proving his own fallibility in Poland and Hungary, he revived doubt in the "leading role of the Soviet Union," and gave a new impetus to "national communism."

The winter of 1956–57 thus brought to a climax the ideological crisis. Outwardly, this was expressed in the defection of a large part of the intellectual periphery and a number of prominent individual members of the Western Communist parties, as well as in a general loss of membership of 20 per cent; in the appearance of opposition to Soviet policy with the "World Peace Council," which necessitated the public admission that no agreement could be reached on Hungary; and in open polemics between the Polish and Yugoslav Communist press, on the one side, and that of the "loyal" part of the Soviet bloc, on the other. The Yugoslavs refused explicitly and officially, and the Polish press implicitly and with some official backing, to accept the Soviet version of the Hungarian events; and when a conference of Soviet-bloc Communist parties under Soviet leadership met in Budapest early in the new year, neither Poles nor Yugoslavs attended.[24]

Even those Communist leaders who officially defended the final Soviet intervention in Hungary were at first divided in their version of the events leading up to it. The Italian Communists as well as those of the United States and of most of the smaller European parties admitted, like the Yugoslavs, that there had been a genuine popular revolt due to the "mistakes" of the former Hungarian leadership; but they claimed that counter-revolutionary elements had gained control of the movement so that Soviet troops had to intervene to "save the achievements of socialism." The French Communist leaders, on the other hand, and those of the "loyal" satellites, unconditionally echoed the Soviet version that the Hungarian rising had been counter-revolutionary from the start, and blamed the Yugoslavs for their support of the Nagy group, which had weakened the cohesion of the regime. Parallel with this dispute, the former group continued to emphasize the need for autonomous leadership of each Communist party and to reject the idea of a single center of authority and organization, while the latter called for the restoration of such a center under Soviet leadership as a condition for international unity based on common principles.[25]

Ideologically even more significant than these disputes was the reappearance of openly anti-Leninist views among the Polish and Yugoslav Communists. In Poland, this took the form not only of a general call for a "humane socialism" as opposed to Stalinism – the formula for the continuing moral revolt of the intellectuals – but also of a specific revival of the fundamental critique of the Bolshevik revolution written in 1918 in a German prison by Rosa Luxemburg, the Polish-born founder of the German Communist Party. Rosa Luxemburg had always been an uncompromising critic of Lenin's centralist party of the Jacobin type and of its tendency to substitute itself for the working class; when the Bolsheviks seized power in the name of the Soviets, she welcomed their victory, but warned at the same time against equating the "dictatorship of the proletariat" in the Marxian sense with a terrorist party dictatorship, which would inevitably end in personal rule. The critique, published only posthumously by her pupil, Paul Levi, after his expulsion from the Comintern,[26] had not been discussed by Communists for thirty-five years. Now Dr. Julian Hochfeld, a former left-wing Social Democrat and a leading member of the Communist Sejm group, applied the salient points to the disclosures about Stalin's regime;[27] he concluded that the only long-run guarantee for a Socialist development was real democracy, including the right of free criticism and organized opposition. These views were not, of course, accepted by the Polish Communist Party, any more than were the philosophical criticisms of orthodox Marxist dogma published by the young Communist philosopher Leszek Kolakowski; but both authors were allowed to remain party members although neither recanted.

From another angle, the theoretical spokesman of the Yugoslav Communists, Vice President Edvard Kardelj, had long sought the cause of Stalin's excesses in the "bureaucratic degeneration" of Soviet society, and the remedy in the devolution of administrative and managerial functions to elected organs of self-government, such as workers' councils, communes, and so forth. But when during the winter of 1953–54 Milovan Djilas had drawn the conclusion that effective self-government was incompatible with the monopoly of a single party whose members in all self-governing organs act under centralized discipline, and had advocated the abolition of this Leninist discipline in the interest of true Socialist self-government,[28] he had been branded as a heretic and deprived of all his functions. Now, under the impact of the Hungarian revolution, Kardelj himself took a major step toward revising Leninism. In a speech to the Yugoslav Federal Assembly, he argued that the political "workers' councils" formed in Hungary would have been the natural organs of a truly Socialist power in contrast to the bureaucratic power of the discredited Communist Party, and that both Kadar and Nagy had been wrong in trying to revive that party — the one with Soviet help, the other with the help of a parliamentary coalition — instead of relying on the organs of the "direct rule of the workers." [29] He thus admitted that party dictatorship might have to give way to such "Soviets without Communists," in some cases, in the interests of socialism; and he even came close to the "Djilasist" conclusion that a state party was in principle an obstacle to the growth of workers' self-government in saying that "any party monopoly at the center, whether exercised by one or several parties, is incompatible with a truly decisive role of the masses of producers in the workers' factory councils and the communes." While no practical conclusions have been drawn from this astonishing statement in Yugoslavia, it has never been withdrawn or disowned, though it was, of course, bitterly attacked in Soviet and other orthodox Communist publications as "anarcho-syndicalist."

As for Djilas himself, he reacted to the Polish and Hungarian events by publishing abroad his final conversion to Social Democratic views:[30] "national communism" of the Yugoslav type, he wrote, might mitigate some evils but could not overcome the fundamental defects of every totalitarian system; true socialism could not be achieved without the freedom of organized opposition, that is, a multi-party system. At this point, the Yugoslav rulers recognized a danger to their own regime, and Djilas was sent to prison for "hostile propaganda."

THE "SAFE" COMMUNIST STATES

In the Soviet Union and in the "loyal" member states of the Soviet bloc, it remained impossible publicly to advocate such "revisionist" political concepts as those of Hochfeld or Kardelj. But even there, the official polemics against these views, as well as contacts with Polish and Hungarian intellectuals and reading of Polish and Yugoslav newspapers (or in some cases of Western Communist newspapers which had to give space to dissident views), broke through the official monopoly of information and stimulated the spread of critical attitudes and sometimes the formation of inner-party resistance groups, particularly among students.

The best-documented case of such a group is that of the circle of East German intellectuals formed in the autumn of 1956 around Dr. Wolfgang Harich in Berlin. They saw the future of the East German Communists in terms of a choice between continuing with the existing "Stalinist" leadership and policy, which must needs lead to a catastrophe as in Hungary, or effecting a timely change "on the Polish model," which would at once bring decollectivization, workers' councils, and a "democratization" of the party. The latter demand went clearly beyond the bounds of Leninism; so did their idea that such a reformed party should accept unification with Western Germany by free elections, provided that the Social Democrats should have won power there and carried out their program, and should eventually merge with the Social Democrats in a united, neutral, and democratic Socialist Germany. After Harich had been sentenced to ten years' imprisonment in March 1957, his platform was published by the West German Social Democrats, with whom he had established contact before his arrest in November 1956.[31] Meanwhile a number of East German professors who had profited from the "thaw" to develop interpretations of "dialectical materialism" that differed from the standard textbooks, or to discuss problems of economic planning in the light of comparisons between Soviet and Yugoslav experience, came under increasingly bitter attack as followers of Hungarian, Polish, and Yugoslav heretics, if not as political associates of the condemned "traitor" Harich. At the same time a general purge of the universities and of cultural life got under way.

In November 1956, a wave of arrests and students' expulsions had also swept the universities of Russia, Czechoslovakia, Rumania, and Bulgaria; they were generally connected with "uncontrolled" discussions about Hungary or demonstrations for greater academic freedom, including freedom to study Western literature, and, in some cases, with the formation of secret opposition groups. On the whole, these measures succeeded in bringing the immediate repercussions of the Polish and Hungarian events in this group of countries under control and banishing the ideological crisis from the surface of their social life. But the more profound effects, both of October 1956 and of "de-Stalinization," on the authority of the ruling parties continued to manifest themselves even in Russia and in the apparently "stable" satellites: they became visible in the stubborn struggle waged by otherwise politically loyal writers and scholars for increased independence from "ideological control" in their work — a struggle that was to bring them victories or defeats according to the advances or setbacks of "de-Stalinization" in the years to come — and in a marked loss of faith among the young generation.

NO ECHO IN ASIA

The critical events in Russia and Russian-dominated Eastern Europe, which shook the faith of so many Communists and fellow travelers both there and in the West, caused no comparable crisis among Communists in the underdeveloped countries of Asia and the Middle East. Broadly speaking, the attraction of communism in Asia did not diminish during those years; on the contrary, events in Indonesia, in Syria, and in parts of India rather suggested that it was on the increase.

In the light of the above remarks about the basic contradictions in Communist ideology which the crisis of 1956–57 brought to the surface, it is not difficult to understand this reaction. Communism in Asia has not, in the main, presented itself as the heir to the Western democratic ideals of liberty and equality; rather has its attraction been based on its proven value as an engine for the speedy industrialization and modernization of an underdeveloped country. Nor has it seriously pretended lately to be a workers' movement. Following Mao's example, the Asian Communists have increasingly claimed to embody an alliance of *all* "anti-imperialist" classes – workers, peasants, petty bourgeois, and "patriotic" bourgeois – and while making obeisance to the "leading role of the working class," they have hardly bothered to disguise the fact that the leading role is in practice exercised by the intelligentsia.

But this means that Communist attraction in Asia, with the possible exception of Japan, is based far less than in the West on fictions that may be destroyed by some dramatic event, and far more on true facts. It is not true that the Communists are the heirs of the ideals of 1789, and the tragedy of Hungary has demonstrated this even to the willfully blind; but it is true that a combination of state-directed industrialization, financed by ruthless dictatorial exploitation, with the ideological monopoly of a revolutionary party opposed to traditional superstitions as well as to traditional values, is a powerful engine of speedy modernization.[32] It is not true that the victory of the Communists in an industrial country would improve the material position and rights of the working class, for Hungary has shown this dramatically; but it is true that their victory in an underdeveloped country would open vast opportunities to the modern-minded intelligentsia to turn itself into a powerful political and economic bureaucracy — in fact, into the new ruling class. Where ideological attraction is not chiefly based on lies, there is no scope for an ideological crisis: in Asia, the lesson of the Sputniks proved more important than the lesson of Hungary.

The weak point of Communist ideology as preached in Asia is, of course, its claim to champion the equality and sovereign independence of all nations. Inasmuch as Hungary had a critical effect on the Asian Communist following at all, it was as a case of oppression of a small nation by a Great Power; but on the whole, the disillusionment of Asian Communists and fellow travelers with Soviet "anti-imperialism" had hardly yet begun at that time, except to some extent in Japan.

More important to the development of Asian communism during the same period was the attempt, and later the failure, of Mao Tse-tung to "liberalize" the Communist regime in China. Though given additional impetus by the spectacle of Soviet "de-Stalinization" and by the Hungarian and Polish events, this effort had its roots in the very features that have always distinguished Chinese Communist ideology from the Soviet variety, and must therefore be discussed in a different context.[33]

THE ROLE OF THE CHINESE COMMUNISTS

What was, however, of the utmost importance for the over-all development of the crisis of 1956–57, and for the later evolution of the world Communist movement, was the gain in international authority that the crisis brought to the Chinese Communist leaders and the manner of their intervention in its course. Even before he took the decisive steps on the road to power. Mao Tse-tung had emancipated his party from Stalin's advice, at least in Chinese domestic affairs, and had developed inner-party methods that differed markedly from those of Stalin; yet he had largely taken over Stalin's interpretation of the international scene and had educated his party in reverence for this "classic of Marxism-Leninism." When Khrushchev began to smash the idol, at the time of the Twentieth Congress, the Chinese Communists were worried by the manner of the attack, even though they welcomed the critical view taken of Stalin's "Great Power chauvinism" and the rise in their own status thereby implied. They were aware that so dramatic a break in the continuity of the Soviet party leadership could not fail to shake its authority — an authority they rightly regarded as the indispensable cement for the unity of the Soviet bloc. Hence the Chinese party leaders were the first, as early as the first days of April 1956, to try to balance the necessary criticism of Stalin with recognition of his abiding merits. They stressed the continuity of basic principles in a way that the Soviet leaders only came to imitate a few months later, under the impact of the first symptoms of the approaching East European crisis.[34]

As the 1956–57 crisis developed, the foresight thus shown by Mao contributed to the growth of his authority in the ranks of the world Communist movement. But quite apart from Mao's own actions, the brutal discrediting of the Stalin cult by an as yet comparatively unknown successor was bound to raise the prestige and influence of the leader who had acquired dictatorial power over the most populous country on earth by revolutionary struggle, and who had not merely inherited power from a predecessor who had himself inherited it. Faced by unfamiliar dangers, Russian, East European, and other

Communist leaders thus increasingly came to ask Mao's advice and to look upon him as the natural arbiter of their ideological problems: the year between the fall of 1956 and 1957 saw the first direct intervention of China in the history of Europe.

The direction of this intervention and the specific use Peking made of the authority that had thus accrued to it were determined in part by its interest in preserving the cohesion of the bloc on a new and more flexible basis, but in part they also represented the contemporary vicissitudes in the evolution of the Chinese regime itself. As has been mentioned,[35] the Chinese seem to have encouraged the Polish Communists' desire for greater autonomy when talking to their delegation at the Chinese party congress in September; after the October crisis, Chou En-lai took the opportunity during his European visit to urge Gomulka to recognize the "leading role" of the Soviet Union, but he also urged the Russians to recognize the independence of the new Polish leadership in domestic affairs.[36] A loosening of Soviet control over the satellites, combined with preservation of the Communist alliance and its common ideological principles, would indeed give the Chinese the best possible opportunities for strengthening their direct economic relations with the Communist states of Eastern Europe. By contrast, an overthrow of the party regime, followed by defection from the bloc, as occurred in Hungary during the climax of the revolution, could only be regarded by the Chinese – just as by the Russians – as a direct menace to their political and economic interests, and even as an ideological threat to their own regime. In condemning the Hungarian "counter-revolution," Peking therefore supported from the start the "hard" Soviet line; and it contributed to the subsequent international discussion by publishing, at the close of 1956, a new theoretical statement which vigorously defended the identification of the "dictatorship of the proletariat" with the party dictatorship against Yugoslav criticism and as vigorously rejected any suggestion of a "bureaucratic degeneration" of Soviet society.[37]

In contrast to later developments, however, this first Chinese critique of Yugoslav "revisionism" was still conducted in a fraternal manner; it seemed intended to convert, not to reject, the "erring brethren." Moreover, the Chinese Communists seem to have supported Khrushchev rather than his "Stalinist" opponents in the Soviet party leadership – who had not then been finally defeated – throughout the critical winter of 1956–57. To Peking, Khrushchev then appeared to offer the best guarantees for a flexible direction of the bloc, hence the best chances for maximizing Chinese influence within it; in addition, this was also the phase when Mao was reacting to the Hungarian shock by an attempt to open more widely the legal safety valves for the expression of discontent inside China itself.[38]

In 1956, the "de-Stalinization" had coincided with the first great experiment of the Chinese regime in permitting some freedom of intellectual discussion – the "Hundred Flowers Campaign." The spring of 1957 actually witnessed an intensification of this "liberal" course, with Mao's famous speech on "contradictions among the people." [39] Mao pointed out that such contradictions could arise even under a "Socialist" regime, but would normally remain "non-antagonistic"; only if the regime committed serious bureaucratic mistakes could such contradictions become "antagonistic" and thus be exploited by the imperialists and counter-revolutionaries, as in Hungary. In order to avoid such mistakes it was necessary to "correct the thinking" of the party cadres by a frank confrontation with all forms of popular discontent. Mao's sharp rejection of "revisionist" doubts concerning the need for the party dictatorship was thus originally coupled with an effort to make the actual conduct of that dictatorship more tolerable for the people. The unexpected strength of the outburst of criticism of the Chinese regime, however, led to a subsequent sharp turn against the "rightist danger" within China from 1957 on.[40]

THE BALANCE SHEET OF THE CRISIS

By May 1957 all the leaders of ruling Communist parties had realized how seriously their ideological disputes might endanger their power, and they were looking for means to restore at least a semblance of international unity. In the Soviet Union, Khrushchev was increasingly successful in defeating those critics who blamed his rash "de-Stalinization" for the disasters of the previous autumn, and he found Tito ready and indeed eager to call a truce of ideological argument and put the emphasis on the common defense of the one-party state against anti-Communist critics, including Djilas. In Poland, too, Russia abandoned its support of Gomulka's "Stalinist" opponents, and Gomulka reciprocated by political attacks on the "revisionists" in his party.[41] From then on, open polemics between Communist parties ceased, and consolidation proceeded rapidly, leading by August to Tito's acceptance of a formula that seemed to bind him to "solidarity" with Soviet foreign policy, short only of joining the military alliance of the Warsaw pact,[42] and by September to the first administrative measures against "revisionist" journalists in Poland. The basis of this consolidation was that Russia, in return for support of its foreign policy and for the definite rejection of "revisionist" views on fundamentals, would allow each Communist leader unquestioned authority in deciding for his own country such major questions as the scope and pace of agricultural collectivization, the forms of economic planning, and the role to be granted to workers' councils.

Yet this was clearly a diplomatic compromise rather than an ideological solution: it rested on the unwarranted assumption that these economic issues had no major ideological significance; it ignored such ideologically ominous facts as Gomulka's concessions to the Church and the continued existence in Poland of the very freedom for writers and scholars for which their Russian colleagues were still vainly striving – that is, freedom from party ideological control; it left the Yugoslav heresy about the possibility of successful "reformist" roads to socialism in advanced democratic countries unrenounced and unforgiven. Above all, it left the crucial question of the ultimate seat of doctrinal authority in abeyance – and because of that, it did not even effectively guarantee that the pledged solidarity in foreign affairs would last.

Khrushchev quickly showed himself aware of these weaknesses. He called the November conference of Communist parties in Moscow and used it not only to re-create the nucleus of an international organization, based on an inner ring of twelve ruling Communist parties, but to gain acceptance for the principles that international communism requires a single center of authority, which could only be the Soviet Union, and that ideological solidarity in a divided world requires allegiance to a military bloc. His success was marred by the renewed refusal of the

Yugoslavs to subscribe to either principle or to join the "inner ring"; but it was nonetheless considerable in that the Chinese Communists actively insisted on the solemn recognition of Soviet leadership and doctrinal authority, that the Poles accepted it, however reluctantly, and that the ghost of "polycentrism" as an officially tolerated doctrine was thus laid at last.[43] In the organizational field, the conference saw the test performance of a new, comprehensive machinery for international liaison, built up within the secretariat of the Soviet party's Central Committee — a machinery that clearly constituted the germ for the reconstruction of a Russian-centered international organization.

Outwardly, then, world communism had withstood the ideological crisis of 1955–57 remarkably well. No territory had been lost to Communist rule; a single center of authority was once again recognized by all parties except the Yugoslav; and the nucleus of a new world-wide organization had been formed. Even the losses suffered by the Western Communist parties were not disastrous in organizational terms, while those of Asia had hardly been affected at all. Yet the course of the crisis seemed to warrant the conclusion that this successful consolidation was primarily due to the growth in Soviet military and industrial power rather than to any inherent resilience shown by the ideology itself.

Underneath the restored organizational façade, the unsolved questions and the awakened doubts persisted. After the disclosures of 1956, the renewed recognition of Soviet authority was an expedient rather than a faith. After Hungary, the "proletarian" character of Communist dictatorship remained an absurdity; after the criticism of Stalin, the justification for its permanence was left unexplained. In the West the fact that communism had lost its aura as a movement embodying ideals of freedom and equality represents a far more important factor than can be measured in terms of loss in party members or votes; in Poland, "revisionist" ideas were still tolerated in fact, however loudly the regime might declaim against them; in Russia itself, the struggle of the awakened writers to maintain their integrity and independence from directives continued in ever new forms. As the instrument of a great power, international communism had recovered; as a faith, it would never be the same again.

4

1956–58: TITO'S GAMBLE ON KHRUSHCHEV

"I do not think the new conflict with the Soviet Communists has been a disappointment to our party or to our people – only to some of our leaders." The words were said with a smile, but the underlying bitterness was unmistakable. The speaker, a Yugoslav Communist with considerable international experience, clearly belonged to those who were relieved rather than surprised when the new break came. I met many of them during a visit to Yugoslavia in July 1958, and one of my most striking impressions was the frankness with which they voiced their criticism of some of the policies pursued by President Tito during the period of the abortive reconciliation with the Soviet Union, or at least during its later part – roughly from September 1956 to October 1957.

Lest this be misunderstood, let me hasten to explain that my informants were loyal Communist Party members and firm believers in a posture of "non-alignment" in the Cold War. (Indeed, I doubt whether even a non-Communist government in Yugoslavia, provided it cared to maintain the unity and independence of the country, could adopt a different posture.) None of them had ever feared that President Tito could be moved to join the Soviet military bloc, or submit once again to the discipline of a resurrected Cominform under Soviet or Soviet-Chinese leadership. None of them was in the least worried that there could be any serious opposition within the party to its renewed stand for political and ideological autonomy. What they did convey, one by one, was a sense of having emerged from a dangerous adventure which had needlessly damaged the international position of their country, and which had exposed both the party in general and each of them personally to intense strain. And, openly or by implication, they put the blame for this adventure on Tito himself.

Their criticism was not, of course, directed against the "normalization" of relations with the Soviet Union, as originally begun after Stalin's death. That, on the contrary, they recognized as a precondition for securing the advantages of a non-aligned position in world affairs. The adventure, in their view, was the later attempt to influence the trend of over-all Soviet policy — domestic as well as external — during its post-Stalin period of flux by "keeping in" with Khrushchev, backing him in his internal struggle for power, and seeking to furnish him political trumps even at the expense of Yugoslavia's immediate national interests.

It was this gamble for high stakes that for more than a year seriously divided the Yugoslav Communist leaders behind their façade of unanimity, and it was its final failure that brought the hidden tension to the surface. For nobody in Belgrade in the summer of 1958 doubted that the failure was final, or that the whole policy had been based on a miscalculation of the mainsprings of

Khrushchev's actions where questions of Soviet-bloc discipline and inter-Communist relations were concerned. Nor did anybody in Belgrade believe any longer that Khrushchev had been forced against his will to adopt this policy — either by a mysterious "Stalinist" opposition in the party Presidium, or even by Mao Tse-tung. Of course, the Yugoslavs were well aware that Peking had in the preceding months exerted its influence to increase the violence and viciousness of the new Soviet campaign against them, just as it had generally been trying to push Soviet foreign policy in the direction of over-confidence and bomb-rattling threats. But the Yuogslavs did not jump to the silly conclusion that because China, the economically and militarily dependent partner, was throwing its weight about and rocking the boat of Soviet diplomacy, it had in fact assumed the political and ideological leadership of the Communist world; nor could they believe that China suddenly, in the spring of 1958, forced a Soviet-Yugoslav break which Khrushchev himself had announced to them as impending in November 1957, during the fortieth anniversary celebrations of the Bolshevik seizure of power!

The "problem" of why Khrushchev excommunicated the Yugoslavs, which had caused so much speculation in the West, did not exercise the minds of the Yugoslav Communists at all. They had realized the failure of their courtship of Khrushchev in October 1957, when he sent them the draft of the declaration that was to be signed in Moscow and that later *was* signed by all ruling Communist parties *except* the Yugoslav. For the essence of that declaration, with its attribution of all the troubles of the world to the "imperialist warmongers," its emphasis on the need to strengthen the Warsaw pact, and its declaration of war on ideological "revisionism," was that nobody could be a good Communist who did not join the Soviet military bloc and accept the Soviet concept of ideological orthodoxy.

It was, in fact, at the very moment when Khrushchev, with the elimination of Marshal Zhukov from the army leadership and the party Presidium, finally achieved complete and undisputed dictatorial power at home that the Yugoslavs had to abandon the illusion of their influence on him. Just when the horse they had backed all along had won the race, they discovered that they would not be paid off after all! Or perhaps I should say that Tito, Rankovic, and a few other leaders discovered it, for many other Yugoslav Communists had suspected it long before. Because of that, the final failure of the gamble for the first time seriously impaired – though it did not, of course, destroy – Tito's personal authority within his party. This has had a number of curious consequences. The political police have increased the harassment of critics and suspected critics – and I do not mean pro-Soviet critics – *after* the break with Russia. Further, officials have been extremely reticent about the secret history of the period of *rapprochement*, even though Khrushchev has deliberately taunted the Yugoslavs by "disclosing" selected half-truths in his speeches.[1] Finally, the official reticence has been partly nullified by the willingness of responsible critics to hint at vital, hitherto undisclosed facts – facts that allow, I believe, a tentative reconstruction of that secret history, and in particular of the role that the Yugoslav attitude to Hungary – before, during, and after the revolution – played in it.

YUGOSLAVIA AND "DE-STALINIZATION"

In his 1958 speech in Sofia,[2] Khrushchev claimed that at no time had he placed all the blame for Stalin's 1948 break with Yugoslavia on Russia's account: he had always told the Yugoslav leaders that, in his view, both sides had made mistakes, but they had not dared to pass this on to their party. The facts behind this claim are intriguing. It appears that Khrushchev's 1955 visit to Belgrade was preceded by a preparatory correspondence between the Soviet and Yugoslav Central Committees, extending over several months, and that in the course of these exchanges Khrushchev indeed proposed that each side should accept part of the responsibility for the past conflict; the Russians would blame their share on Beria, and the Yugoslavs should blame theirs on Djilas (who by then had already been expelled from the party). This brilliant proposal was not, of course, kept secret by Tito; it was put before a meeting of the Yugoslav Central Committee late in 1954, and was turned down at his own suggestion. (As one critic put it, "Tito would not be such a fool as to give Djilas all the credit for the struggle for national independence.") Tito's famous scowl when Khrushchev publicly dished out the Beria story on arrival at Belgrade airport was thus due to a realization that Khrushchev intended to stick to a formula that Tito had already rejected. No agreement seems to have been reached on this point during the Belgrade discussions, which was one of the reasons why the joint declaration that finally emerged was signed on behalf of the governments rather than the parties; and when Khrushchev defended his action against Molotov's criticism before the Soviet Central Committee on his return, he still maintained internally – as he later stated publicly – that the first Cominform resolution of 1948 which excommunicated the Yugoslav party was "basically correct." [3]

Nevertheless, the Yugoslavs had been highly satisfied with the result of that visit. By confining the first stage of the public *rapprochement* to the sphere of state relations, they had succeeded in establishing their right to sovereign equality and independence before accepting party ties. The fact of the visit and of their treatment as brother-Marxists had the moral effect of a unilateral admission of Stalin's fault, whatever the formula; and the Soviet acceptance of the right of each country to determine its own road to socialism, though it might mean less in Khrushchev's mind than in Tito's, was bound to encourage all those Communists in the satellite countries who wished to get out of the Stalinist mire and to learn from the Yugoslav example, whether the Russians liked it or not. Yet the very extent of the new possibilities opened by their success brought to the Yugoslavs a new problem.

Even before Khrushchev's visit to Belgrade, there had been hopeful stirrings among the surviving victims of Stalin's "anti-Titoist" purges in Eastern Europe because of the beginning devaluation of Stalin, the loosening of Soviet police supervision in the satellites, and the first moves toward a normalization of Soviet-Yugoslav relations. Watching these developments with keen interest, the Yugoslavs felt that nowhere were they more promising than in neighboring Hungary. There, a surviving advocate of a policy of internal autonomy and popular reform, Imre Nagy, had actually come with Soviet consent to hold office as Prime Minister – though not power as party leader – since the summer of 1953, and had followed the Yugoslav example in permitting the peasants to leave the collective farms. And when by the winter of 1954–55 the counter-offensive of the old Stalinist leadership around Rakosi led to bitter disputes in the Hungarian Central Committee, the Yugoslavs were optimistic about the outcome and about Nagy's eventual chances of winning a broader mass basis for an independent Communist regime through further reforms. Even when Nagy was overthrown by the "old guard" in March 1955, apparently as a by-product of Malenkov's fall and the campaign for the primacy of heavy industry in Russia, the Yugoslavs were inclined to regard this as a merely temporary setback to the forces of progress, just as Nagy himself continued to prepare memoranda defending his policy for the Hungarian Central Committee and the Soviet leaders.[4]

Nor was Yugoslav interest in developments among the Hungarian Communists purely ideological. For years, the Yugoslavs' hard-won independence had been perilously close to isolation; and while Russia's new emphasis on peaceful co-existence encouraged them to proclaim the ambitious goal of an ultimate dissolution of the two hostile military blocs in world affairs, their practical diplomacy patiently pursued the more modest aim of extending the area of bloc-free nations, and preferably creating a belt of neutral territory in their neighborhood. For that reason, Khrushchev's agreement to sign at last the "state treaty" which guaranteed the withdrawal of both Russia and the Western powers from a neutral Austria was viewed by the Yugoslavs as a vital proof of his good will, far outweighing any awkward remnants of doctrinaire rigidity he might show. It owed its special importance in their minds to the hope that eventually an independent Communist Hungary might also become neutral with Russian consent. We know today, from Imre Nagy's papers, that by the beginning of 1956 he, too, had committed himself to the vision of close Yugoslav-Hungaro-Austrian co-operation on the basis of neutrality; [5] and though by that time he had been expelled from Rakosi's party (and the fact that he held these views and communicated them to the Yugoslavs later figured in his indictment for treason), the Rakosi regime was so obviously unstable that the Yugoslavs could well count on his eventual comeback. The rehabilitation of Laszlo Rajk – executed in 1949 for alleged treasonable co-operation with Yugoslavia – and the dropping of Rakosi had been the only specific changes in satellite policy urged by Tito on Khrushchev from the start, and he obtained the former in April 1956 – after the disavowal of Stalin at the Soviet party congress – and the latter in July of the same year, after his own triumphant journey through Russia.

Yet Khrushchev, in fact, never intended to permit Hungarian neutrality, or even full political autonomy in internal affairs. When he finally sacrificed Rakosi because the pressure had become too strong and the discredit brought on the regime by Rakosi's known share in Stalin's crimes too intolerable, he appointed as successor not Nagy but Enroe Geroe, who had been Rakosi's closest associate throughout. By then, the Poznan rising and the outburst of free discussion in both Poland and Hungary had warned Khrushchev that further "de-Stalinization" might easily go far beyond his intentions. Worried about Yugoslav moral backing for "anti-Stalinists" in the satellite countries, Khrushchev now faced Tito with a demand that he should switch his support to Geroe in the interest of stability: otherwise, his own new course in Russia might be in danger from "Stalinist reaction." At that time, such a danger was not wholly fictitious: the pro-Stalin riots in Georgia which followed circulation of the "secret speech" in the spring had not been confined to Tiflis, and some of the demonstrators had called for Molotov, then still a member of the party Presidium and a first deputy premier of the Soviet Union.

This, then, was the decision confronting Tito: whether to continue backing his anti-Stalinist friends in the satellites and above all in Hungary, at the risk of incurring Khrushchev's displeasure and possibly weakening the "progressive" elements in the Soviet party Presidium — or whether to abandon his real friends in order to keep Khrushchev's confidence and perhaps help keep him in power. Some might have viewed it as a decision between ideological and moral principle and cautious opportunism; from another angle, it implied a choice between the regional interests of an independent Yugoslavia, which had inspired the backing of Nagy, and the dream of influencing Soviet policy from outside. In fact, Tito chose Khrushchev and invited Geroe to Yugoslavia — though he gained for Nagy readmission to the party as a consolation prize. The choice was made against the advice of many of his closest colleagues, and of all the Yugoslavs most intimately concerned with Hungarian affairs. That was the moment when the adventure began.

TWO TENDENCIES AMONG THE YUGOSLAV COMMUNISTS

At this point, a word must be said about the alignment within the Yugoslav leadership. The one group that wholeheartedly backed Tito's bid for Khrushchev's friendship were those conservative party bureaucrats who had long been uneasy about Yugoslavia's own "unorthodox" reforms, especially since Djilas's evolution had shown how easily these reforms, if pursued consistently, might become a threat to the party's power. As good Yugoslav patriots, these people were as determined as Tito to defend their country's independence against all comers; but because they hoped that better relations with Russia would stop the dangerous drift toward "liberalization" at home, they were only too willing to believe that these better relations could be secured without danger to their independence, simply by talking less about ideological differences. This group was dominant in the Serbian Central Committee; it also included the leading Serb among Tito's Politburo colleagues – Aleksandar Rankovic, creator of the political police and controller of the party's organization and personnel. It was, in fact, from about this time that Rankovic came forward as Tito's effective deputy in all party matters, and began to be discreetly boosted as his designated successor.

Conversely, the leaders opposed to concessions to Khrushchev, and particularly to dealings with Geroe, were the same who had shown most zeal in promoting Yugoslavia's internal reforms, from the workers' councils to the dissolution of Soviet-style *kolkhozes*, and from the planned market economy to the growth of organs of decentralized self-government. These people did not belittle the importance of the process of social change that had started in post-Stalinist Russia, but they refused to regard it as dependent primarily on Khrushchev's influence, or to believe that Yugoslav efforts to support him could have a decisive effect on the broad trend of Russian development. In their view, Yugoslavia could contribute most to that trend by continuing her own experiment and seeking to win increased diplomatic elbow-room by support for like-minded elements in neighboring countries.

Not surprisingly, this group had its main strength among the Slovenian and Croatian leadership – that is, in the most advanced parts of the country. To them, the vision of closer co-operation with a neutral Hungary and Austria was both historically plausible and politically welcome as a recipe for diluting the retrograde "Balkanic" influences within Yugoslavia, while preserving the unity of the Yugoslav nation. They also enjoyed the warm support of all those younger elements in the party who feared that closer relations with Russia would produce the very thing that the conservative disciplinarians hoped for — an end to reform and experiment, a tightening of control from above, an attempt to shut the windows and to restore the stuffy climate of an orthodoxy they had outgrown during the years when Yugoslavia first discovered the non-Communist world.

Between these groups, the aging leader was apparently swayed by motives all his own. There is no reason to assume that he then shared the preoccupations of the petty bureaucrats, their fear of further reforms and dangerous ideas; but neither was he much concerned to spread the ideology of "Titoism" within a limited regional framework. For years, he had become accustomed to bestride the world stage; now the evolution of post-Stalinist Russia seemed to present him with the chance of a new "historic role." Perhaps we in the West have come to take Marshal Tito too much for granted as a national leader, and to underestimate the emotional importance of his long years as a professional international revolutionary. However genuinely and successfully he filled his national role, the separation from the comrades of his youth must have been a severe psychological strain — and the chance to return into that brotherhood, not defeated and contrite but proudly triumphant, an immense temptation. During his Russian journey in the summer of 1956, when enthusiastic crowds hailed him at every station as the symbol of their own new hopes, that temptation assumed flesh and blood, became vivid, exciting experience. Russia, and with

Russia the whole Communist world, seemed to lie at his feet, willing to follow his road if only he was patient and careful. So when Khrushchev, having failed to obtain Tito's return to the Soviet bloc, sent to the satellite parties a circular warning them against Yugoslav heretical influences,[6] and then offered reconciliation if Tito would shake hands with Geroe, how could he refuse?

TITO AND THE HUNGARIAN UPRISING

Before the Hungarian party delegation under Geroe came to Yugoslavia, Vlajko Begovic, a member of the Yugoslav Central Committee, had warned in a long report from Budapest that Geroe enjoyed no authority and that events were moving toward a revolution.[7] While the visit was in progress, Gomulka assumed power in Poland and defied Khrushchev's attempt to intervene; the news was enthusiastically received in Hungary. The delegation itself turned out to be divided: Kadar, once a victim of Rakosi and now a member of the Hungarian Politburo, was clearly in favor of further changes,[8] but Geroe continued to defend his record; and the Yugoslavs, faithful to their agreement with Khrushchev, "did not intervene in Hungarian party affairs." Directly on his return from Yugoslavia, Geroe made the provocative broadcast that turned a peaceful students' demonstration into a revolt, and during the following night asked for the intervention of Soviet troops, which turned the revolt into a rising supported by the bulk of the Hungarian armed forces.

The Yugoslav leaders were naturally shocked by this "Stalinist" behavior of their supposed protégé, Geroe, and extremely worried about the consequences. When, after a few days, the success of the rising led to the replacement of Geroe by Kadar with Soviet consent, and Nagy took over the government in fact as well as in name, they hoped — as did the Soviet representatives on the spot — that Kadar and Nagy would succeed in stabilizing the situation under a reformed Communist regime.[9] But it quickly became clear that the revolutionary movement had gone beyond that stage, that the people and the armed forces were calling for a revival of democratic political parties, a withdrawal of all Soviet troops, and immediate neutrality, and that Nagy was willing to meet these demands. At that point the Soviets lost confidence in Nagy — and so did Tito.

The motives of that decision have been obscured by a flood of lies about the alleged danger of "Fascists" and "counter-revolutionaries" getting control of the movement — a fiction that Tito still maintained in his Pula speech.[10] The more honest Yugoslav spokesmen have always said that the crucial argument for the second Soviet intervention was one of power politics rather than ideology. The Soviet leaders had, in fact, never intended to allow a Communist Hungary to leave the Warsaw pact; they could not possibly permit a non-Communist Hungary to do so in an atmosphere of violent rebellion against Soviet control, and at the moment of the international crisis produced by the Suez expedition. In Soviet language, which the Yugoslavs understood only too well, the term "counter-revolutionary" simply expressed the fact that the movement was no longer in Communist hands and the fear that a new democratic government would in fact assume a pro-Western orientation, whatever its formal neutrality. What was at stake, from the Soviet point of view, was the loss of an important territory to their potential enemies, without compensation and with incalculable repercussions on other members of their bloc, at a moment of high international tension. To prevent that, they were prepared to use force.

The Yugoslav leaders were thrown into a panic. They seriously feared an East-West clash on their borders; most of them also feared that anti-Communist revolution might spread to engulf their own regime. For a day or two, some of them considered the idea of marching in before the Russians did, to ensure both the survival of communism and "real" neutrality; at any rate, Yugoslav diplomats sounded Nagy's advisers on how they would react to such a move, but nothing came of it. Instead, there is now evidence that before their decisive second intervention, the Soviet leaders informed and consulted the Yugoslavs, and that Tito, while disagreeing on some points with the Soviet analysis, gave his advance consent to the crushing of the Hungarian revolution.

This advance consultation is the background to the charge, made in the Kadar government's reply [11] to the Yugoslav protest against Imre Nagy's execution, that "during the night of November 3–4, when the responsible Yugoslav authorities, *on the basis of confidential information received by them,* had learned that at dawn on November 4 the revolutionary worker-peasant government and the Soviet troops would, with joint forces, launch a counter-attack to crush the counter-revolution, Minister Soldatic telephoned the leaders of the Imre Nagy group and, with reference to the expressed request of Belgrade, appealed to them to avail themselves at once of the right of asylum" [my italics]. The reference to confidential information clearly implies something more official than the reports about the approach of returning Soviet forces which were generally known in the Hungarian capital during its last days of freedom.

I was first told about this consultation — by a critical

Yugoslav Communist — two weeks before the above hint was published by the Hungarians. According to my informant, it took the form of a flying visit by Khrushchev (straight from Moscow) and Mikoyan to Tito at Brioni Island on one of the first days of November; the Soviet leaders had by then made their decision, but were anxious to obtain Yugoslav political support for their action in order to ease Kadar's future work in rebuilding the regime, and to contain anticipated reactions in Poland and other satellites. I am not certain that the details about the flying visit can easily be reconciled with what is otherwise known about Khrushchev's and Mikoyan's timetable in those crowded days,[12] but I am satisfied that Yugoslav advance agreement was solicited in *some* form, and was obtained. Apart from the hint in the Hungarian note, this is confirmed by the immediate Yugoslav reaction to the second Soviet intervention: it was one of complete approval. This was shown in a circular sent out by the Yugoslav Central Committee on November 5; in the attitude taken, clearly on instruction from home, by the Yugoslav observer at the Asian Socialist conference then meeting at Rangoon; in the behavior of the Yugoslav chief delegate to the United Nations, who turned his back when Anna Kethly, the Hungarian Socialist leader, was introduced to him; and not least in the grossly misleading confidential information sent at the time by Tito to Pandit Nehru, which was the principal basis for the unsympathetic attitude initially taken by the Indian leader toward the revolt of the Hungarian people.

It would be unjust to accuse Tito and his team of having betrayed the cause of Hungarian democracy. They are Communists, not democrats, and they cannot betray principles which they have never professed. But they did betray their own dream of a neutral, progressive Hungary when it could no longer be reconciled with the preservation of Communist Party rule, and they sided with Kadar against Nagy, who clung to the dream. As a last service, they tried to save him by granting him temporary asylum in the Yugoslav Embassy, but they were not strong enough. If the Yugoslavs were ever deceived by the Kadar government's promise of safe-conduct for those who would leave the building, their envoy at least must have learned the truth at the last minute. For the Hungarian officer who headed the escort for Nagy – he is now a refugee abroad – reported to him with the words: "Mr. Prime Minister, it's not home we are going"; and that was still before Nagy boarded the fateful bus and took leave of his Yugoslav friends.

THE INTERNATIONAL DEBATE ON HUNGARY

The critical reaction of the Yugoslav Communist rank and file to the Soviet intervention in Hungary proved unexpectedly strong. For the first time, Tito had publicly to admit a mistake. Within a week of the final crushing of the revolution by Soviet tanks, he conceded in his Pula speech that he had been unwise to receive Geroe, who had proved himself an unrepentant Stalinist and had brought about the Hungarian tragedy by his incompetent and provocative behavior.[13] In a further circular he sought to explain the nature of the pressure from Khrushchev to which he had yielded in September. Moreover, he publicly emphasized the issue on which he now disagreed with the official Soviet view – that the rising had started as a genuine working-class movement with the active participation of many good Communists, and had only come under the leadership of the "reactionary elements" later on.[14] A month later, Edvard Kardelj, the leading idealogist of the party and the architect of many of its anti-Stalinist reforms, who had been silent since the September agreement to support Geroe, went even further in a speech to the Federal Assembly.[15] He argued that the Hungarian revolution had shown how completely estranged from the working class a monopolistic party could become by merging with the state machine and relying on its power — regardless of whether or not it called itself Communist and claimed to be the vanguard of that class; and he explicitly drew the conclusion that the Yugoslav Communists should show more boldness than hitherto in detaching themselves from the state machine and relying chiefly on their influence in the organs of self-government. But even now neither Tito nor Kardelj could condemn the second and decisive Soviet intervention; the formula adopted by them was that it *might* prove historically justified *if* it led to a better new start of the Communist regime.

Meanwhile, Khrushchev had really suffered a temporary weakening of his domestic position, owing not to Tito's action, but to the actions of the Polish and Hungarian peoples, who were subject to no such subtle tactical calculations. Even though the Soviet leaders now shared Tito's contempt for Geroe's incompetence, they could not swallow his view of the total bankruptcy of the Hungarian Stalinist regime and the revolutionary character of the rising; the speeches of Tito and particularly Kardelj gave rise to bitter polemics in the Soviet and international Communist press.[16] The Yugoslavs answered back for a time, most outspoken when Bulganin hinted — at the beginning of April 1957 — at a possible trial of Imre Nagy in which they would be compromised. But the knowledge of the Yugoslav leaders that they had approved the second and decisive Soviet intervention in advance caused them to pull their punches. Indeed, even in the summer of 1958, when I asked whether they still considered the second intervention as "historically justified" in the light of subsequent development, including the execution of Nagy, I could not get a single Yugoslav spokesman, whether government official or Central Committee member, to answer on the record with a clear No.

For, while the first after-effect of the Hungarian tragedy within the Yugoslav party had been to make Tito yield somewhat to the indignation of the rank and file, second thoughts soon made him veer in a different direction. Clearly, the *élan* of the forces of reform within the satellite countries had been broken by the frightful object lesson of Hungary, and Yugoslavia's own independent ideological influence would henceforth be limited by the ambiguity of her position at the critical moment. In Russia herself, Stalinist reaction seemed once again in the ascendant, and if it finally triumphed all the gains of the post-Stalin "thaw" might be lost. Thus, the one overriding task, after Hungary even more than before, seemed to be to support Khrushchev against the "Stalinists." At the end of April 1957, Tito sent him a personal message offering a renewal of the ideological truce, which was gladly accepted; the press polemics stopped abruptly, and the reformers within the Yugoslav leadership fell silent once again.

Khrushchev, however, did not fail to spot the weakness underlying the move. In a speech in a Prague factory, shortly after his triumph over Malenkov, Molotov, and Kaganovich, he talked of the Yugoslavs in a tone of condescension verging on friendly contempt: he felt sure that the remaining differences would be overcome by frank talk, as he had no objection to the Yugoslavs' retaining their own peculiar institutions such as workers' councils — but he would no longer tolerate their setting themselves up as a rival international model.[17] Frank talks subsequently took place in Bucharest at the beginning of August — and they marked the closest point of the *rapprochement*.

BEFORE THE MOSCOW CONFERENCE

By that time, Khrushchev was fully embarked on plans for some new form of organized co-operation among at least the ruling Communist parties, which was to consolidate once again the unity of the Soviet bloc and to help restore the international authority of its leading power; and he wanted to make sure that the Yugoslavs, despite their bitter memories of the Cominform, would help rather than hinder the new project. The Bucharest meeting took place in great secrecy, and the final communiqué was ambiguous, talking, on one side, of obstacles to complete agreement which were still to be overcome, but, on the other, of the particular importance both sides attached to "the strengthening, in all its aspects, of the unity and fraternal co-operation of the Communist and Workers' parties of the peoples of all socialist countries." [18] Since the break, Khrushchev has claimed that at this meeting Tito agreed to come to the fortieth anniversary celebrations in Moscow in November and to sign a joint declaration of principles of the ruling Communist parties; [19] while the Yugoslavs say they left under the impression of having convinced Khrushchev that they could be more useful to the cause of peace by staying, contrary to his original wish, outside the Soviet bloc. The two versions are not really in conflict, and each of them contains some truth — but hardly the whole truth.

The question of Yugoslavia's joining the Soviet camp in the military sense, by becoming a member of the Warsaw pact, was not a major subject of discussion at the meeting. Yugoslavia's unwillingness to do so was, of course, a permanent sore point with Khrushchev, and he probably raised it again. But when they declined, he had no need to insist in the light of two considerations: their growing willingness to be "useful to the cause of peace" by supporting Soviet foreign policy all along the line — including, evidently, the promise of an early recognition of the East German government; and their agreement to accept much closer party ties than before.

In fact, the talks were held strictly on a party level, with the international secretaries of both parties present and without any government ministers or officials; and the principal subject was the forthcoming Moscow conference of all the Communist parties of the world, and the need to issue a joint declaration of principles. If the Yugoslavs agreed to that, they would automatically have to abandon the attitude, first defined by Kardelj in his Oslo speech in 1954, that Eastern Communist and Western "reformist" parties were both making valuable contributions to the cause of socialism, with its corollary that the Soviet bloc had no monopoly of Socialist progress; and they would contribute to rebuilding an international Communist authority whose influence would eventually compel them to rejoin the military bloc as well. That was at least how Khrushchev saw it. Yet Tito did not see it that way; and he agreed to attend the Moscow celebrations and to help prepare a joint declaration of principles without fully realizing the inevitable consequences of such a move.

For the Yugoslav leader was now back in the same mood as a year previously, before the Hungarian revolution; and he envisaged the forthcoming Moscow celebrations as the second act to his triumphant tour of Russia – again with Khrushchev as his guide, but this time with the whole elite of international communism, including Mao Tse-tung, welcoming him back to the fold and listening to his words. The brilliance of the prospect somehow blinded the 65-year-old man to the change in the situation brought about by the Hungarian tragedy, the impending end of the Russian succession crisis, the weakening of his own position, and the hardening of Khrushchev's outlook. Once again, as at the time of his visit to Yalta and his agreement to back Geroe, he was willing to stake the future of Yugoslavia on the chance of influencing Khrushchev; and once again he overruled the voices of caution, of which there were many.

During the weeks that followed, Yugoslav non-alignment rapidly disappeared in all but the formal sense. In September, during Gomulka's visit, Tito publicly subscribed to the Soviet formula of "proletarian internationalism" as a guide to foreign policy, and even gave his own interpretation of the "leading role of the Soviet Union" – in a sense that would recognize its special responsibility for the common cause without impairing the right of each Communist state to its sovereign equality and independence.[20] Soon afterwards, recognition of the East German government followed – a unique act among "non-aligned" states.[21] There remained only one meaning to the refusal to join the Soviet "camp," but that an important one: so long as Yugoslavia was not tied by a higher discipline, its support of Soviet foreign policy, however, complete, remained conditional – it could still be withdrawn if Khrushchev tried to interfere with Yugoslav independence or relapsed into a policy of aggressive threats.

It was the Russian attempt to eliminate that last but vital reservation which brought the turning-point. Yugoslavia's new policy had increasingly isolated her from the West: her recognition of Eastern Germany had led to a break in relations with Bonn [22] and to public attacks in the United States, while the new heavy sentence on Djilas and the trial of prewar trade union leaders had alienated the sympathy of Western democratic Socialists. In that situation, Khrushchev clearly believed that the time had come to increase the pressure. Suggestions for military arrangements, made through diplomatic channels and through Marshal Zhukov during his visit,[23] became more importunate. There were attempts to interfere in party matters as well: the new Yugoslav program promised for the next party congress, which was to codify the specific outlook of Yugoslav communism – including, inevitably, its differences from the Soviet variety – had been all but shelved after the Bucharest meeting so as to avoid new disagreements; but now the Soviets asked to see the draft so that they might suggest amendments even before it reached the Yugoslav party members! The decisive moment came when the Soviet draft for the declaration of principles to be signed by the ruling Communist parties in Moscow arrived in Belgrade. For though Khrushchev has told the truth in that this draft did not yet contain the formula recognizing Soviet leadership (that was only put in later on Mao's suggestion), it was a harsh and uncompromising Cold War document, and clearly faced the Yugoslavs with the implicit choice of either unconditionally joining the Warsaw pact or being attacked as "revisionists" and expelled from the Communist family.

THE RELUCTANT HERETIC

When Tito saw that draft, he knew at last that the gamble on his influence with Khrushchev had been lost. The dream of his triumphant return to the Communist world general staff was ended, and his own visit to the Moscow celebrations had to be called off. His deputies, Kardelj and Rankovic, had to make it clear from the start that they would not sign the declaration, and they were promptly treated in Moscow as outcasts, despite their readiness to sign the almost equally absurd "Peace Manifesto" as a gesture of good will; and when Khrushchev saw them at last, he clearly warned them that they would be attacked. After that, the Yugoslavs had to prepare for the new break – and the first measure of preparation consisted precisely in getting the programmatic codification of their own theories ready for their party congress.

Even then, Tito still seems to have entertained the hope that the inevitable disagreement could be contained in the forms of a fraternal discussion among comrades. After the draft had been published and circulated to all Communist parties in February 1958, and the opening blasts of Soviet criticism had been received by correspondence between the Central Committees, he had some amendments adopted so as to mitigate those criticisms of Soviet "hegemonism" and of the Warsaw pact at which the Russians seemed to take particular offense. Given these concessions, Tito clearly expected that those East European leaders who wished to preserve some degree of internal independence from Moscow – and among them he included not only Gomulka but Kadar – might, in the interest of their own autonomy, prevail on Khrushchev to avoid an outright break. At the end of March, Kadar's wish for an invitation to Yugoslavia – uttered long ago in a very different situation – was suddenly fulfilled, and the need for a joint stand for the autonomous rights of all Communist parties, whatever their theoretical differences, was broached to him.[24] Kadar's reaction seemed friendly enough; but when Khrushchev came to Hungary immediately after Kadar's return, he concluded from Kadar's report that Tito was trying to form an "autonomist" bloc with Hungary and Poland. He reacted not only by sanctioning the public attack on the Yugoslav program, but by demanding from all the satellites what amounted to an immediate break of party relations with the Yugoslavs – a decision not to send fraternal delegates to the Yugoslav congress.[25] It was Kadar's immediate compliance and Gomulka's hesitation which accounted for the lavish praise of the former and the thinly veiled insults against the latter (as well as against Tito) in the somewhat high-spirited speech Khrushchev made on his return to Moscow.[26]

But even apart from these last-minute incidents, it was only logical that Khrushchev, who viewed the Yugoslav program as a counter-document to his own twelve-party "declaration of principles," would take it as the occasion for an all-out attack and final excommunication. For the Yugoslav document justified in a programmatic form the right of an independent Communist state to remain neutral between the military blocs, by denying, in an elaborate analysis of the contemporary social scene, the Soviet bloc's claim to a monopoly of Socialist progress. But if these arguments were valid for Yugoslavia, they were equally valid for any and every satellite; if a good Communist could hold these views, it followed that a good Communist was entitled to take any member country out of the Warsaw pact and declare it neutral. For their own sake, the Yugoslav Communists had finally had to proclaim in a general form the right to neutrality which they had failed to support at the critical moment in Hungary. The Soviets showed their understanding of what was at stake by demonstrating that the right to neutrality did not exist in the Communist world: they excommunicated the Yugoslavs – and they executed Imre Nagy.[27]

THE MORNING AFTER

This end of the adventure did not solve the long-standing disagreements among the Yugoslav leaders but made it more difficult to hide them. The critics were naturally inclined to say, "I told you so." The conservative bureaucrats, just as naturally, sought to defend their positions by tightening up discipline within the party and by police measures against those critics who had been expelled from it in 1954 because they refused to support the wholesale condemnation of Djilas. The resulting atmosphere can be gauged in an off-the-record outburst of one member of the top party leadership when asked by a Western journalist whether he regarded the execution of Nagy as a sign of strength or of weakness on the part of the Soviet government. "It was a sign of fear," he replied, "just as our treatment of Djilas was a sign of fear."

The speaker was very far indeed from sharing Djilas's views about the need for an opposition party; he was merely utterly fed up with the harm done to his country and party by the stupid meddling of the political police with party affairs. On no previous visit had I heard party members complain about the activities of the police; this time it happened again and again. The reason was not, so far as I can judge, that the police had become more powerful, but that they were trying to become more active in many petty ways because they felt threatened. After the break with Russia there were quite a number of cases of prolonged interrogations of loyal party members, ranging from their personal relations with expelled critics to questions concerning their reservations during the height of the Tito-Khrushchev flirtation; there was systematic police interference with the attempts of party leaders in good standing to bring some of the expelled critics back into the party; and there followed a real orgy of petty harassment against the expelled men themselves. Most serious of all was the withdrawal of prison privileges from Djilas – which also occurred *after* the break.

Part of the political importance of all this pettiness was that the blame for it was widely attributed, not indeed to Tito, who was believed to get very little information on these matters, but to Rankovic. Though he had abandoned direct control of the political police years ago, he was generally regarded as its ultimate political chief and protector; and while even critics who know him well described him as honest and straightforward and did not believe that he would personally stoop to inspire acts of vindictiveness against his old comrades, they claimed that his outlook was essentially rigid and narrow and that he was covering the stupidities of his subordinates in the belief that he was shielding the regime from the spreading of "hostile influences." But Rankovic's power within the party has steadily grown in recent years; and while there is no formal basis for the general assumption that he is Tito's designated successor, it finds indirect confirmation not only in the unofficial talk of official spokesmen, but in the changes made in the party secretariat after the 1958 congress, when its work was subdivided into a number of commissions: Rankovic was put in charge of the political commission and thus made effective head of the secretariat in Tito's absence, while Kardelj, though formally still a member of the secretariat, got no commission and began to concentrate more and more on running the administration and developing the organs of self-government.

Clearly, the intended division of labor was that Kardelj, the ideologue, should decentralize the administration, while Rankovic, the disciplinarian, would re-centralize the party, whose power remains ultimately decisive. In practice, however, things do not seem to work out wholly in accordance with this classical Leninist recipe. On one side, the tasks of the various self-government organs, from workers' councils through local communes and producers' councils to the parliaments of the national republics, are now so varied that it is practically impossible for the party leadership to give its members in these various organs concrete directives on more than the broadest issues; on the other hand, decisions must be taken in the light of the local situation, and that means – even with party members – often in the light of local and regional interests. The party regime does not remain untouched by the growth of a decentralized society; and that growth, stimulated by the economic successes of 1957, by the new tax concessions then granted to the more advanced factories and regions, and by certain efforts to revive the trade unions, could be expected to continue even more vigorously now that its underlying principles had been sanctioned in the new party program.

This whole evolution tends to limit the authority of the top leadership, and that limitation may also prove effective in the question of Tito's succession. It is not a question of personal rivalry: Kardelj, the obvious alternative to Rankovic within the present inner ring, would from all accounts be perfectly content to continue as No. 2 man after Tito's death — which may anyhow still be a long way off. The trouble comes from below: the idea of Rankovic as policy-making leader does not seem to catch on with the party cadres, at any rate not outside Serbia. He is not regarded as a unifying national figure; he has not lost the odor of the police; and he represents a conservative outlook whose supporters among the party rank and file were rather declining in numbers by 1958. And while formerly the fact of Tito's personal confidence could easily have silenced all these doubts, Tito's own authority within the party was, after the unhappy adventure with Khrushchev, no longer as absolute as it used to be: it was still amply sufficient for the "old man" to carry on, but he seemed no longer strong enough to commit the party's future by picking his own successor.

The future belongs to the new postwar generation, which for the first time appeared in numbers at the 1958 party congress; and that generation seems in Communist Yugoslavia as much less ideologically-minded than their elders as are their counterparts in Western Europe. Having grown up during the years of conflict with Russia and gradual relaxation at home, most of them seem to have felt as uncomfortable during the pro-Soviet episode as the older reformers, but — at least partly — for different reasons: their criticism attacks the whole illusion of "Yugocentrism," of trying to influence world history from their small and still comparatively poor country; and while they strongly disapprove of a policy that risked the loss of Western confidence and aid in an attempt to wrestle for the soul of Khrushchev, they do not see much sense either in losing Soviet aid because of an ideological program outlining alternative roads to socialism. They would like to follow their own road, to concentrate on cultivating their own garden, without permitting anybody to interfere but also without pursuing a grandiose dream of Yugoslavia's international mission. They believe that a cautious and modest neutrality that does not unfold any flags but seeks friends wherever possible is what best befits a small Balkan nation, and that a slow but steady expansion of internal freedom will be best for a multi-national country with a bitter history of civil war and revolution. And eventually they will have their way.

5

THE DISTINCTIVE CHARACTER OF CHINESE COMMUNISM

When in 1949 the Chinese Communists established their rule over the whole of mainland China, they changed not only the world-wide relation of forces between the Communist "camp" and its opponents; they also transformed the nature of that camp itself. For the new state they had created was not merely one more satellite of Stalin's Russia, but an independent power born out of an independent revolution; and its founders were conscious of owing their victory chiefly to their own efforts and wholly to their own decisions – decisions taken, sometimes against Stalin's advice, by the first Communist leader who had, in Stalin's reign, won control of his party without Stalin's investiture: Mao Tse-tung.

Henceforth there existed two Communist Great Powers. For though only the Soviet Union was a world power, Communist China soon established herself as a great regional power in Asia. Her intervention in the Korean War demonstrated quickly how formidable a military force the new dictatorship had built up in a country that had for decades been helpless in the grip of foreign aggression and civil strife. Her appearance at the Geneva conference of 1954 showed that, whether diplomatically recognized or not, Peking's delegates could confront the representatives of other Great Powers as equals when Asian affairs had to be settled, and did in fact exert a major influence on the terms of the Indochina armistice. By state visits to neutral Asian countries and by Chou En-lai's performance at the Bandung conference in 1955, the Chinese Communists achieved a considerable impact on the public opinion, and even on the foreign policy, of the emerging "Third World" of ex-colonial nations. Finally, when Khrushchev's overthrow of the Stalin idol was followed by a grave crisis of the Soviet's European empire, by popular revolt in Hungary and by the popularly backed change in the leadership of the Polish Communist regime, an astonished world watched how the Chinese Communist leaders during 1956–57 threw their intact authority into the scales to preserve the cohesion of the Communist bloc and world movement under Soviet leadership – the first effective intervention of China in the history of modern Europe. Poor and backward China, so obviously dependent on Russian military and economic aid, had seemingly demonstrated to its powerful protectors in the Kremlin that they in turn had become dependent on Chinese ideological support.

It was natural that so impressive a display of Chinese independence should give rise to Western speculations about the possibility of eventual conflict between the two main Communist powers; and these speculations increased interest in the accumulating evidence that the Chinese Communists under Mao's leadership had a way of solving their problems that differed persistently from the Russian Bolshevik model. Moreover, the Chinese Communists themselves had increasingly come to emphasize these differences in their strategy for conquering power, in their style of inner-party work, and in their methods for "building socialism," as achievements due to Mao Tse-tung's creative adaptation of "Marxism-Leninism" to the conditions of an underdeveloped, semi-colonial Asian country; and they had also proclaimed the Chinese road as the appropriate model for the Communists of other parts of the underdeveloped world.[1] Hence when clear evidence of Sino-Soviet disagreements – both over questions of foreign and military policy and over the new Chinese "people's communes" – began to reach the West during 1958 and 1959, the question naturally arose as to what extent these disagreements reflected not only differences of national interest or personal and national rivalries for leadership within the Communist bloc and world movement, but also differences of ideological emphasis and inner-party style rooted in the different histories and conditions of development of the Soviet and Chinese Communist parties.

IS THERE A "MAOIST" IDEOLOGY? *

By now, this question ought to have been settled by events. For as the half-hidden Sino-Soviet disagreements of 1958 and 1959 have grown into open, full-scale conflict, both sides have formulated their positions on each disputed issue in ideological terms, until finally two complete rival systems of interpretation of the Marxist-Leninist doctrine have come to be developed by Moscow and Peking.[2] This does not, of course, prove that the historic differences

* The next two sections do not appear in the German edition of this work.

between the outlook and approach of the two ruling Communist parties, and even the tendency to erect them into rival models for the revolutionaries of other countries, would by themselves have been sufficient to cause the present conflict; as I have argued elsewhere,[3] I believe that it was an increasingly acute divergence of national interest that brought about the first critical change from differences of opinion to conflict of policies. But the further crucial transformation, by which these practical conflicts of interest gave rise to an ideological schism between two rival versions of the creed, seems hardly conceivable without that historic difference of outlook and approach: clearly, it was that pre-existent difference that made it possible for either side to erect a coherent ideological structure out of the materials furnished by various practical disagreements.

Yet in Western specialist discussion, the recognition of this historical and structural element in the present Sino-Soviet conflict is still to some extent obstructed by the long-standing controversy about "the originality of Mao Tse-tung" or about the existence of a specifically "Maoist" strategy for the conquest of power. While one group of scholars has from an early stage emphasized the new features by which Mao adapted his strategy to Chinese conditions and the differences between this Chinese version of Leninism and the Soviet version as interpreted by Stalin, another school has attempted to prove that in all his practical innovations Mao has kept strictly within the framework of Leninist, and indeed Stalinist, orthodoxy.[4]

It is clearly not possible to discuss the historical background to the Sino-Soviet schism without taking sides in this controversy. This does not, however, require that we should enter into a detailed examination of the various disputed historical facts; for a study of the relevant literature shows that the heart of the matter is not in historical disagreements about the relation between Soviet and Chinese Communist policies at particular times, but in methodological differences about the relation between political decisions and their justification in terms of doctrine.

THE RELATION OF POLICY AND DOCTRINE

Those who deny Mao's "ideological originality" apparently believe that the Leninist doctrine is by itself sufficient to determine the proper strategy for any given situation; hence statements justifying a major policy decision in doctrinal terms may be taken as adequately indicating the actual motives of that decision. This method of interpretation is dogmatic in the sense that the understanding of the actions of Communist leaders is reduced to the immanent exegesis of the dogma they profess.

By contrast, those who regard Mao as an innovator assume that no political doctrine can possibly anticipate all the major choices by which its followers may be faced: at crucial moments, "ideological" politicians are forced to give preference to one element of the doctrine over another with which, owing to unforeseen circumstances, it has come into conflict. Whichever decision has been taken will henceforth be justified by emphasizing the corresponding aspect of the doctrine; hence it is not the unchanging doctrine that has determined the decision but the decision that determines the further evolution of the doctrine. This method of interpretation is functional and critical in the sense that the doctrine is seen as a justifying ideology as well as a motivating force, and it is truly historical in focusing attention on the preferences that determine the crucial choices – even if those preferences may not yet have found a mature formulation.

In siding with the latter view, I do not have to assume that Mao was ever consciously heretical, or even that he clearly saw himself as an innovator as soon as he actually started to explore new roads. He was confronted with situations unforeseen by the orthodox theory, and he took new decisions in meeting them; whether his decisions were "orthodox" is therefore a secondary, and in some cases a strictly meaningless, question. What cannot seriously be disputed is that, in taking new decisions to meet new problems, Mao imparted to Chinese Communist strategy and organization, and *therefore* also to Chinese Communist ideology, new characteristics differing from those of Soviet communism. Our concern here is to try and identify these distinctive characteristics, to trace their origin in the conditions in which Chinese communism rose to power, and to point to their consequences for the later course of relations between the two leading Communist parties.

NEITHER "LIBERALS" NOR "EXTREMISTS"

When a wider non-Communist public first became aware of the existence of major differences of outlook and approach between the Soviet and Chinese Communists, the impression was contradictory and confusing. Thus when the Chinese Communists advised Khrushchev during the winter of 1956–57 to tolerate the new leadership of the Polish Communists headed by Gomulka and to grant its demand for increased autonomy in shaping the Polish state and the Polish economy in return for a pledge of bloc discipline in foreign policy,[5] this was generally viewed as proof that Mao represented a more "liberal" type of communism than the Soviet leaders. At the time, this interpretation seemed to be confirmed by Mao's famous instruction to his party machine to "let a hundred flowers bloom, let a hundred schools contend" in intellectual discussion, and by his sensational admission of the existence of "contradictions between the leadership and the masses" within his regime, which were to be kept in a "non-antagonistic," that is, non-explosive, framework by opening safetly valves for the expression of legitimate grievances. Yet as early as the summer of 1957, this period of domestic relaxation was followed in China by a new drive to purge the critical intellectuals, which in turn considerably exceeded by its ruthlessness the corresponding post-Hungarian reaction period in the Soviet Union. During the following year, the Chinese Communists took the most intolerant and aggressive position in the Soviet bloc's new conflict with Yugoslavia;[6] and finally, in trying to achieve a sudden total revolution in the living and working conditions of hundreds of millions of Chinese peasants by means of the "people's communes," they acted with a degree of doctrinaire utopianism that provoked the criticism of the Soviet leaders and produced results that soon forced a partial correction.

Clearly, then, our alternatives of tolerance or intolerance, liberalism or dogmatism, relaxation or rigidity do not get to the root of the underlying ideological differences. To uncover this root, we have to go back to the historic beginnings of Chinese communism as an autonomous movement — beginnings which we may date from Mao Tse-tung's stepping forward as leader of an independent unit of Communist partisans toward the close of 1927.

THE PARTISAN TRADITION

At that time, Stalin's Chinese policy of the 'twenties had ended in a catastrophic defeat.[7] On Stalin's instructions, the Chinese Communists, while maintaining their separate party organization, had individually entered the revolutionary nationalist party, the Kuomintang, and had systematically supported the organization of its Canton power base and its Northern expedition for the unification of China; by this "united front from within," they had aimed to develop mass organizations of the workers and peasants under their own control, to occupy key positions in government and army, and to cement the alliance between the Soviet Union and the emerging Chinese nationalist government. Yet with the victorious advance of the nationalist armies and with the unfolding of the revolutionary peasant movement, conflicts between the Kuomintang leadership and the Communist-directed workers' and peasants' unions had multiplied. While the Communists were still following Stalin's orders in searching for compromise, Chiang Kai-shek, as commander in chief of the nationalist army, had suddenly broken with them and begun to destroy their organizations and exterminate their cadres. After a period of confusion, the Communists reacted with desperate attempts at insurrection in several South Chinese cities; but the discouraged workers no longer followed their slogans, and the isolated little bands of armed Communists were defeated everywhere without difficulty.

It was in this situation that Mao, then no more than an

important Communist Party official in Hunan province, led the remnants of his armed followers – rebel units from the nationalist army, proscribed Communist workers, and uprooted peasants – to temporary safety in the mountain stronghold of Chingkanshan. At first this was hardly more than an act of self-preservation; instinctively the peasant's son fell back on the ancient Chinese tradition of peasant risings. Even before the final break with the Kuomintang, Mao had warned the party against underestimating the elementary force of the peasant movement; now, in defeat, he chose the road of rural partisan warfare for which few other Communists saw a future. But Mao knew as well as his comrades that China's traditional peasant risings had never been victorious unless leaders from outside, that is, from the educated classes, had enabled them to overcome their limited local horizon and to merge into a nation-wide movement: now, he developed the concept that this would have to be the role of the Communists in Chinese conditions. Lenin had built up his Bolshevik Party as a centralized organization of professional revolutionaries, in order to "introduce" the conscious revolutionary struggle for political power into the young Russian labor movement; just so, the Chinese Communist cadres were henceforth to give political leadership and military unity and mobility to the peasant partisans. The eventual fruit of this concept was not only the creation and expansion of large "Soviet areas" deep in the rural hinterland of China, but the successful "mobilization" of many thousands of uprooted peasants, their transformation into an army of partisans who were to prove their ability to fight far from their native region in the ordeal of the now legendary "long march" from the Southern "Soviet areas" to Yenan in the far Northwest.[8]

A decade later, Tito was to copy the organization and strategy of Mao's "Red Army," consciously and successfully, in his partisan campaign against the German and Italian occupation forces in Yugoslavia.

Yet in order to create a disciplined, mobile army from his peasant partisans, Mao required – just as Tito after him – trained Communists, intellectuals and workers coming from the cities; and here he at first encountered the opposition of the leaders of the Chinese Communist Party and the Comintern.[9] For years, the official Chinese party leaders argued, with Moscow's backing, that a Communist Party must necessarily have its main strength in the cities where the industrial workers are concentrated: there alone, the victory of the revolution could be decided – there alone, too, the party itself could preserve its fundamental character as a party of the working class. The Russian example had proved, in their opinion, that even where the industrial proletariat formed a small minority of the population, its concentration in the big cities would enable it to determine the outcome of a national crisis; after that, the peasant masses were bound to follow. Even when it gradually became apparent that Mao's partisans had grown into a much stronger force than the remnants of the Communist underground in the cities, this realization at first resulted only in new troubles for him: the party leaders now demanded that he should conquer important provincial capitals in order to provide the missing "proletarian center" for the movement! Yet the occupation and static defense of fortified localities are contrary to the basic rules of partisan warfare; and the attempt to comply with the demand, for the sake of party discipline, by the occupation of Changsha in July 1930, ended in one of the partisans' most serious defeats. Only in 1932, four years after the beginning of Mao's partisan warfare, did the Central Committee finally transfer its seat into his "Soviet area," because continuation of its work in Shanghai had been made all too hazardous by the police; only in 1935 was Mao elected leader of the Chinese Communist Party; and another three years were to pass before a Soviet publication officially mentioned him in this capacity.[10] His strategy had prevailed in the Chinese party not because it had the backing of Moscow – it was eventually approved by Moscow because it had prevailed.

SEEING THROUGH THE "PROLETARIAN" FICTION

Naturally, the fact that the Chinese Communists followed a different road to power was also noticed by many Western observers at an early stage; and just as many Communist doctrinaires, both in Russia and in China, doubted for years the "orthodoxy" of Mao's strategy, many of those Western observers at first believed that Mao and his men were not "real" Communists, but were merely leading a militant movement for agrarian reform. The underlying error, common to both views, consisted in defining a modern Communist Party in Marxian terms as a representative organ of the industrial working class, and not in Leninist terms as a centralized party organized for total power. In fact, the Russian Bolsheviks' pretense of being a working-class party had never been true either, even when industrial workers constituted the majority of their membership – because their form of organization made them independent of the actual support of the bulk of the working class and enabled them to change their "social basis" as occasion required: only parties with a democratic structure can truly be class parties, for only they are permanently tied to the particular social soil from which they have grown and from which they draw their nourishment. Rather, the Bolsheviks are a modern totalitarian cadre party, led by "professional revolutionaries," which originally relied on the support of a section of Russia's industrial working class, but as a ruling party has long since merged with the bureaucracy of the Soviet state and mastered the totalitarian art of balancing between the various classes of Soviet society and manipulating them all. Just so, Mao's Chinese Communist Party never was a class party of the peasants; it is a totalitarian cadre party which during the civil war relied primarily on peasant support, but as a ruling party has long since proved its ability to manipulate and, if necessary, oppress the peasants no less effectively than it manipulates and oppresses China's other social classes.

And yet there remains an important difference. Orthodox Leninist theory has always insisted on the fiction that the Communist Party was "the class-conscious vanguard of the proletariat," that is, that it embodied the true historic interests of that class even at times when the actually living workers were too short-sighted and prejudiced to follow its lead. There are, moreover, many indications that Lenin himself believed in this fiction — that he never came to realize fully how fundamentally his form of organization differed from Marx's idea of a proletarian party, and his state from Marx's concept of a proletarian dictatorship.[11] With Stalin, under whose rule the social composition of the Bolshevik Party changed beyond recognition, it seems far less probable that he managed to preserve this part of his early Marxist faith. Mao, finally, could hardly have performed his historic role without consciously casting off the proletarian fiction and clearly realizing the strictly classless character of the modern totalitarian party. Yet in a country where the industrial working class still constitutes a small minority of the population — and where this minority was even tinier during the years of the struggle for power — such ability to see through the traditional Marxist fiction gives to a Communist leader an incomparably greater freedom of maneuver than is enjoyed by his more doctrinaire rivals: it is Mao's real *arcanum regni,* his secret prescription for the conquest and preservation of power.

THE STRATEGY OF "NEW DEMOCRACY"

The organization of rural partisan warfare, though a decisive first step in the development of Mao's independent strategy, was not to remain the only consequence of his emancipation from the proletarian fiction. He proved himself an innovator for the second time during the years of the international "Popular Front" strategy before World War II, and of the Communist policy of wartime "national unity." In Stalin's mind, the aim of this policy was the winning over of non-proletarian classes and non-Socialist governments for an alliance against the dangers threatening from Hitlerite Germany and Japan; the means consisted in coalitions between the Communists and bourgeois parties, concluded on a platform combining resistance to the "Fascist aggressors" and friendship for the Soviet Union with democratic economic and social reforms, but carefully avoiding any demands of a specifically Socialist, let alone revolutionary, character. Mao Tse-tung, too, during that period concluded an alliance with Chiang Kai-shek against Japan; and by the end of 1939, he proclaimed under the slogan of the "New Democracy," a program of moderate reform intended to appeal to all patriotic classes —not only the workers and peasants, but also the urban petty bourgeois and the so-called "national bourgeoisie," that is, the capitalist groups not linked by their interests with the foreign imperialists. But in contrast to the European Communists, he did not attempt to bring about this alliance of classes by coalition between different parties but boldly pretended, in sovereign disregard of Marxist dogma, that his own Communist party was representing the interests of all these classes.[12] True, for the sake of national unity he had for the duration of the common struggle against Japan to accept the rule of Chiang Kai-shek and his Kuomintang on part of the national territory, pressing only by propagandist means for its "democratization"; but in his own "anti-Japanese base areas," he shared power with no other party, but organized their government on the principles of "democratic cantralism." [13] (The much-quoted "three-thirds" rule, under which positions in these areas were to be shared equally between organized Communists, non-party progressives, and moderate "middle-of-the-roaders," was not a coalition rule, since the last group, though including where possible locally known Kuomintang members, was not based on any regular Kuomintang organization; the Communists were quite openly told that while forming a numerical minority in the organs of government, they must use their advantage as a disciplined faction to ensure party leadership of those organs.[14]) Thus Communist concessions to the "allied classes" remained confined to the economic contents of Communist policy for the given period; the "partners" were not allowed any form of independent political representation.

But where power remains undivided, the contents of policy may easily be changed in a changed situation; where concessions to the "allies" are not embodied in a coalition pact, they may be withdrawn without a coalition crisis once the time is considered ripe. When the Communists broke with Chiang after 1945, Mao's "New Democracy" thus proved far superior to the West European coalitions as a road to Communist power; and that superiority was ultimately rooted in the original and useful fiction by which the Communists' party had identified itself not with one class only but with a broad "alliance of classes."

RE-EDUCATING THE CLASS ENEMY

But what was to become of such a fiction after the seizure of national power, once the transformation of society according to the Communist program was begun and the bases of existence of all non-proletarian classes became subject to a permanent revolution from above? How could the ruling Communist Party liquidate the very classes whose interests it had pretended to represent only yesterday? Here lies the third strategic innovation of the Chinese Communists: the term "liquidation of classes" is not to be found in Mao's political dictionary. According to his theory, it is only the old class *situation* that is liquidated – the function, but not necessarily the persons: the aim is to force the bulk of the latter, by a mixture of administrative pressure (including, of course, terror against "die-hard" recalcitrants) and intensive persuasion, to accept a transformation of their functions. The manner in which the countless small entrepreneurs in the Chinese cities were first turned into "partners" sharing the profits of their enterprise with the state, and then, after their complete expropriation, into state-employed managers, may serve as an illustration: the entire pressure of state and party was not directed toward driving them away but to getting as many as possible to agree "voluntarily" to this change in their situation. Even the collectivization of Chinese agriculture was started off by similar easy stages and at first with similar methods.

All this, of course, is not to deny that the pressure was often severe and the loss of economic independence bitter for the victims; nor is it to suggest that the enthusiastic declarations, say, of "reformed" entrepreneurs – how much happier they now feel, serving the community as state-employed managers, than they ever did as capitalists working for private gain – should be taken at face value. But it is relevant for an understanding of Chinese communism that its leaders have sought to ease their tremendous revolutionary tasks by not treating large classes of the population as irreducible enemies from the start, and that instead they have conceived the bold aim of transforming, along with the material conditions of existence of those classes, their attitudes to the state and the economy, to individual and national interest. To put it in Marxist language, they have attempted to transform the social consciousness of all these millions along with their social being.

The three new departures of the Chinese Communists that we have so far discussed – the seizure of power by means of a partisan army mainly recruited from peasants; the replacement of the coalition strategy of the "Popular Front" type by the fiction of an alliance of classes represented by the single Communist Party; the preference for "re-educating" rather than liquidating the urban and rural middle class after victory — all point to the same conclusion: that Mao has never seriously allowed himself to be guided by the doctrinaire premise that a Communist Party aspiring to dictatorial rule must be a class party of the proletariat. The same applies also to the great innovation of 1958 — the institution of the rural "people's communes," into which a hundred million peasant families, constituting the overwhelming majority of the Chinese people, were driven within a few months.

THE "PEOPLE'S COMMUNES" AND THE CLASS DOGMA

The crucial new element in these communes was not simply the merging of many collective farms into much larger units, nor even the more far-reaching replacement of family property by collective or "communal" property, but the organization of a new rural division of labor on the new, larger scale and under quasi-military discipline — the attempt to exploit all the hitherto unused time of the peasants and their families for the massive launching of what might be thought of as collectivized cottage industries.[15]

The technique of these new "industries," including the much-publicized rural furnaces and toolsheds, was generally extremely primitive and, by our standards, "unproductive"; yet in an overpopulated country suffering from extreme shortage of capital that could not possibly build modern industrial plant at the rate needed for absorbing its agricultural surplus population, even the most primitive methods for getting additional industrial output directly from the peasants might appear as offering a net increase of the national income.

But from the class point of view, this Maoist innovation was as un-Marxist as the preceding ones. For while the classical Soviet method of industrialization amounts to a technique for driving the agricultural surplus population into the new towns by the whip of hunger, thus rapidly increasing the share of the industrial proletariat in the national total, the "people's commune" method seeks to mobilize this surplus population for part-time industrial production on the spot, without uprooting them from the soil, hence without directly increasing the ranks of the industrial proletariat. Of course, this experiment had its compelling reasons in the lack of the amounts of capital needed for an industrialization of the Stalinist type—just as the strategy of partisan warfare had its compelling reasons in the lack of a strong, militant labor movement, and as the comparatively "mild" methods used in transforming the lives and thoughts of the urban and rural middle classes had their compelling reasons in the fact that these classes still constitute the enormous majority of the Chinese people. The Chinese Communists are perfectly conscious of this continuity in the special character of their problems and of the solutions devised by them; in forming the "people's communes," for example, they explicitly harked back to the methods of improvising industrial production for their military needs that they had worked out in the rural "Soviet areas" during the civil war.[16] But like Mao's earlier innovations, the decision to launch the "people's communes" was only possible because to him the total transformation of society in a Communist direction has always been more important than the dogma that only a rapid increase in the strength of the industrial proletariat can ensure lasting stability for Communist rule.

It is primarily by casting aside this proletarian dogma that Mao has been able again and again to adapt Communist strategy creatively to the problems of an underdeveloped and overpopulated country — a country that started its revolution on a far lower level of industrialization than Russia in 1917, and with an incomparably higher population pressure. But this adaptation has not been directed toward the temporary acceptance of more modest targets in view of the backwardness of initial conditions but, on the contrary, toward attempting the forcible transformation of these unfavorable objective conditions, by the use of political power and by the re-education of the entire nation, at a pace that would have seemed impossible not only to Marx, but also to Lenin and even to Stalin.

LEAPING OVER OBJECTIVE CONDITIONS

If it is accepted that the Chinese Communists could not have conquered and retained power without Mao's emancipation from the dogma that Communist strategy must be founded on the proletarian class struggle — an emancipation that, though silent, seems too consistent not to have been conscious — it follows that Mao's "deviation" from Marxism was necessary rather than accidental. Indeed, all the "objective preconditions" for the achievement of socialism, let alone communism, in a Marxian sense are obviously absent in China. Marx had argued that the ending of exploitation and the possibility of a classless society depended on the achievement of material abundance and on the attainment of a high cultural level by all; he expected these conditions to be brought about thanks to the tremendous productivity of modern industrial mass production. It follows that in underdeveloped countries, where modern industry exists only as an island in a sea of peasants vegetating on the border of starvation, the achievement of socialism in the Marxian sense cannot seriously be regarded as an immediate task: by nationalizing the means of production and introducing dictatorial economic planning, such countries may put a new class of state-capitalist bureaucrats in the place of the old privileged classes of private owners, but they cannot bring a classless society or a democracy of the toiling masses into being. This is precisely the warning that was uttered prophetically, even before the Russian Bolsheviks seized power, by their Menshevik critics; and the complete political failure of the Mensheviks ought not to blind us to the intellectual honesty and accuracy of their predictions – predictions that have been fully confirmed by the history of both the Soviet Union and Communist China.

There is true historical irony in the fact that during the winter of 1958–59, the Russian Bolsheviks began to use against their Chinese comrades the very same Marxist arguments that their Menshevik critics had used against them forty years previously. The Chinese Communists, dizzy with the pace of their "permanent revolution," had started to advertise their new "people's communes" as a short cut or leaping directly on to the higher stage of the classless Communist society and thus catching up with their Russian elder brothers and even surpassing them with a single gigantic jump. If the peasants in the communes were now spending part of their working time on primitive industries – was not that the eventual disappearance of the contrast between town and country foreseen by Marx? If the commune members got no money wages but, apart from a little pocket money, only "free supplies" – that is, rations in kind, and equal rations at that, regardless of the work performed – was not that the fulfillment of the Marxian formula for the "higher stage" of communism, "from each according to his abilities, to each according to his needs"? It was left to the Soviets to point out, drily and somewhat acidly, that this formula refers to a state of abundance and not of rationing, that abundance cannot come about without the most highly developed techniques of production, and that the high productivity required cannot be achieved without a prolonged period of wages offering material incentives – which means unequal money wages – and an equally prolonged period of strict occupational division between agriculture and industry: [17] the contrast between town and country cannot be transcended in the Marxian sense before it has been developed to the full by the parallel advances of the division of labor and the technique of production.

The Chinese Communists did, in fact, accept some of this sobering and realistic advice a few months later – owing partly to the difficulties and setbacks caused by the hasty execution of their over-ambitious program, and partly, it seems, in exchange for the promise of more substantial deliveries of Soviet capital goods. Yet the basic tendency that had become visible on that occasion – the desire to leap over the "objective material conditions," in the Marxian sense, even more boldly than the Bolsheviks had done, thus pushing the Bolsheviks to assume the role of their own erstwhile Menshevik critics – was to remain characteristic for the Chinese Communists even after that temporary retreat.

STANDING KARL MARX ON HIS HEAD

Nor is this tendency wholly absurd. For the classical Marxian criticism of the utopian illusions harbored once by the Bolsheviks and now by the Chinese Communists has always overlooked one politically crucial point. It is indeed impossible for an underdeveloped country, suffering from backward techniques and shortage of capital, to accomplish the leap into the classless society of Marxian vision simply by means of state economic planning. But as Stalin has shown, it is perfectly possible for a bureaucratic dictatorship by means of such planning to accelerate enormously the process of industrializing and generally modernizing such a country. The social and political order that is thus brought into being will certainly be anything but classless or democratic, hence anything but Socialist in the Marxian sense; but it may accomplish in a few decades some of the basic changes – the accumulation of capital for the modern apparatus of production, the disciplining of the masses for industrial labor, the rationalization of the general culture – which in the old industrial countries of Europe took centuries. The reason is that in the totalitarian dictatorships of the Communist type the ruthless, concentrated use of political power and ideology – two factors that are not economic in the narrow sense – is playing a far greater role in this process of "modernization at a hothouse pace" than Marx could ever have imagined; [18] and this applies even more to Communist China than to Russia, with the result that the Chinese Communist leaders seem far more conscious of it.

If one looks in retrospect for the crucial points at which Lenin's political concept deviated from classical Marxism, one is left with two basic ideas: Lenin's conviction of the indispensable function of a centralistic party of a new type for introducing his sense of the historic urgency of the struggle for political power into the working class; and his belief that such a party could and should seize dictatorial power even in a situation where the industrial preconditions for a Socialist order were lacking, and could retain such power without abandoning its Socialist aims. If one goes on to ask where Stalin went beyond Lenin, the answer must be that he applied this party power with a historically unprecedented degree of violence for enforcing ever new changes in the structure of society. The originality of Mao Tse-tung, who is pursuing a similar aim in even more backward conditions, consists in the fact that besides the use of violence, he has, far more deliberately than the Russians, used as a weapon of his permanent social revolution the modern totalitarian techniques for transforming the consciousness of the masses.

Karl Marx once wrote that the dialectic in its Hegelian form was standing on its head, because Hegel had understood it as the form of a process of thought; it was necessary to put it on its feet, that is, to reinterpret it as the dialectic of productive forces and relations of production, "in order to discover the rational core within the mystic garb." But the longer and further Marxism proceeded on its eastward migration, away from the old industrial countries, the less there was left of the economic materialism of its Western founder, and the more the emphasis shifted to the active role of consciousness as a revolutionary factor – until today it may truly be said of Mao Tse-tung that he has stood the Marxian dialectic on its head again.

REMOLDING THE PARTY CADRES

In the course of time, this tendency toward an "idealistic" reversal of Marxism has increasingly expressed itself also in the Chinse Communists' inner-party style of work, giving it a distinctive character of its own. That character first became visible in the so-called Cheng Feng campaign of 1941–42.[19] Cheng Feng means the straightening-out of minds, the correction of unorthodox tendencies in thought, and it was used here with special reference to the education of party cadres. The campaign was started during the wartime period when Mao's headquarters were still in Yenan in the distant Northwest, but his forces were expanding their control in various parts of North China, while an uneasy truce, concluded to ensure the concentration of all armed forces against the Japanese enemy, linked him with Chiang Kai-shek's government in Chungking. The Chinese Communists were thus simultaneously faced with the political problems of a ruling party in their own "base areas," and with those of a complicated diplomatic relation with Chiang, their temporary ally but permanent enemy – quite apart from the military problems of anti-Japanese guerilla warfare. Not surprisingly, the pressure of these heterogeneous problems gave rise to considerable inner-party tensions, disagreements, and rivalries; and many responsible party officials were apparently inclined to settle these issues by the methods familiar from Stalin's practice – by branding their inner-party opponents of the moment as "enemies of the party" and "traitors," and by calling for the use of police measures against them.

Against these tendencies, Liu Shao-ch'i, who has since been elected to become Mao's successor as chief of state, first inveighed in an essay "On Intra-Party Struggle," written in 1941.[20] Inner-party discussions, he argued, were necessary to defend the party against the influence of the ideas of non-proletarian classes – a concession to the fiction of the party's proletarian character which was not to be repeated in Mao's own lectures and writings of the following year. But, Liu continued, the inner-party struggle must not be conducted with the same methods as the struggle against the foe outside the party: its aim was to convince erring comrades, not to destroy enemies. When Mao himself officially opened the Cheng Feng campaign in 1942,[21] the subject was considerably broadened to include the training of cadres and the proper relationship between them and the ruled population as well as the methods of inner-party struggle. Mao warned against the tendency to rely on the party's power and order the people about instead of endeavoring patiently to convince them; and he specially criticized the mechanical learning by rote of texts from the Marxist classics, demanding that party training should instead be aimed at enabling the cadres to apply the ideas of Marx and Lenin to the particular conditions of China. The Chinese Communists themselves have later correctly described the Cheng Feng movement as an important stage in their emancipation from mechanical imitation of the Soviet model; and indeed one may observe how in the course of the campaign, even when ideas familiar from Russian party history were expressed, the terms used tended to become specifically Chinese.[22]

A NEW INNER-PARTY STYLE

For, of course, the Russian Bolsheviks had long had their own campaigns against sectarianism, their warnings against mechanical learning by rote, and so forth. But the Chinese Communists were now putting a new emphasis on the idea that the whole success of the party depends on training the cadres in the right way of thinking, and expressing a new belief that the tendencies to stray from it toward rotten liberalism on one side or toward narrow "commandist" sectarianism on the other are not just due to the influence of non-proletarian classes, but represent the natural temptations of human weakness from which the party collective must protect each individual member by untiring puritan vigilance. More and more, a moralizing, idealist tone thus comes to dominate inner-party work; more and more, the party insists not only on criticizing the sinner and removing him when necessary from his position, but on truly "straightening him out," improving him by using moral and ideological pressure to make him admit his mistakes and accept the justice of the correction received. It is a fact that while Chinese Communist history, like that of other Communist parties, knows the institution of the regular "purging" of unfit members, Stalin-style liquidations of Communist "traitors" have so far remained exceptional among the Chinese leaders.

This technique of intense ideological and moral pressure, directed from above but carried out by the collective from below, which Mao had developed in the wilds of Yenan as a new style for controlling and remolding the party cadres, was transferred after 1949 to the remolding of the entire Chinese nation, particularly the urban and rural middle classes. It explains why, despite the obvious brutality of Chinese collectivization, police terror operating by physical violence played a so much smaller role than in the corresponding Russian phase, and "neighborhood terror" operating by ideological and moral pressure a so much bigger role. Ultimately, the fact that China has become the classic land of "brain-washing," of the manipulation of the individual soul by the ideological machinery of the totalitarian state, reflects this special Maoist emphasis on changing the social consciousness in the attempt to leap over the backwardness of objective conditions.

Never have these distinctive characteristics of Chinese communism been manifested more strikingly than in the crisis of the Communist world movement which was started by the repercussions of Khrushchev's secret "de-Stalinization" speech in 1956. The admission of Stalin's crimes caused hitherto believing Communists throughout the West to raise the anxious question of how such degeneration of the regime could have occurred in a Socialist society. Even so faithful a champion of the Soviets as Palmiro Togliatti, the Italian Communist leader, openly flirted with Trotsky's and Tito's thesis that Stalin's rule of terror had only become possible as an expression of the power of the new privileged caste – the state-capitalist bureaucracy. The official reply of the Bolshevik leaders, claiming that Soviet society had continued to advance all the time in a Socialist direction despite Stalin's "errors," and treating the extermination of an entire generation of revolutionaries as merely a regrettable by-product of the "cult of the individual," satisfied nobody. Only the Chinese Communists found an explanation that was perfectly meaningful within their system of thought: it was wrong, they argued, to look for the roots of Stalin's mistakes in the class structure of Soviet society – they had been caused merely by his abandoning the "correct" way of thinking in favor of a wrong, "subjectivist," and "commandist" approach.[23] True, this was not a Marxist explanation, but it fitted smoothly into the Chinese version of Communist theory – that of a dialectic standing on its head.

MAO'S 1957 EXPERIMENT

It was therefore logical that the Chinese Communists should react to the crisis of "de-Stalinization," and particularly to the shock of the Hungarian revolution, by starting a new Cheng Feng campaign in 1957. But this time, Mao went even further in his idealistic reversal of Marxism than he had gone fifteen years before. He now stated explicitly that it was normal that "contradictions" would continue to exist even in a so-called Socialist Society – in other words, that there would be discontent and conflicts of interest even in countries ruled by a Communist Party dictatorship. Those contradictions, however, would remain "non-antagonistic," that is, non-explosive, so long as the party applied the "correct" methods in dealing with them; this meant so long as it kept enough safety valves open to notice the manifestations of discontent and conflicts in good time, and so long as it reacted to such symptoms with sufficient tactical flexibility and power of persuasion to ensure that the discontented elements would express their grievances within the limits of loyalty toward the regime. Only where the party leadership did not think and act in the "correct" way would there be a danger of such conflicts being successfully exploited by the external class enemy and finally assuming an "antagonistic" character, that is, endangering the regime, as in Hungary.[24]

The second Cheng Feng campaign of 1957 thus led to the deliberate opening of opportunities for criticism in the press, in meetings, and in petitions, and even for occasional legal strikes – all based on the expectation that the Chinese Communists' ideological hold on their people was strong enough to enable them to cope with any expression of discontent either by concessions in detail or by benevolent talk. In practice, however, the limits of this Communist form of moral rearmament soon became apparent: the sufferings of the Chinese masses were far too bitter, the conflicts of interest much too serious to be cured by mere persuasive talk, once they had come to the surface. Within a short time, Mao found himself compelled to put the lid back on the overheated kettle and to decide that critics who had responded too eagerly to his invitation to speak their mind must be enemies in disguise, after all. The experiment had proved that the manipulation of the social consciousness by a totalitarian state can only supplement, never replace, the use of force.

Just as the Chinese Communists' tendency to overemphasize the role of consciousness had been underlying their unlucky "rightist" experiment in encouraging free criticism for a few months in 1957, it also explains their "leftist" excesses during the creation of the "people's communes" in the following year. This time, the Communist cadres seem to have believed that ideological pressure and "remolding" would be sufficient to make hundreds of millions of peasants work a twelve-hour day without incentive wages, and to get them at the same time to give up the accustomed forms of family life – and all this as a long-term policy. Once again, only enormous practical setbacks were able to convince them that they had gone too far, and that the cynical materialist criticism voiced by the Russians had been closer to reality than their own splendid vision.

Yet neither of these corrections has been able to affect the basic idealist tendency that produces ever new differences with the Soviets, because that tendency has profound roots in the history and ideology of Chinese communism. As we have seen, these roots lie ultimately in the poverty and technical backwardness of China, which demand from a Communist regime even bolder "leaps" than Russia has experienced. But these conditions are not, after all, confined to China: they exist more or less in all underdeveloped countries — particularly where the combination of material backwardness with rapid population increase and traditional resistance to industrial modernization forms a kind of magic circle of seemingly insoluble problems. This combination still prevails in large parts of Asia and the Near East, and in somewhat different forms in a number of Latin-American countries. It is precisely in these countries that the attraction of communism is today far greater than in the old industrial nations with their strong and stably organized working class — particularly its attraction for the modern-minded, nationalistic intelligentsia, whose ambitious activism is impatiently searching for ways to break out of the magic circle of stagnation and backwardness. Communism appeals to this stratum not as a type of working-class movement nor as a system designed to achieve social justice, but precisely as a way out — as a prescription for violently wrenching their countries out of the rut of stagnation and for quickly building a powerful, modern state.

CHINA AS A MODEL FOR ASIAN REVOLUTIONS

But for people attracted to communism for these reasons, the Chinese example is not only nearer home than that of the Soviet Union but more immediately applicable at first sight and hence more impressive. It was therefore inevitable that both the Communists and the pro-Communist intellectuals of Asia should increasingly look to China and try to learn from her example. Yet in view of the historical differences between the Soviet and Chinese versions of Communist ideology, this attraction of the Maoist model also contained a potential of conflict: the rapid growth of the authority of China, the younger and weaker but now politically more dynamic partner in the alliance of the two Communist empires, constituted a potential challenge to the traditional claim of the Soviets, the older and still incomparably more powerful partner, for world-wide authority.

Both parties have certainly endeavored to avoid such conflict. Just as they tried for years, in the interest of their joint struggle against the non-Communist world, to settle their material conflicts of interest – about the exploitation of raw materials in Sinkiang, about their respective influence on Outer Mongolia, about the scale of Russian capital aid for China's industrialization, or about the future production of Chinese atomic weapons – in secret without allowing them to come to the surface, they have also attempted for a long time to avoid any visible ideological rivalry for influence on the world Communist movement. In the beginning, this was made easier by the effects of the Chinese Communists' prolonged isolation from the outside world; for while Mao and his team had followed their own road to power without heeding Stalin's advice in Chinese affairs, they had during their long years in the wilderness utterly relied on Soviet sources for all information on and interpretation of world affairs. The domestic strategy of the Chinese Communists was independent and original, but their image of the world scene was 100 per cent Stalinist – and this is one reason why Khrushchev's brutal attack on Stalin's authority in his "secret speech" at the Twentieth Congress seemed unacceptable to Mao.[25]

Stalin, in his turn, had by 1948–49 been willing to adjust,

within certain limits, to the fact that the Chinese Communists were winning a victory in which he had not believed: he wanted no second Tito-conflict with a far stronger opponent, who could be far more valuable as an ally on the world stage. Even while Mao was winning his final battles, a whole series of Asian Communist parties — in Burma and Malaya, in Indonesia, the Philippines, and even in India — made attempts at copying the Chinese partisan tactics. Though these attempts were hasty and generally unsuccessful, they were certainly not discouraged by Moscow at the time; and when Liu Shao-ch'i, at the Peking conference of the WFTU held in November 1949, explicitly proclaimed the Chinese Communist strategy as a model for the Communists of Asia, the claim was endorsed in the Soviet and Cominform press.[26] Liu was then putting his main emphasis not on the need for forming Chinese-style revolutionary partisan armies where conditions permitted, but on the need to form throughout Asia broad anti-imperialist and anti-feudal fronts of all "patriotic" classes, from the workers and peasants to the petty bourgeois and intellectuals and the "national bourgeoise," under the leadership of the Communist parties. He also emphasized the value of a moderate democratic program for creating this broad alliance of classes and thus facilitating the Communist seizure of power. Soon afterwards, an attack on this program as insufficiently proletarian and Socialist, published by the left-wing leaders of the Indian Communist Party, was explicitly rejected by Moscow and its authors removed from their positions.[27] In the following years, the mechanical imitation of Mao's partisan strategy in non-revolutionary situations was gradually abandoned, but Mao's program of the "New Democracy," based on a bloc of all patriotic classes under Communist leadership, remained the recognized model for the Asian Communists.

CHINA AS PIONEER OF ASIAN DIPLOMACY

It was inevitable that the Chinese Communists' influence on Soviet-bloc policy toward Asia should even increase after Stalin's death. The year 1954, during which China's premier, Chou En-lai, appeared at the Geneva conference of the Great Powers and helped to shape the Indochina armistice, also saw the activation of China's diplomacy toward the neutral nations of Asia — the promulgation of the "five principles of peaceful co-existence and non-interference" by a joint statement of Chou and Nehru (ironically enough, occasioned by an agreement on Tibet), and Chou's first state visits to his neutral neighbors.

Underlying all this activity was clearly a first revision of the Stalinist view of the world. Peking had come to realize that the great ex-colonial states like India, Burma, and Indonesia had not acquired a merely nominal independence while in reality remaining tools of the Western imperialists (as the Cominform had so far insisted), but possessed genuine freedom of maneuver in foreign policy, and that it was therefore worth China's while to keep them neutral and not to push them into the new SEATO alliance. When Khrushchev, Bulganin, and Mikoyan visited Peking in the autumn of that year, they found themselves agreeing with their hosts not only on the correctness of the new diplomatic tactics based on this new analysis but on the need to change the attitude of the Communist powers toward Japan: no longer was Japan to be taken for granted as an enemy but to be wooed in the hope of detaching it one day from the American alliance. During the following year, the new Asian diplomacy of the bloc reached a visible climax with the remarkable success of Chou's participation in the Bandung conference of Asian and African governments on one side, and with Khrushchev's and Bulganin's Indian journey on the other. Finally, one of the major results of the Twentieth Congress of the CPSU was Khrushchev's explicit revision, in February 1956, of Stalin's dogmatic view about the continued dependence of the ex-colonial nations, and the proclamation of a new foreign political strategy that aimed at creating beyond the borders of the "Socialist camp," that is, the Soviet bloc, a neutral "zone of peace." [28]

MAO AND THE CRISIS OF THE SOVIET BLOC

Throughout this development, the Chinese Communists acted as the pioneers of a new, successful Asian policy for the whole Soviet bloc; yet their "vanguard role" did not then take organizational form. As far as we know, the technical links of most Asian Communist parties continued to be with Moscow rather than Peking, and Peking does not seem to have asked for more direct organizational control at that time – except over parties whose members were of predominantly Chinese nationality, as in Malaya. But the formal dissolution of the Cominform in April 1956 was bound to revive debate over the proper form of international contacts among Communists; and it occurred at a time when Khrushchev's disclosures about Stalin's crimes had shaken the authority of the Soviet Union throughout the world Communist movement, and when many a major leader of European communism took the road to Peking in order to find comfort and ideological assurance in the unbroken authority of Mao — the victorious leader of a great revolution and not a successor's successor like the men in the Kremlin. As the year proceeded and the Polish and Hungarian events made the crisis of Communist ideology and Soviet authority increasingly manifest, those Communist pilgrimages to the Peking oracle became more and more frequent.

By the winter of 1956–57 it appeared that the overcoming of the crisis and the future cohesion of the bloc might depend to a considerable extent on the intervention of Mao's intact authority; and the Chinese Communists had far too large a stake in the working of the economic system of Soviet-controlled Eastern Europe to think of withholding such intervention. In the theoretical debate, it took the form of their second statement on Stalin's errors, in which they acquitted the Soviet Union of any charge of structural degeneration, thoroughly condemned the Hungarian popular revolt as "counter-revolutionary," and rejected the cautious and hesitant doubts raised by the Yugoslavs about Soviet military action in Hungary; [29] in the field of practical diplomacy, it was supplemented by Chou En-lai's European visit and his assumption of the role of mediator between Khrushchev and Gomulka's new team in Poland.[30]

The Chinese Communists had ventured for the first time actively to influence the destinies of the Communist world movement beyond Asia, and had done so successfully. But they were still conscious of the disproportion between the increased authority conferred upon them by events and their comparatively inferior material power, and correspondingly cautious. Hence in November 1957, when the fortieth anniversary of the Bolshevik seizure of power was made the occasion for a world-wide conference of Communist parties in Moscow, it was Mao who insisted that the leading role of the Soviet Union and the Bolshevik Party should be explicitly recognized in the joint declaration of the twelve ruling Communist parties; and as his reason for such recognition he cited the superiority of Soviet technique and material power, naming the Sputniks as its symbol. "The Soviet Union," he was reported to have exclaimed, "has two Sputniks, while China has not even a quarter Sputnik!" Peking's determination to hide its own light under a bushel in order to avoid any appearance of ideological rivalry with its powerful ally could hardly have been expressed more naïvely, nor more graphically.[31]

TOWARD OPEN IDEOLOGICAL RIVALRY

Yet less than six months after that November celebration, the Chinese Communists had begun to prepare for such ideological rivalry. In April 1958, they founded their first experimental "people's commune," and they ominously baptized it "Sputnik"[32] – as if, by alluding to Mao's words, they now wished to stake a claim to equality in leadership after all.

We may only speculate about the reasons for this change. We know that the "people's communes" were formed in an attempt to solve the urgent problems of Chinese industrialization despite an extreme shortage of capital; and we also know that one of the causes for that attempt was that the Soviet Union, though willing to sell China considerable amounts of new industrial plant, had offered no new loans for that purpose since 1956.[33] It was thus partly the Soviet Union's fault that China had to rely on her own resources for her "Great Leap Forward" and to devise her own original methods for that purpose. Hence this leap really originated as an effort to increase China's economic capacity and power more rapidly than the Soviets considered possible – or even desirable. When, in August, the Chinese leaders decided that the first unpublicized pilot communes had been a success and proceeded to proclaim a policy of transferring the entire rural population into these new units,[34] their ideological enthusiasm made it seem natural to present this revolutionary emergency measure as a direct short cut to the higher stage of communism. It seemed natural because of the Chinese Communists' traditional inclination to leap over objective conditions and to believe that nothing was impossible to a determined will guided by a clearly conceived aim; but it also seemed natural because resentment against the slowing down of China's development by insufficient capital aid from Russia increased the appeal of an idea that implied that China, thanks to the genius of Mao Tse-tung, was about to catch up with the Soviet Union and even surpass it on the road to the higher stage of communism.

Thus by the last four months of 1958, the ideological rivalry between Peking and Moscow had become fairly open. While Peking's campaign for the new communes was at its climax, Moscow at first kept silent about the affair, then published some remarkably detached reports stressing the heroic primitivity of the rural furnaces and the "war Communist" atmosphere of work in the communes, and finally began a theoretical discussion about the Soviet road to communism. Its participants never mentioned China but emphasized in article after article that progress toward the higher stage of communism was only possible on the basis of the highest technical productivity.[35]

The reports and comments of most of the East European satellites followed the same line; only for the most primitive among the Communist countries of Europe, Bulgaria and Albania, did the Chinese experiment have an obvious appeal. In Albania, the Chinese device of making leading bureaucrats do occasional physical work as a demonstration of "classlessness" was quickly copied,[36] and the Bulgarians even announced the founding of a first people's commune" – only to revoke their announcement promptly.[37] The Russians, having found that the heretical Chinese prescription was making converts among the Communists of the most backward European countries, had clearly intervened to stop the infection.

THE INITIAL SOVIET RESPONSE

The chief counter-action by the Soviets, apart from the unpublicized intervention in various Communist-governed countries at which we may guess, was taken in the context of preparations for the Twenty-first Congress of the CPSU; and there are indications that this Congress – an "extra-ordinary" one, that is, one not yet due under the party statutes – was called chiefly for this purpose. The only point on its agenda, the new seven-year plan, could just as well have been decided on and popularized by different means; the plan only became a subject for a party congress because it was treated not as a purely economic project, but as the first step in laying the foundations for the higher stage of communism, and the Congress itself was announced as "the Congress of the builders of communism." The preparations thus furnished to the Soviet leaders ample opportunity for explaining again and again their orthodox Marxist version of the interdependence between the raising of productivity and the standard of living and the transition to a classless society, and also for stressing both the need for maintaining differential incentive wages and the role of money as a yardstick of cost and return all along the road to communism. Every one of these arguments was a blow aimed against the claims of the Chinese Communists and against their idealistic tendency to leap over the objective conditions – even though the Chinese were never mentioned by name.

By December 1958 the combined pressure of this Soviet criticism and of the practical difficulties that had manifested themselves in the working of the "people's communes" forced the Chinese party leaders to decide on a partial retreat. At a meeting of their Central Committee, the ideas of jumping directly into "communism" were corrected; the new official view was that only the building of "socialism" and the creation of certain "germs of communism" were on the agenda so far, and that the transition to a really classless society would take many years.[38] In February 1959, when the Twenty-first Congress of the CPSU met, the new Sino-Soviet understanding was sealed – by the admission of Chou En-lai, the Chinese delegate, on the one hand, that the Soviet Union was the only country that had actually begun to build communism,[39] and by the first substantial agreement for the delivery of Soviet capital goods to China since 1956, on the other.[40]

Yet the settling of this first public argument had clearly not removed the roots of ideological rivalry. The Chinese Communists, after all, continued to cling to their belief that the "people's communes" contained at least germs of communism and thus represented the starting-point of an original Chinese road to the classless society – while the Russians continued to reject that view. And behind that disagreement stood the whole historically conditioned difference between the Soviet and Chinese Communist styles of thinking, which was bound to lead to new arguments and rivalries again and again.

But just as surely as the distinctive characteristics of Chinese Communist ideology and strategy are rooted in the difficulties of modernizing an underdeveloped and overpopulated country, so the utopian hopes raised among the Chinese Communists by the campaign for the "people's communes" must have found an echo in the hearts and minds of many other Communists throughout Asia. In future debates, these Asian Communists would find the Chinese of Mao and his followers easier to understand than the Russian of their Soviet comrades – a language that to their ears has become Westernized with the progress of Russia's industrial technique.

6

1958: FIRST RIFTS IN THE ALLIANCE

In 1958 there emerged, for the first time in the history of the Russo-Chinese alliance, clear evidence that Soviet policies toward the non-Communist world (not merely within the "Socialist camp") and in both European and world-wide affairs (not merely within a region where Chinese interests were directly affected) had been modified by the impact of Chinese pressure. The principle of a world-wide partnership in the formation of policy, and the resulting obligation to regular and all-round (as distinct from occasional and regionally restricted) advance consultation, was formally recognized in the joint Soviet-Chinese communiqué published after Khrushchev's Peking talks in August 1958.[1] At the same time, the Chinese Communist leaders not only demonstrated anew their determination to seek their own solutions to their own peculiar domestic problems, but boldly underlined the originality of these solutions in a manner that was clearly intended to present them as a potential model for other Asian countries, and that thus constituted a first implicit challenge to Russia's ideological leadership of the international Communist movement.

We were thus confronted, on the one hand, with the symptoms of a major shift in the relation of forces between the Soviet Union and China and of a growing Chinese demand for real partnership in world affairs, and, on the other, with the first visible manifestation of conflicts of interest between the two allied Communist powers. The evidence for this thesis can be found in the record of the Soviet-bloc campaign against Tito's Yugoslavia, in the history of Khrushchev's abortive proposal for a "summit conference" on the Middle East crisis of the summer of 1958, and in the development of the Chinese campaign for the formation of "people's communes" as the new, quick road to "the building of socialism and the transition to communism." But before such evidence is submitted, two possible objections must be met.

The first of these is that the power shift of 1958 was not a wholly new development: on the contrary, it was only the latest stage in a process that had been going on steadily at least since the death of Stalin. Indeed the imitation of "Maoist" strategies by some Asian Communist parties began shortly after the Chinese Communists' domestic victory – thus within Stalin's lifetime and with his apparent agreement. China's full status as an Asian Great Power was recognized in the arrangements for the Geneva conference of 1954, which negotiated the Indochinese armistice, and in the modification of the terms of the Soviet-Chinese alliance including Moscow's renunciation of its remaining occupation rights) during the Peking visit of Khrushchev, Bulganin, and Mikoyan later that year. China was the pioneer of the new Soviet-bloc attitude toward the uncommitted countries of Asia, as embodied in its sponsorship of the "five principles" of co-existence and in Chou En-lai's role at the Bandung conference – an attitude which culminated in Khrushchev's explicit revision (in his report to the Twentieth Congress) of the doctrinaire view that these countries were still governed by "imperialist stooges."

In addition, the crisis of Soviet authority in the international Communist movement, brought about by the shock of "de-Stalinization" and, in particular, by the events of October 1956 in Poland and Hungary, had created a situation in which international unity and discipline could only be restored by mobilizing the intact authority of the Chinese Communist leaders; and the latter, vitally interested in the economic, diplomatic, and military cohesion of the bloc, used their prestige among European Communists to restore respect for the "leading role of the Soviet Union" – first by their New Year's Eve pronouncement of 1956–57 on the lessons of Hungary,[2] then by their "mediating" intervention in Poland, and finally by Mao's speech at the Moscow conclave of ruling Communist parties in November 1957.[3] What was new in 1958 was not the growth of Chinese influence on bloc policies as such, but the extension of that influence beyond either the regional affairs of Asia or the internal affairs of the Communist movement – and the indications that this latest extension was achieved at least partly in conflict with the Soviet leaders, and was accompanied by preparations for far-reaching ideological rivalry.

This last point gives rise to the second objection. In 1958 the interests that the Communist regimes of Russia and China had in common clearly still far outweighed any causes of conflict between them: one could then speak only of limited conflicts within an overriding community of interests – just as one should when studying the relations between the major partners of the Western alliance. Nevertheless, a rift had become visible during 1958, and it was based on genuine and important, if still subordinate, conflicts of interest as well as on a deeply rooted divergence of ideological development.

DIFFERENCES OF NATIONAL INTEREST

One cause of conflict is that Communist China was vitally dependent on the Soviet Union and its European satellites, both militarily and for its industrial growth, but naturally wished to reduce that dependence as quickly as possible; while the Soviet Union had a major interest in having a great Asian power as its ally, but could not wish that ally – which is also its chief Eastern neighbor – to become more powerful too quickly. Another source of disagreement is that the Soviet Union is in a phase of development where, while not averse to using local threats and occasionally force to gain foreign policy objectives, it wants to assure its citizens that they may go about their business without fear of a major war. China, on the other hand, is in a phase where the Communist leaders, though probably as unwilling to provoke world war as their Soviet colleagues, need the atmosphere of the "beleaguered fortress" and of war hysteria as much as Russia needed it twenty or thirty years ago in order to dragoon their peoples into exceptional efforts.

Combined with the facts of geography and the differences in diplomatic status, these different views of the desirable pace for the growth of Chinese strength and of the relative uses of tension or relaxation in world affairs were bound to find expression in different estimates of the relative urgency, say, of a "summit conference" without Communist China or of a diplomatic crisis to force a solution of the "Taiwan question"; of the relative priority to be given in Soviet economic planning to capital aid for the Chinese ally as against uncommitted neutrals; and—least publicly discussed and most important among these critical issues—of the desirability of agreement on the banning of atomic tests under international control, which would result in a closing of the "nuclear club" and hence in the permanent dependence of China on Russia for obtaining nuclear weapons. Nor is it surprising that under the pressure of these conflicts the Chinese Communists' tradition of self-reliance in working out their own strategy without regard to foreign models has given rise to an ambitious and explosive new concept of a specific road to communism for overpopulated and underdeveloped countries unable or unwilling to rely on foreign capital aid, whether from "capitalist" or "Socialist" sources.

Given Moscow's and Peking's undoubted awareness of their overriding community of interests as against these important differences, and given the total control of the published word exercised by both, it is understandable that up to the end of 1958 no explicit arguments and only a few implicit disagreements on these critical issues were to be found in the public record. Nevertheless, it was possible to trace their impact in a number of symptoms of wavering and apparent indecision which appeared in Soviet foreign policy that year and which were difficult to account for otherwise.

These symptoms have been widely noticed in the West, and have led a number of observers to make conjectures about new divisions within the Presidium of the Soviet Communist Party. Yet while it is, of course, perfectly possible that some of the Presidium members incline to differ from Khrushchev and from each other on tactical questions of foreign policy, all the evidence suggests that Khrushchev's control of the party and government machine had become virtually unchallengable since the successive elimination first of the "anti-party group" and then of Marshal Zhukov in 1957 (none of Khrushchev's Presidium colleagues any longer controls any power apparatus of his own), and whatever rivalry now survives in the policy-making inner circle is merely in the nature of competition for influence with the new dictator and for his eventual succession. Repeatedly during 1958, Khrushchev publicly proclaimed new domestic policies — from the dissolution of the Machine Tractor Stations to the educational reform — apparently without bothering to obtain the advance approval of any of the constitutional organs of the party. If, then, he did show symptoms of uncertainty in foreign affairs, it would seem logical to look for the cause not in any weakness of his domestic position, but in a diplomatic tug of war due to divergencies between his own conceptions and those of his major ally.

TWO POLICIES TOWARD YUGOSLAVIA

The first case where sudden changes in the emphasis of Soviet policy became apparent was the new break with Tito's Yugoslavia in the spring; and here the violence of Chinese participation in the conflict was so striking that a number of Western students were led to attribute the whole break to Chinese initiative, and to assume that it was somehow forced on a reluctant Khrushchev by pressure from Peking. In this extreme form, the theory is contradicted both by the public chronology of events and by what limited inside knowledge is available from Yugoslav sources. The Yugoslav leaders insist that they had expected the break ever since they first received the draft of the "declaration of principles" that came to be adopted by twelve ruling Communist parties – but not by them – in Moscow in November 1957, with its emphasis on the obligation of all Communists to support the Warsaw military pact and its doctrinaire condemnation of "revisionism." The Yugoslavs have also stated that Khrushchev himself warned their delegates that they would be politically attacked when they refused to sign that document.[4] Thus the final draft of the new Yugoslav party program, which became the formal pretext for the attack in the spring, was prepared and published in the knowledge that the break was coming.

The Soviet decision not to send fraternal delegates to the Yugoslav party congress and to "advise" the other ruling parties not to send any – a clear step toward formal excommunication – was transmitted to Belgrade on April 5,[5] that is, while Khrushchev was in Hungary, and as soon as he had heard Kadar's report on the results of his efforts to get the program changed in essentials; we now know from Gomulka that a similar attempt was undertaken, apparently at the same time, by two members of the Polish Politburo.[6] During the same days of early April the first public attack on the new Yugoslav program – a joint article by Fedoseyev, Pomyalov, and Cheprakov in No. 6 of the Moscow *Kommunist* – was passed for publication; it came out in time for distribution before the Yugoslav party congress, and while formally still couched in "comradely" language, condemned the draft, root and branch, as a "revisionist" document. On April 21, still before the Yugoslav congress but after the publication in Belgrade of some amendments to the passages that had caused most offense in Moscow, Pyotr Pospelov, secretary of the Central Committee of the CPSU, said in an official Lenin Memorial speech that "objectively speaking, the draft program of the LCY looks like a document intended, in effect, to weaken the unity of the Communist and workers' parties, to weaken the unity of the socialist states." [7] And while he formally expressed the hope that the Yugoslav party congress would substantially revise the draft, the refusal to send fraternal delegates made it clear that no such hope was really entertained and that the formal breaking off of party relations was being prepared. With the determined rejection of Soviet interference and the adoption of the program by the congress, the break became inevitable.

The first Chinese intervention in the public discussion — an editorial published by the Peking *People's Daily* on May 5 — did not take place until a week after the conclusion of the Yugoslav congress, and a full month after the basic Soviet decision had been taken. There is thus no evidence whatever to back the hypothesis of "Chinese initiative" in provoking the break. Nevertheless, the Chinese intervention marked an important new development — the partial extension of the break to the field of state relations. Up to that moment, all indications were that the Soviet leaders wished to excommunicate the Yugoslav Communists from the international Communist movement as heretics, but to demonstrate at the same time that, in contrast to Stalin's practice, they would not allow the ideological conflict to interfere seriously in their diplomatic relations with a friendly neutral state. Even while the Yugloslav congress was in progress, public statements to this effect were made by two members of the Soviet party Presidium who happened to be abroad — Mikoyan in Bonn and Furtseva in Warsaw.[8]

The *People's Daily* article went much further, however: it was the first to state publicly that the original condemnation of the Yugoslav party by the Cominform in 1948 had been "basically correct"; it reintroduced the Stalinist method of appealing to the Yugoslav rank and file over the heads of the "leaders"; and it charged bluntly that "the program put forward by the Yugoslav revisionists fits in exactly with what the imperialists, and particularly the American imperialists, want." In short, it prepared the atmosphere for treating the Yugoslav leaders not as friendly if ideologically misguided neutrals, but as agents of the imperialist enemy—a conclusion explicitly drawn in later Chinese Communist documents.[9]

This shift of emphasis was all the more important because the *People's Daily* article was published on the eve of a meeting of the Central Committee of the CPSU. No resolution on Yugoslavia was published after that meeting, though the obvious fact that the subject was discussed has since been confirmed.[10] Even while the meeting was in progress, *Pravda* belatedly published Khrushchev's and Voroshilov's congratulations to Tito on his re-election as President of Yugoslavia and his reply. But immediately afterwards (May 9), a *Pravda* editorial condemning the Yugoslav program labeled as "naïve" the view that state relations might remain unimpaired by ideological differences, suggested that American aid to Yugoslavia was given as a reward for services rendered in disrupting the "Socialist camp," and hinted that Soviet credits to Yugoslavia might be canceled if the dispute continued.

During the following weeks, the Soviet press reprinted criticism of the Yugoslav program by various Communist parties, ranging from the still fraternal admonitions of the Poles to the bitter attacks of the Chinese. The latter were also the first to charge that the Yugoslavs had already engaged in disruptive activities in 1956 by supporting the "traitorous Navy clique" in Hungary — a charge that came to be repeated in the official indictment published after Imre Nagy's execution in June.[11] On May 27, just as the Chinese party congress was adopting a resolution on the level of the previous press attacks, the Soviet embassy informed the Yugoslav government of the "suspension" of promised credits; on June 2, Khrushchev, speaking at the Bulgarian party congress in Sofia, personally endorsed most of the anti-Yugoslav charges as well as the "correctness" of the 1948 Cominform resolution — while still talking, almost in the same breath, of the desirability of maintaining "normal" state relations.[12]

The history of this singularly confused campaign seems to justify three conclusions: first, that the Soviet leaders initiated the break with Yugoslavia, despite the hopes Khrushchev had once invested in a *rapprochement*, because they could not persuade the Yugoslav leaders to renounce their "non-bloc" position outside the Warsaw pact, and because the restoration of discipline within the bloc required the condemnation of any ideology that could serve as a justification for "neutralism"; second, that they wished to keep the campaign within the limits of an ideological excommunication, because they were well aware that to bring state pressure on one neutral country might alienate many other neutral countries, particularly in Asia; third, that they were reluctantly driven to adopt measures exceeding their original intention by the pressure of their Chinese allies. The question remains what interest the Chinese Communists could have had in sharpening the conflict; their interest in the cohesion of the bloc, while obvious, cannot explain why their zeal should have exceeded that of the Soviet leaders, who were even more immediately concerned.

The answer, in my view, must be found partly in Peking's general interest in heightening rather than relaxing international tension as discussed above, and partly in specific Chinese discontent with the distribution of Soviet credits. According to the best information available, Soviet credits to China all but petered out after 1956, and the vital deliveries of Soviet and satellite equipment in subsequent years had to be fully paid for.[13] The CPC's decision at its May 1958 congress to try to achieve a "Great Leap Forward" toward industrialization by the large-scale creation of primitive rural cottage industries was a desperate response to China's appalling shortage of capital goods, which had so far limited the pace of industrialization efforts and was leading to growing unemployment in the towns; in this situation the continued granting of Soviet credits to uncommitted nations must have been fiercely resented, and the execution of the credit pledge to the Yugoslav "renegades" would have seemed unbearable.

But beyond that the Chinese leaders clearly considered the Yugoslav view that a Communist country could be on friendly terms with the United States as particularly dangerous, because they could not help worrying whether the diplomacy of co-existence might not eventually lead the Soviet leaders to adopt a similar attitude – to the incalculable disadvantage of Communist China. By treating the Yugoslav revisionists not as erring brethren to be led back to the right path but as bought enemy agents to be discredited and eventually destroyed, the Chinese were seeking deliberately – and not without success – to set a limit to Khrushchev's efforts to reach an international *détente*. An indirect confirmation of this hypothesis may be found in the fact that a few months later, after a greater degree of foreign policy co-ordination had been promised to the Chinese, and after international tension had been increased through a succession of crises, Khrushchev felt free to return to his own preferred methods of fighting the Yugoslav deviation by "ideological struggle," while seeking to promote "friendly relations" between the governments, acknowledging Yugoslav diplomatic support on many issues, and favoring the extension of trade and cultural exchanges.[14]

CHINA AND THE "NUCLEAR CLUB"

On the far more central issue of the ending of atomic tests under international control, no contemporary direct evidence of differences between the Soviet and Chinese attitudes is available. One possible glimpse is afforded by the fact that on May 11, 1958, Chinese Foreign Minister Chen Yi stated in an interview that China intended to become a nuclear power, without specifying whether she would do so only with the help of Soviet deliveries or eventually by her own production also.[15] At that time, discussions concerning the Western proposal for a conference of technical experts to examine possibilities of effective control were still in progress; soon afterwards that conference met and reached positive conclusions, leading in time to a conference of the three nuclear powers on the diplomatic level.

Considering the failure of all previous Soviet proposals for a "summit meeting" and the breakdown of all disarmament discussions conducted under the aegis of the United Nations, this conference on tests appeared by the end of

1958 much the most hopeful outcome of "co-existence diplomacy" so far. The obvious fact that agreement on a prohibition of further tests under effective international control would result in a closing of the "nuclear club" constituted both its main political importance and its main inherent difficulty, as control to be effective would have to be extended to the territory of powers that, having no nuclear arms production yet, were not parties to the negotiation. China was one of these.

Now while Peking had not voiced any specific views on the subject so far, the Soviet attitude showed a striking degree of wavering and inconsistency: its record, in fact, is neither wholly compatible with the assumption that the Russians were seriously concerned to reach an agreed ban on atomic tests, nor with the opposite assumption that they merely aimed to score a propaganda success by putting the Western powers in the wrong. Up to the very opening day of the conference of technical experts, the Soviet government threatened to refuse participation under a threadbare pretext; yet without any change in Western policy, their experts came at the last moment and co-operated constructively in working out the possibilities of control. Again at the political conference, the Russians started by obstructing any discussion of controls by means of procedural wrangles, while accusing the West of unwillingness to accept any binding obligation on the cessation of tests; yet repeatedly they showed themselves ready to accept procedural compromises rather than risk complete breakdown.

The result of these contradictory tactics was for years neither to fulfill nor to destroy the hopes set on the test negotiations by world opinion – including, presumably, Soviet opinion – but to postpone the day when the critical problem of obtaining the agreement of outside parties as a precondition of world-wide control would have to be faced. It is permissible to wonder whether this was the real purpose of the wrangling, and whether the underlying cause of the inconsistency was simply that the issue still remained unresolved between the Russians and the Chinese.[16]

CHINA AND THE "MIDDLE EASTERN SUMMIT"

The link between Russian wavering and Chinese interest was far more obvious in connection with the proposals during the Middle Eastern crisis of the summer of 1958, to hold a "summit conference" within the framework of the Security Council of the United Nations. The assumption that Chinese pressure changed Moscow's view on these proposals has been challenged on the basis of documentary evidence that Chinese and Soviet public statements during the late July phase of the crisis were at no point out of step, and that Khrushchev started backtracking on his acceptance of Macmillan's proposal for such a meeting several days before his journey to Peking.[17] Yet this does not alter the fact that the backtracking itself took place under an absurd pretext and is explicable only in terms of Chinese pressure, and that the Peking meeting between Khrushchev and Mao which followed these events in early August resulted in a new Soviet commitment to "all-round co-ordination" of policy.

Indeed, both Khrushchev's own original proposal for a "summit conference" on the Middle East, including India, and his subsequent acceptance of the British counterproposal to hold such a conference within the framework of a special session of the Security Council, were so clearly injurious to the interests of Communist China that the real problem is what moved him to take these steps at all rather than what caused him to reverse them. The general Soviet campaign for a "summit conference" had lost most of its original impetus by mid-July, and Khrushchev must have been fully aware that the West was not going to accept such a conference on terms that amounted to an implicit recognition of the *status quo* of Communist rule in Eastern Europe — his principal purpose in advocating one.

The sudden demand for a "summit conference" on the Middle East with the inclusion of India was thus not a simple modification of a continuing campaign for "a summit meeting, somehow or other"; it was a panic reaction. There is little doubt that the Allied landings in Lebanon and Jordan (July 15–17) were at first genuinely viewed by the Soviet leaders as preparations for armed intervention against General Kassem's new revolutionary government in Iraq; during the first few days, they were, after all, interpreted in this way by a great many non-Communists as well. Yet if that expectation had come true, the Russians would have been faced with the choice of using force against American troops, with all the risks involved, or appearing impotent in the face of American intervention in a crucial, contested area.

Rather than confront this dilemma, Khrushchev was evidently determined to use every conceivable political pressure to prevent the Western powers from carrying out their supposed intention, while still eschewing military commitment: although he hurried to recognize the new Iraqi government and promised Nasser support in the unlikely event of a Western attack on the United Arab Republic, he sent no "volunteer" fighters and instead issued his appeal for an emergency summit meeting with Indian participation (July 19). When the British counter-proposal was made on July 22, the danger was not yet over in the Soviet view; it should be remembered that the first Western states to recognize the new Iraqi government acted only on July 30, and Britain and the United States only on August 1 and 2. Even unofficial indications that recognition was intended – the sure sign that the danger feared by Moscow had passed – did not emerge until the London Meeting of the Council of the Baghdad Pact on July 28.

Thus Khrushchev's decision on July 23 to accept a Security Council meeting with the interested states, and to suggest July 28 as the date for it, was still made in a crisis atmosphere; the air of hurried improvisation surrounding this decision is attested to by the fact that comment on the British proposal in that morning's *Izvestia* was still hostile, using the same arguments about the Council's "unrepresentative" character that were being marshaled in China, and that – as it subsequently transpired – Foreign Minister Andrei Gromyko had gone (or been sent) on leave at this of all times. Clearly the routine reaction of Soviet diplomacy to the idea of a Security Council meeting was negative, largely out of regard for Communist China's well-known susceptibilities; but the routine was overridden by Khrushchev's sense of an emergency – or, if you prefer, his panic.

The first preparations for getting out of the commitment to a Security Council meeting emerged in the Soviet and Chinese press on July 27–28 in the form of warnings against Western "delaying maneuvers" and crystallized in Khrushchev's note of the 29th, rejecting the Western proposal for a meeting of the permanent Security Council representatives to prepare for the special session. Ostensibly, the reason for this rejection was that the Western powers were trying to substitute a routine meeting of the Security Council in place of the special summit session; but this was clearly untrue. The real reasons must have included the growing realization that the acute danger was apparently past, and that at any rate the Council meeting would no longer come in time to make a difference to it; but none of this would have caused Khrushchev to default on a commitment he had already accepted if there had been no positive reason arguing *against* such a meeting which now, in the changed situation, gained decisive weight — and that positive reason was the interest of his Chinese ally, whom he flew to visit two days later.

The Chinese Communists had never, so far as is known, objected to the settlement of European questions by four-power conferences; it was the Russians who had lately begun to object to this forum because they felt that the relation of three to one in favor of the West no longer corresponded to the realities of power, and also because they wanted to force the West to deal with some of their satellites on major international issues. But the attempt to settle a major crisis on Asian soil by a "concert of powers" including an Asian government other than Peking — be it Delhi or Taipeh — was quite a different matter: it was bound to injure Peking's prestige and to prejudice its diplomatic future. Moreover, the mere fact that such an attempt was possible drastically showed Mao both the dangers of imperfect consultation on Soviet policies and the risks of leaving the unsolved problems of China's diplomatic status and of Taiwan for too long in a state of quiescence, however comfortable this might be for his Russian allies. He could not, therefore, be content merely to make Khrushchev withdraw from his rash commitment; he had to ensure better consultation and higher priority for his own problems in the formation of joint policies in the future. Hence the need for a conference.

This interpretation is confirmed by the text of the Soviet-Chinese communiqué of August 3, with its perfunctory demand for "the immediate summoning of a conference of the heads of government of the great powers" (without mention either of India or the Security Council), and with its emphasis that "both parties have decided to ensure the continued all-round development of the comprehensive co-operation between their two countries and to strengthen still further the unity of the socialist camp."[18] The words "all-round co-ordination," which recur elsewhere in the document, were plainly intended to prevent a repetition of major Soviet improvisations anywhere in the world without advance consultation with Peking; but by the same token, they would also prevent Peking from starting a new crisis over Taiwan — which necessarily involves Soviet backing in the game of atomic blackmail — without advance consultation with Moscow. The subsequent launching of the new attack on Quemoy, but also the limitations of that attack, may thus be taken as the first fruits of the "complete identity of views" reached in "all-round discussions" on "the urgent and important problems of the international situation, on further strengthening the relations of friendship, alliance, and mutual assistance between the USSR and the Chinese People's Republic, and also on problems concerning the joint struggle for a peaceful settlement of international questions and concerning the safeguarding of world peace." The moving up of the Formosa problem in the scale of Soviet priorities, if only to a limited extent, was still another reflection of the shift in the balance of influence inside the bloc.[19]

PEKING'S MEANS OF PRESSURE

So far, a number of symptoms have been listed that indicate that such a shift was taking place in 1958; yet the question remains what underlying factors enabled the Chinese Communists to exert such effective pressure? After all, their dependence on Soviet military aid and on Soviet-bloc industrial equipment was still very great; in case of a major conflict, it would be absolute. How, then, did they manage to influence the foreign policies of the world power on whose support they ultimately depend?

The first condition for a realistic answer is to get the dimensions of the problem in perspective. At no moment were the Chinese "dictating" policy to the Soviets; they were still the junior partner, though a partner that had to be taken more seriously every year. The impact of their partly divergent interests on Soviet policy had become visible, but it remained limited. The Soviets wavered over the best tactics for dealing with the excommunicated Yugoslavs; they wavered over the prohibition and control of atomic tests; they gave in over the special session of the Security Council on the Middle Eastern crisis when the crisis was all but over; they backed a limited campaign against Quemoy. The most serious Chinese gain at that stage was the principle of "all-round co-ordination"; which meant in essence that the views of Moscow, the more powerful partner, would still prevail most of the time – but not all of the time. In other words, the outcome of any particular disagreement was no longer a foregone conclusion; that is as far as Peking had got by the end of 1958.

Within these limits, the shift was to some extent an automatic reflection of the real growth in the power of the Chinese – above all, their industrial growth and their increased influence over their Asian neighbors. To some extent it also reflected China's growing power to embarrass the USSR: as long as Russia felt she could not afford to see her one major ally defeated and destroyed, Mao's greater willingness to incur risks of war gave him a power of blackmail over his protector. His recklessness may not be as absolute as his propaganda and some of his private utterances quoted by the Yugoslavs suggest; it probably contains an element of bluff.[20] But not even the Soviet leaders can be sure just how large that element is: and when every reasonable deduction has been made, there remains one real factor that must be frightening to the successor of Lenin's successor — the unrelenting determination of a younger revolution, which even now seems to have entered its most extreme utopian phase.

This brings us to what is probably the most important factor of change in the Soviet-Chinese balance: the unbroken authority of Mao Tse-tung, and the determined use he is making of it as an ideological innovator. When that authority was first invoked in the course of 1957 to repair the ideological damage done throughout the Soviet bloc and the Communist movement by Khrushchev's "secret speech," it was unreservedly and willingly thrown in to promote renewed recognition of the "leading role" of the Soviet Union.[21] But while this formula continued to be repeated in China on festive occasions like the anniversary of the Bolshevik seizure of power, the revolutionary reorganization of the country on the basis of "people's communes" had by late 1958 come to be recognized in both China and Russia as an implicit challenge to the Soviet monopoly of ideological leadership — a claim to the discovery not only of a specific Asian road to "socialism" but of an Asian short cut to the higher stage of "communism." The immediate Soviet response was an equally implicit, but unmistakable denial of the claim.

The "people's communes" had their origin in the "Great Leap Forward" on which the second session of the Eighth Congress of the CPC embarked in the spring of 1958. The effort to overcome China's desperate shortage of the capital goods needed for the classical type of industrialization – a shortage aggravated by the drying up of Soviet credits – through the massive development of primitive, rural cottage industries, raised problems of labor rationalization for which the creation of these large militarized units seemed the only solution. In organization and spirit, they consciously hark back to the long tradition of the civil war – to the military communism that was the "mode of production" of a self-sufficient army confined to the countryside.[22]

Both the "Leap Forward" and the revival of the civil-war tradition carried distinct overtones of the Chinese Communists' pride in their ability to stand on their own feet, if necessary without Soviet aid. But added to this there now emerged a new ideological superstructure: the claim that the partial replacement of wages by the organized distribution of food rations and other necessities in the communes was a step toward the realization of the "higher stage" of communism with its principle, "to each according to his needs." This claim constituted a challenge to the monopoly of the Soviet Union as the first and so far the only country where the "Socialist state" had been completed and the "transition to communism" had begun.[23]

In fact, of course, the challenge was based on ideological sleight-of-hand. In the Marxian vision, the Communist stage is based on productive abundance: "to each according to his needs" means according to whatever needs the individual may feel, because society produces enough for all. In Chinese reality, distribution in kind is based on rationing: "to each according to his needs" means according to whatever minimum needs the authorities decide can and must be satisfied. Every army is "Communist" in this sense, and every prison; so was every Pharaonic household. The Soviet ideologues, who no doubt saw through the trick, at first refrained from exposing it. But the Soviet press gave no publicity to the claims, while theoretical articles ostensibly dealing with Soviet problems explained at length that communism can only be built on the basis of real abundance and the most advanced technical methods, and "friendly" reports from Soviet correspondents in China stressed the ingenious use of medieval production techniques in the industrial self-help of the communes.[24] One Soviet party philosopher even put forward the explicit doctrine that the "Socialist" countries of Asia would enter the Communist stage only after the "Socialist" countries of Europe.[25]

Yet even if the exuberant ideological claims of the Chinese Communists are left aside, there remain two facts of crucial importance for the future of China's position in the world Communist movement. One is that the Chinese Communists, however much their official statistics are to be discounted, are at any rate making enormous efforts to increase both agricultural and industrial output through large-scale labor rationalization and the development of cottage industries – methods that are utterly different from those used during the corresponding phase in Russia, and that seem more naturally adapted to the conditions of overpopulated countries with an extreme shortage of capital. The other is that they are doing so, for the time being at least, by using social and ideological techniques that contrast directly with those of both the Stalinist and the present phase of Soviet development. In contrast to Stalinism, they are not relying on the quick creation of new, materially privileged groups but are seeking to revive some of the early egalitarian appeal of the revolution; in contrast to present-day Russia, where Khrushchev is seeking to replace payments in kind throughout agriculture by the yardstick of money (in order to promote rational cost-accounting as a basis for the steady improvement of output per man),[26] the Chinese tend to increase the scope of distribution in kind. The resulting atmosphere is utterly different from that of Soviet society, but far closer than the latter to the utopian dreams that may inspire primitive Communist mass movements elsewhere.

Now it seems highly improbable that the new Chinese concept of communal organization will seriously influence Khrushchev's ideas about the future development of Soviet collective farms (despite the superficial resemblance between the "people's communes" and the "agro-towns," to the creation of which he is still committed), or, conversely, that Khrushchev's ideas will divert the Chinese Communists from their new road, though experience may cause modification of some utopian excesses: for both policies are rooted in utterly different conditions. But if the two different models continue to "co-exist" within the "Socialist camp," other ruling Communist parties will be forced to take a choice, and the outcome is likely to be a division on geographical lines. The trend is toward a Chinese ascendancy over Asian communism – and that in turn must intensify the shift in the Sino-Soviet balance of power and the tensions produced by that shift. For in the long run, the unity of an alliance of totalitarian states requires the ideological unity of the ruling parties, and the latter can only be maintained if the right of a single authority to interpret the ideology in the face of changing conditions and problems is recognized by all. Diplomatic consultation and compromise may be a very effective method for adjusting differences of interest within an alliance so long as its members agree that their common interests are more important. But if historical experience is any guide, synods and councils are not equally effective in maintaining the doctrinal unity of a Church.

POSTSCRIPT: THE COMPROMISE OF DECEMBER 1958

The above had been written before the sixth plenary session of the Central Committee of the CPC, held between November 28 and December 10, marked a new phase in the developments here discussed. The Central Committee communiqué[27] showed marked concessions to the Soviet point of view on several of the controversial issues. Instead of war hysteria, there was now emphasis that time was on the side of the Communists and that growing decay and divisions among the "imperialists" would permit the maintenance of peace. The "Quemoy crisis," which had been allowed to peter out since the end of October, was quietly buried, and the issue of Taiwan treated as a problem that would be solved by time and the people rather than by outside force. Finally, the danger of international "revisionism" got no more than one perfunctory reference, and Yugoslavia none at all; in fact the resumption of Sino-Yugoslav trade negotiations was reported at that time.

The most significant change of line, however, was contained in the long and detailed resolution on the "people's communes" adopted by the same plenum.[28] While the essential program of this revolutionary transformation of the Chinese countryside was maintained, the resolution marked a limited but substantial retreat on two fronts — practically, before the Chinese peasants, and ideologically, before Soviet criticism. The practical retreat, dictated, above all, by the need to stop the wholesale encroachment on the peasant's family life, his small private possessions, and his spare time, cannot be discussed here in detail, except to mention the convincing comparison drawn in the resolution itself with Stalin's 1930 warning against "dizziness with success"; it is difficult to estimate the severity of the symptoms of discontent and disorganization that may have necessitated this partial return to realism.

The ideological retreat, on the other hand, is directly relevant to the present analysis. It centered in the warning that while there was a connection between the creation of "people's communes," the transformation of co-operatives into all-national property, and the transition to communism, these were nevertheless three distinct processes, of which the second would take years longer than the first, and the third a much longer period yet. This amounted to a complete disclaimer of any rivalry with the Soviet Union in the speed of the transition to communism, and a renewed recognition that Russia was so far the only country to complete the construction of "socialism" and to start the transition to the "higher stage" — a claim that constitutes the doctrinal foundation of Russia's "leading role." In addition, the resolution's practical injunctions against a hasty treatment of communal property as state property, against a primitive egalitarianism at a time when skilled cadres are scarce, and against an exaggerated reduction of the (differentiated) money portion of wages in favor of the (equal) rewards in kind, tended to reduce further some of the contrasts in the social atmosphere analyzed above. The resolution even stated that in the immediate future, the cash portion of wages would have to grow faster than the "free supply" portion, thus leading to greater differentiation.

Yet, while the resolution accepted a more modest and realistic estimate of the *stage* that China had reached, it maintained the principle of her own original *road* to communism. This applied not only to the essential combination of agriculture and rural industries in the communal units but also to the "free supply system" itself. If the latter was no longer viewed as an egalitarian short cut for the immediate transition to communism, it was still valued as a "germ" of Communist relationships to be preserved for another day. This remained in direct contrast to Khrushchev's insistence that there was no road to communism without abundance, no road to abundance without the highest productivity, and no road to higher productivity without "the yardstick of the ruble"; and it therefore remained the "germ" of a concept for a different "Asian road" which might sooner or later be brought to flowering. Thus the new shift in the relation of forces within the Communist alliance – for once, clearly a shift in Russia's favor – had failed to close the ideological rift.

7

1959–60: DIPLOMACY AND REVOLUTION

The policy statement and the appeal to the peoples of the world adopted in December 1960 by the Moscow conference of eighty-one Communist parties marked the end of one phase in the dispute between the leaderships of the ruling parties of China and the Soviet Union – the phase in which the followers of Mao for the first time openly challenged the standing of the Soviet Communists as the fountainhead of ideological orthodoxy for the world movement. But the "ideological dispute" which began in April of that year was neither a sudden nor a self-contained development: it grew out of acute differences between the two Communist Great Powers over concrete diplomatic issues, and it took its course in constant interaction with the changes in Soviet diplomatic tactics. Hence the total impact of that phase on Soviet foreign policy on one side, and on the ideology, organization, and strategy of international communism on the other, cannot be evaluated from an interpretation of the Moscow documents alone, but only from a study of the process as a whole, as it developed during that year on both planes.

To say that the 1960 Chinese challenge to Soviet ideological authority grew out of pragmatic disagreements over foreign policy is not to take the view that the varieties of Communist ideology are a mere cloak for conflicts of national interest. The profound differences in the history of the Soviet and Chinese Communist parties, both in the strategy by which they conquered power and in the methods they used afterwards for transforming society, have clearly produced a different ideological climate, different forms of inner-party life, and a different "style of work"; and the fact that Mao Tse-tung could only win control of the Chinese party and lead it to victory by repeatedly defying Stalin's advice has contributed to the formation of a Chinese Communist leadership that is highly conscious of those differences. In their essence, these distinctive characteristics have always amounted to an exaltation of faith and will over all "objective conditions" of the productive forces and all given class structures which exceeds that shown by the Bolshevik model, and is even more remote from the original Marxian doctrine than the latter.[1]

A party leadership conditioned by this ideological climate will obviously perceive both the internal problems and the national interests of the state it governs in a peculiar way; to that extent, the ideological difference constitutes a kind of permanent potential for rivalry between the two Communist Great Powers. Yet it does not by itself explain the timing and content of any particular dispute between them. For given the manifestly overriding importance of their common interests, the potential rivalry could only became actual when concrete policy disagreements arose that could not be settled by the ordinary means of intra-*bloc* diplomacy, and that the weaker and dependent ally regarded as sufficiently vital to take recourse to the public use of the ideological weapon. This was done by China in muted hints during the 1958 disagreements, and much more openly in 1960.

FROM CONFLICT OF INTERESTS TO "IDEOLOGICAL DISPUTE"

In both cases, Chinese misgivings seem to have been based on a sense of insufficient Soviet diplomatic and military support in their long-standing conflict with the United States, and to have been acutely aggravated by Khrushchev's efforts to achieve a Soviet-American *détente* — by his repeated bids for a "summit conference" without Communist China and by his visit to the U.S. in September 1959. The Chinese leaders apparently feared, probably not without reason, that such a *détente* would further diminish Soviet interest in taking serious risks on their behalf, and increase Soviet interest in preventing them from taking any such risks themselves. Above all, Soviet willingness to make disarmament one of the main items on any summit agenda, combined with the agreed temporary ban on nuclear test explosions and the continued negotiations for a permanent ban, must have given rise to Chinese anxiety lest the Russians might be willing on certain conditions to enter a commitment to close the "nuclear club." The mere fact of negotiation on that subject apparently precluded them from receiving Soviet aid in developing nuclear weapons of their own, and thus helped to delay their becoming a world power of the first rank; an actual Soviet commitment would face them with the choice of either accepting permanent inferiority in this field, or — if they went ahead successfully in developing and testing the weapon themselves — of defying an agreement of the world's leading powers in isolation.[2]

Whatever the Chinese may have said in their private representations to Moscow, they did not then think it advisable to spell out these fears in public. But during the winter of 1959–60 – roughly from Khrushchev's visit to Peking, on his return from his talks with Eisenhower, at the beginning of October to the Moscow conference of the Warsaw pact states in early February – they openly attacked the assumptions on which the effort to achieve a Soviet-American *détente* was officially based.[3] The core of their argument was that the policy of American "imperialism" and of Eisenhower, its "chieftain," could not change in substance even if it was temporarily disguised by peace-loving phrases; hence nothing could be gained by seeking an understanding with the U.S. in an atmosphere of *détente,* only by isolating this "main enemy" and putting maximum pressure on him. A period of quite visible, concrete disagreement on policy toward the Eisenhower administration thus preceded the Chinese Communists' generalized, ideological attack on Soviet authority.

The most striking characteristic of that period is the apparent unconcern with which the Soviet leaders pursued their preparations for a "summit conference," despite the increasingly outspoken Chinese protests. The impression that Mao Tse-tung had refused to approve the concept of a *détente* based on "mutual concessions" as advanced by Khrushchev was confirmed when the latter, addressing the Supreme Soviet on his return to Moscow, coupled his advocacy of that concept with blunt warnings against the "Trotskyite adventurism" of a policy of "neither peace nor war,"[4] and when the theoretical organ of the Chinese Communists developed an analysis of American foreign policy directly opposed to Khrushchev's optimism in the following months.[5] Nevertheless, Khrushchev announced to the Supreme Soviet in January 1960 a substantial reduction of Soviet conventional forces and military expenditures as his advance contribution to the ten-power disarmament negotiations, and also indicated willingness to help overcome the deadlock in the negotiations on an inspection system for a permanent ban on nuclear test explosions – a most sensitive issue from the Chinese point of view.

Within a week, the standing committee of the Chinese National People's Congress, in a resolution formally approving the Soviet disarmament proposals, solemnly announced to the world that China would not be bound by any agreements to which she was not a party; but when this stand, together with warnings against illusions about a change in the character of American policy, was repeated at the conference of Warsaw treaty ministers in early February by the Chinese observer, his speech was not published in any European member state of the Soviet bloc, and the declaration adopted by the conference showed virtually no concessions to his point of view.[6] To cap it all, Khrushchev spent most of the remainder of February, including the tenth anniversary of the Sino-Soviet alliance, in India and Indonesia, two countries with which China was involved in acute conflicts of national interest, and showed throughout the journey an almost ostentatious detachment from Chinese claims and actions.

All during the winter, the Chinese thus experienced the inherent weakness in the position of a dependent ally who urges the stronger partner to pay more heed to his interests, but is unable to switch sides if the latter turns a deaf ear: none of their objections, raised first in secret and then with increasing publicity, were able to deflect Khrushchev from his course. There remained to them one weapon – to interfere directly, not with the

Soviet policy of *détente* but with the *détente* itself, by urging on Communist and revolutionary nationalist movements in the non-Communist world a bolder forward policy than was compatible with the plans of Soviet diplomacy. But this meant that the Chinese Communists must set themselves up as rivals to their Russian comrades in advising these movements – in other words, that they must generalize the dispute and raise the question of ideological authority.

PEKING AND THE "INEVITABILITY OF WAR"

During the later part of the winter of 1959–60, a number of cases became known in which Chinese representatives had opposed Soviet delegates in closed sessions of the directing organs of such international "front organizations" as the World Peace Council, the Afro-Asian Solidarity Committee, the World Federation of Trade Unions, and so forth.[7] The central issue in these clashes was whether the "peace campaign" was the priority task to which all other forms of revolutionary struggle must be subordinated, as the Russians maintained, or whether it was only one among many forms of the struggle against imperialism, which must in no circumstances be isolated and "set in opposition" to more militant forms of revolutionary action, as the Chinese argued. It was as a platform for these discussions in the international movement that the Chinese Communists published in April their ideological statements on the teachings of Lenin – documents that, despite all later elaborations and modifications, have remained basic for that phase of the dispute.[8]

It has been implied in subsequent Soviet polemics against "dogmatists and sectarians," and innumerable times spelled out in Western comment, that the central thesis of those Chinese statements was the continued validity of Lenin's belief in the inevitability of world war. That is not so. Every one of the Chinese documents in question quoted with approval the sentence in the 1957 Moscow declaration (based in turn on the resolution of the Twentieth Congress of the CPSU) that, owing to the growth of the forces of peace, "it is now realistically possible to prevent war." [9] What none of them approved, however, is the formula of the Twenty-first Congress on the emerging possibility "even before the full victory of socialism in the world, while capitalism continues to exist in part of the world, to banish world war from the life of human society." The difference is that, in the Chinese view, the latter phrase implies the disappearance of any serious *danger* of world war while capitalism still exists; the Chinese Communists felt that this presupposed a change in the nature of imperialism – and that they had to deny such a possibility in order to contest the Khrushchevian hope of converting the ruling circles of the U.S. to a genuine acceptance of "peaceful co-existence" from realistic motives.

The picture drawn by the Chinese was that of an unchanged, though weakened, imperialism which would resort to war whenever it could to defend its sphere of exploitation, but might be prevented from doing so in any particular case by the "forces of peace." In practice, they agreed with the Soviets in regarding an all-out attack on the Soviet bloc as unlikely, but argued that inter-imperialist war was still possible, and insisted that colonial wars against national liberation movements were virtually inevitable: the latter could only be "stopped" by vigorous support for the revolutionary movements. But the Communists would fail to give support if they were "afraid" of another world war, if they "begged the imperialists for peace," or if they tolerated or even spread illusions about the warlike nature of imperialism, instead of mobilizing the masses everywhere for an all-out struggle against it.

This analysis implied three charges of "muddle-headed concessions to revisionism" against Khrushchev's policy: exaggeration of the dangers of nuclear war, which might paralyze the will to resist imperialism or at any rate lead to excessive caution; illusions about the growth of a "realistic" tendency toward peaceful co-existence among such "chieftains of imperialism" as Eisenhower, which might lead to a relaxation of vigilance among the Communist governments and movements; and, as a result, excessive reliance on diplomatic negotiation as a means to avert war, causing a desire to restrain revolutionary movements and "just wars" of liberation, instead of welcoming them as the best means to weaken the imperialists and stop *their* wars. Accordingly, the Chinese ideologists argued that it was all right for a Communist to seek a meeting with Eisenhower, but wrong to say that he believed in the latter's peaceful intentions; all right to propose "general and complete disarmament," but wrong to tell his own followers that there was a real chance of obtaining it; all right to propagate peaceful co-existence, but wrong to advise the Algerian nationalists to try and negotiate a cease-fire with President de Gaulle. They accepted peace *propaganda* as a means of revolutionary struggle against imperialism, but not peace *diplomacy* of a kind that might even temporarily mitigate the forms of that struggle.

THE ABORTIVE "SUMMIT"

The Russians, aware that there could be no serious negotiation without an atmosphere of *détente* and at least the pretense of believing in the peaceful intentions of the other side, recognized that this was an attack on their whole co-existence diplomacy; but they had to answer it on the ideological plane. Through the mouth of Otto Kuusinen, a member of the secretariat of the Central Committee of the CPSU who had begun work in the Comintern in Lenin's time, they insisted [10] that Lenin had differentiated between militarist die-hards and possible partners for peaceful co-existence in the imperialist camp, and had foreseen that changes in military technique might one day make war impossible. They argued that the growing strength of the "Socialist camp" and the destructive potential of nuclear weapons and long-range rockets had in fact provided a realistic basis for a diplomacy based on similar differentiation at the present time, and they claimed as telling proof of their thesis the success of Khrushchev's personal diplomacy in general, and of his "historic visit" to the U.S. in particular, in largely dispersing the climate of the Cold War and restoring businesslike relations between the two different social systems. Yet only a few weeks later Khrushchev himself, even while maintaining this position in theory, reversed himself in practice to the extent of wrecking the summit conference on the grounds that negotiation with Eisenhower had become impossible after his assumption of responsibility for the U 2 incident.

Western discussion of the causes of this *volte-face* has necessarily remained inconclusive in the absence of direct evidence of the motives of the Russian rulers and the course of their deliberations in the critical period. But a coherent analysis of the Sino-Soviet dispute is impossible without at least venturing a hypothesis. I have elsewhere stated my reasons for rejecting the theory that a decisive weakening of Khrushchev's position by some combination of "neo-Stalinist" or "pro-Chinese" elements in the Soviet leadership took place at the time; [11] indeed, I know of no convincing evidence for the assumption that such a grouping exists at all. On the other hand, Khrushchev's Baku speech of April 25 showed his anxieties, following a number of authorized American policy statements, lest the summit meeting might fail to yield the Western concessions on Berlin that he expected, and his desire to increase the pressure in that direction; and his initial reaction to the U 2 incident is consistent with the assumption that he regarded it not as a reason for evading the summit conference but as an occasion for making the pressure more effective by driving a wedge between Eisenhower and his "die-hard militarist" advisers.[12]

By marking the complete failure of this crude attempt at differentiation, the President's assumption of personal responsibility for the spy-flights, whatever its other merits or demerits, must have been a double blow to Khrushchev: it deprived him of the last hope of obtaining substantial concessions at the summit, and it put him clearly in the wrong on one important part of his public argument with his Chinese allies. A failure to reach his summit objectives thus became certain at the very moment at which, from the viewpoint of his prestige in the "Socialist camp" and the Communist world movement, he could least afford such a failure: hence it seems natural that, with the full support of his colleagues, he decided rather to wreck the conference in advance unless he could still force a last-minute differentiation by obtaining a public apology from Eisenhower.

Within a few days, Khrushchev demonstrated by his refusal to go ahead with an East German peace treaty, pending a possible summit conference with Eisenhower's successor, that he had not abandoned the "general line" of his diplomacy but only intended to change the time schedule. But the Chinese Communists not only were not content with that, but felt that now they had been proved right by events, they were in a strong position to force a broad change of policy by pressing home their ideological attack.

The attempt was made officially, and in fact publicly, at the beginning of June at the Peking session of the general council of the WFTU by the Chinese Vice President of that body, Liu Chang-sheng. Liu's speech [13] went beyond the April documents in demanding a "clarification" of the Communist attitude toward war, denouncing "indiscriminate" opposition to war, and calling for active support for "just wars" of liberation; in sharply opposing the formulation of the Soviet Twenty-first Congress about "eliminating war forever while imperialism still exists" as "entirely wrong" and leading to "evil consequences of a serious nature which, in fact, we already see at present," though he too admitted the possibility of preventing a new world war; and in condemning any belief that proposals for general and complete disarmament could be accepted, and that the funds formerly earmarked for war purposes could be used for the welfare of the masses and for assisting underdeveloped countries while imperialism still existed, as "downright whitewashing and embellishing imperialism" and thus "helping imperialism headed by the U.S. to dupe the people."

Yet the Chinese had misjudged their chances of forcing a change of the Soviet line. At the WFTU session, they found themselves vigorously counter-attacked by both the Russian and the major European movements, and finally isolated, with only the Indonesian trade unions on their side. Moreover, this seems to have been the point at which the Soviet leaders decided to give battle in defense of their ideological authority, and, first of all, to whip into line those European satellite parties that had in the past shown signs of sympathy for Chinese intransigence. They took the initiative in calling a conference of all ruling Communist parties to meet on the occasion of the Rumanian party congress later that month; and in the meantime the Soviet press began to publish warnings against the dangers of "dogmatism" and "sectarianism" in the international movement,[14] while the Italian delegates returning from Peking published the fact that the Chinese had been isolated and defeated in a major international discussion on the problems of the struggle for peace and disarmament.[15]

THE BUCHAREST CONFERENCE

Now that the issue of authority was out in the open, the field of the dispute kept broadening. Already in April, the speaker at the Peking celebration of Lenin's birthday, Lu Ting-Yi, had claimed for Mao's creation of the communes the succession to Lenin's concept of "uninterrupted revolution," and had attacked people who in Socialist construction "rely only on technique and not on the masses" and deny the need for further revolutionary struggle in the transition to the higher stage of communism.[16] Now *Pravda* quoted Engels and Lenin for their criticism of the Blanquist wish to "skip all the intermediate stages on the road to communism" in the illusion that "if power were in their hands, communism could be introduced the day after tomorrow."[17] Yet the original Sino-Soviet disagreement about the communes had been ended in the winter of 1958–59 with the withdrawal of the Chinese claim that this institution constituted a short cut to the Communist stage, and with an understanding that the Chinese would go on developing and the Soviets and their European satellites rejecting that institution without further debate. The revival of the issue now only made sense as part of the attempt by each side to throw doubt on the other's ideological orthodoxy.

On the eve of the Bucharest conference, a *Pravda* editorial stated bluntly that "among Socialist countries, there cannot be two opinions on the question of peace or war. Socialists believe that in present conditions there is no necessity for war, that disarmament is not only needed but possible, and that peaceful co-existence between nations is a vital necessity." [18] Coupled with a quote from Khrushchev's December speech to the Hungarian party congress about the need for all Communist governments to "synchronize their watches," and his warning that "if the leaders of any one of the Socialist countries would set themselves up to be above the rest, that can only play into the hands of our enemies," this indicated the Soviet leaders' intention to force a clear decision that would be binding on all ruling parties.[19]

But at Bucharest this intention was at least partly foiled by the Chinese. Khrushchev's public attack [20] on people who quote the words of Lenin without looking at the realities of the present world, and whom Lenin would set right in no uncertain manner if he came back today, was plain enough for all the satellite leaders to understand that the time for maneuvering between the two colossi was over, and for all but the Albanians to rally round. His account of how Soviet strength and Soviet skill had again and again foiled the war plans of the "imperialists," from Suez in 1956 to the Turkish-Syrian crisis of 1957 and the U.S. landing in Lebanon after the Iraqi revolution of 1958, if historically dubious, was propagandistically effective as a demonstration of the meaning of his "peace policy" for a Communist audience. But the Chinese delegate P'eng Chen was clearly instructed neither to submit nor to carry the ideological debate to a conclusion at this point: he evaded a decision by a skillful withdrawal to prepared positions.

In public, P'eng Chen appeared as the advocate of Communist unity at almost any price, to be achieved on the basis of the 1957 Moscow declaration to which all but the Yugoslavs had agreed.[21] This committed the Chinese once more to recognition of the possibility of preventing or "checking" imperialist wars – a possibility that, P'eng claimed, could only be fulfilled by the united strength of the "Socialist camp" and the determined mobilization of mass action against the imperialists. But it was also intended to commit the Russians once again to the 1957 thesis that the aggressive circles of the U.S. were the main enemy of peace and all popular aspirations, and that "revisionism" was the main danger within the ranks of the Communist movement. Having said that much, the Chinese representative spoke no word about *détente*, disarmament, or the "elimination of war from the life of mankind" before the disappearance of capitalism.

Behind the scences, he seems to have argued that the 1957 conference of ruling Communist parties had been called chiefly to settle problems of Communist power and "Socialist construction"; the questions now in dispute, being concerned with world-wide revolutionary strategy, could only be decided by a conference representing the whole Communist movement. Khrushchev might well complain about Chinese "factional" methods of carrying the quarrel into the ranks of other parties; in the end he had to agree to put up the dispute officially for world-wide inner-party discussion in preparation for a November conference in Moscow, and to content himself with a brief interim communiqué which, while stressing the primary importance of the "peace campaign," did not go beyond the 1957 declaration on any controversial point.

This fell far short of what the Soviet leaders had expected. The decisive showdown was not only postponed for several months, but it would take place before an audience of revolutionary parties many of whose members were less closely tied to Soviet control than the East European satellites and might well regard the Chinese slogans of unconditional revolutionary solidarity as more attractive than the Soviet readiness to subordinate their struggle to the needs of co-existence diplomacy whenever that seemed expedient. Thus an Algerian Communist might prefer Chinese offers of aid for the F.L.N. to the repeated Russian advice favoring negotiation with de Gaulle; an Iraqi Communist might recall that neither Soviet support for Kassem's regime nor his own party's Soviet-ordered retreat from its earlier offensive policy had obtained for it a legal, let alone a dominating, position under that regime; an Indonesian Communist might resent the manner in which Khrushchev had ignored his party during his official visit, and the general Soviet wooing of the "bourgeois nationalist" regime of Sukarno that limited the democratic rights of the Communists, although less than those of other parties and favored a neutralist bloc with the "renegade" Tito. And would not the Communists of Latin America be sensitive to the Chinese argument that, as Yankee imperialism was the main enemy, any attempts to relax Soviet-American tension were bound to weaken Soviet support for them as well as for China?

Yet without the co-operation of these movements, Khrushchev's co-existence diplomacy could not be carried through: he needed their discipline, and the Chinese had launched their ideological attack on his authority precisely in order to undermine that. Now they had created a situation in which the objects of the struggle, the Communist movements *in partibus infidelium,* were to act to some extent as its arbiters. True, the Russians still had the advantages of the prestige and resources of a world power as well as of older organizational ties: all the foreign Communists knew that the Soviets *could* help them more – financially, diplomatically, and ultimately militarily – than the Chinese, yet they were less certain that the Soviets *would* always help them to the limits of their ability. Hence Khrushchev seems to have felt that, in preparation for the November meeting, not only the circulation of new Soviet documents and the dispatch of new emissaries to the wavering parties were needed, but, above all, new proofs of the spirit of revolutionary internationalism animating his foreign policy.

SOVIET FOREIGN POLICY HARDENS

The fact that he had already decided to postpone his new summit approach until after the U.S. presidential elections, made it easier for him to furnish that proof: for he could now afford to increase rather than relax tension for a time without serious damage to his future diplomatic chances, and perhaps even in the hope of improving them by creating a dark backdrop for the next display of his sunny smile – provided only that he did not allow matters to get really out of hand. The weeks after Bucharest thus offered the strange spectacle of the Soviet leaders conducting themselves on the world stage in the very style that Peking's ideological theses had seemed to demand, while at the same time launching a vigorous campaign against those theses throughout the Communist world movement!

The Bucharest communiqué had not yet been published when Russia demonstratively walked out of the ten-power disarmament talks at Geneva, just before the Western counter-proposals for which she had been calling so insistently were officially submitted. There followed within a few days the shooting down of an American plane over the Arctic, the first Soviet note on the Congo accusing all the Western powers of backing Belgian military intervention as part of a plot to restore colonial rule, and, as a climax, Khrushchev's personal threat to use intercontinental rockets against the U.S. if the latter should attack Cuba. Yet during the same period, Khrushchev used his visit to Austria to insist again and again on the horrors of nuclear world war and on the need to avoid even local wars because of the risk that they might spread; and even in his most reckless gestures he took care not to do anything irrevocable. The Geneva test negotiations were *not* broken off; the Cuban rocket threat was soon "explained" as symbolic, while in the Congo the Russians refrained from backing their policy with force; and a proposal for taking the disarmament negotiations out of the U.N. and for calling instead for a disarmament conference of "all governments" including China, which the Chinese managed to get adopted by a Stockholm session of the World Peace Council in July, was promptly dropped down the memory hole by Moscow in favor of Khrushchev's suggestion that all heads of government of the member states should personally attend the next U.N. assembly session in order to discuss the Soviet plan for general and complete disarmament.

The same contradiction between the desire to keep the lines of negotiation open and the need to pose constantly as an uninhibited revolutionary agitator also dominated Khrushchev's subsequent behavior at the U.N. assembly. He did not back the neutrals' initiative for a new summit meeting but left the onus of killing it to the West. He depreciated the importance of his own proposals for "general and complete disarmament," for the sake of which so many heads of government had come, by devoting far more energy to his attack on "colonialism" in general and on the U.N. secretariat in particular, and by choosing a language and style of behavior more apt to inspire revolutionary movements outside than to influence delegates inside the assembly hall. He followed his attack on the secretariat by proposals for a reform of the latter and of the Security Council which appealed to the natural desire of the new African and Asian member states for stronger representation in the leading organs of the U.N., but then suggested that any such changes in the charter should be postponed until the delegates of the Chinese People's Republic had been seated. These inconsistencies are incomprehensible unless the fact is borne in mind that during all that time Khrushchev was engaged in an effort to prove his revolutionary zeal and international solidarity in preparation for the Moscow conference.

MOSCOW'S NEW PLATFORM

Meanwhile the line for the ideological campaign itself had been laid down by a meeting of the Central Committee of the CPSU in mid-July, which had approved the conduct of its delegation at Bucharest, led by Khrushchev, oddly enough after a report by secretariat member F. R. Kozlov, who had not been there. As developed during late July and August in the Soviet press and the statements of pro-Soviet leaders of foreign Communist parties, the campaign showed some significant changes of emphasis.[22] It was more uncompromising than ever in its emphasis on the need to avoid the horrors of nuclear war, and in its rejection of all attempts to belittle them or to regard any kind of international war as desirable. It insisted that good Marxist-Leninist revolutionaries were entitled and indeed obliged to adopt on this matter conclusions different from Lenin, both because of the new techniques of destruction and because of the change in the relation of world forces to the disadvantage of imperialism. It vigorously defended the possibility not only of stopping each particular war, but of altogether "eliminating war from the life of society" with the further growth of the strength of the "Socialist camp," even while capitalism still existed on part of the globe, as the Twenty-first Congress had laid down; and it claimed that the Soviet program of general and complete disarmament was a realistic policy goal that could be achieved, even though this might require time, "mutual concessions," and compromises. Any opposition to this general line of peaceful co-existence was to be eliminated from the Communist movement as "Trotskyite adventurism."

But the new campaign no longer laid stress on Khrushchev's differentiation between "realistic statesmen" and "die-hard militarists" in the enemy camp, and no longer mentioned "relaxation of international tension" as a condition of co-existence diplomacy. Instead, the goals of peace and disarmament were now put forward, in language first used by the Chinese critics, as having to be "imposed" on the imperialists by the strength of the "Socialist camp" and the relentless struggle of the masses. Peaceful co-existence was now described as "the highest form of the class struggle," and justified as leading not to an even temporary weakening, but to an intensification of revolutionary movements everywhere, including civil wars and colonial revolts whenever the imperialists attempted to hold back the rising tide by force. It was only international wars, wars between states, that should be avoided by the policy of peaceful co-existence; and it was explicitly admitted that imperialist intervention against revolutionary movements might lead to "just wars of liberation," and that in that case the duty of the Socialist camp was to support the latter — though not necessarily with troops — and to seek to end the intervention. In short, it was now claimed that there was no contradiction at all between the diplomacy of co-existence and the policy of unconditional revolutionary solidarity: both had become compatible in an age where, owing to the growing strength of the "Socialist camp," the "dictatorship of the proletariat had become an international force," as once predicted by Lenin.

This interpretation of Soviet policy evidently placed its authors in a very strong position to meet the Chinese ideological challenge; yet as the Chinese had intended, and as Khrushchev's simultaneous actions illustrated, it was bound greatly to reduce the credibility and effectiveness of the co-existence campaign in non-Communist eyes. The Soviets could hope to succeed in restoring their international ideological authority to the exact extent to which they were prepared temporarily to weaken the political impact of their diplomacy. This dilemma became evident when Vice President Edvard Kardelj, the chief ideological spokesman of Yugoslav communism, published a pamphlet in defense of co-existence and against the Chinese cult of revolutionary war: [23] *Pravda* immediately accused him of all the revisionist sins of which the Chinese had accused the Soviets [24] – because he had not only been so tactless as to name the Chinese as his target, which the Soviets had never done, but had also taken a consistent position with which they could not afford to identify themselves. For Kardelj had argued that real peaceful co-existence between states with different social systems required that these systems should not become the basis of permanent "ideological blocs" in foreign policy; and this concept was, of course, as incompatible with Soviet practice as with the new definition of co-existence as "the highest form of the class struggle."

During the same period, the Chinese Communists were also shifting their ground. They stopped belittling the horrors of nuclear war and claiming that only cowards could fear them,[25] and repeatedly protested their willingness to fight for peaceful co-existence and the prevention or stopping of wars. But they kept calling attention to the formula of the Moscow declaration of 1957 about the role of the aggressive U.S. circles as the center of world reaction and the need for vigilance against its war plans camouflaged by peace talk, which they felt had been borne out by Khrushchev's experience with Eisenhower; and they pictured peaceful co-existence and disarmament as goals that could be "imposed" on the enemy only "to some extent" and for limited periods, without the slightest assurance of permanence or completion before the final, world-wide victory of the Communist cause.[26] In other words, they remained adamant in their rejection of the thesis of the Twenty-first Congress about "eliminating war from the life of mankind" before that final victory.

THE QUESTION OF ROADS TO POWER

Parallel with that, the Chinese concentrated on extolling the importance of revolutionary violence, including revolutionary war. While the Russians now *admitted* that peaceful co-existence did not *exclude* colonial uprisings and civil wars, and that imperialist intervention in these cases *might lead* to "just wars of liberation," the Chinese stressed revolutionary violence as the *normal* and *classical* road for the advance of the Communist cause, and support for just wars as the *criterion* of true internationalism. In fact, they abandoned the safe ground of the 1957 Moscow declaration (on which they were otherwise relying in that phase) to the extent of attacking its thesis, taken over from the Twentieth Congress of the CPSU, that the Communist seizure of power might take place in some countries without violent upheaval and civil war, as a peaceful revolution carried out with the help of the legal parliamentary institutions. Ignoring the examples given by the Russians at the time – such as the annexation of Estonia and the Czechoslovak coup of February 1948 – the Chinese now insisted that the bourgeoisie would never and nowhere abandon power without resorting to violence, and that it was "muddle-headed" at best to confuse the peaceful construction of socialism *after* the seizure of power with the necessarily violent conquest of power itself.[27] To this, the Soviets replied with renewed charges of "Blanquism."[28]

Of all the differences raised in the 1960 dispute, this

argument on the violent and non-violent roads to power seemed most artificial, at least in its generalized form. The Soviets had started talking about the "parliamentary road" in order to ease the tactical position of the Communist parties in the West, and it was chiefly the latter that made propagandist use of the formula. But in the weeks before the crucial Moscow meeting, the Chinese effort was chiefly directed at those Communist parties in underdeveloped countries for which the Chinese experience had long been regarded as a natural model; and most of these had developed alternately in co-operation or conflict with nationalist dictators, but had certainly no prospect of gaining power by "parliamentary" means. Only in the case of the faction-ridden Indian Communist Party – a party operating legally in an underdeveloped country with effective parliamentary institutions – was there a serious struggle going on between a "right wing" advocating and a "left wing" rejecting the "parliamentary road" to power; and it may have been largely with an eye to the Indian "left wing" that the Chinese now engaged in a public denunciation of the Soviet concept of that road as "revisionist." [29]

The Soviets replied to this twist by a similar piece of demagogy – implicitly accusing the Chinese of a sectarian refusal to work with broad nationalist movements against imperialism unless these movements subscribed in advance to Communist principles and leadership.[30] As a general charge, this was as untrue as the Chinese attack on the alleged "revisionism" of Moscow's "peaceful road"; the close contacts maintained by Peking with the Algerian and many African nationalists proved that every day. But Peking's conflicts with the Indian and Indonesian governments, actually the result of Chinese chauvinism rather than doctrinaire prejudice, and its support for leftish malcontents in several Asian Communist parties against Moscow's wooing of nationalist dictators gave to the charge a semblance of substance.

THE CRISIS OF STATE RELATIONS

Soviet-Chinese relations seem to have reached a low point in August and early September. It was during that period that an unusually large number of Soviet technicians left China, while many Chinese students returned from Russia; that the organ of the Soviet-Chinese Friendship Society disappeared from the streets of Moscow; and that the expected Chinese scholars failed to turn up at the Orientalists' Congress there. It was then, too, that a number of Soviet provincial papers printed an article explaining that in contemporary conditions, not even a huge country like China could build socialism in isolation and without the aid and backing of the Soviet Union,[31] while Peking's theoretical voice published a statement of the need for China to rely chiefly on her own resources for the fulfillment of her plans.[32] It was not clear at the time whether Moscow had really tried to apply economic pressure and failed, or whether Peking had made a gratuitous demonstration of her capacity for "going it alone."[33] Chinese criticism, at any rate, had not been silenced by October 1,[34] when the Russians used the eleventh birthday of the Chinese People's Republic to make again a show of friendship; on the contrary, some of Peking's most polemical utterances came in the last weeks before the Moscow conference,[35] whereas the Soviet ideological campaign had rather abated since the middle of September. But by then the Soviets could afford to stop arguing in public, for the Chinese had been largely, though not completely, isolated in the international movement: early in September even the North Vietnamese party fell in line with the Soviet position.[36]

The mere duration of the Moscow conference – almost three weeks of argument behind closed doors – showed that agreement on a new common statement of principles was anything but easy. This time, the Chinese had sent the strongest possible team short of exposing Mao himself to the risk of defeat – a delegation led by Liu Shao-ch'i and the party secretary Teng Hsiao-p'ing; and reports that he fought for every clause and comma, and finally yielded to the majority view on some crucial points only under the threat of an open ideological breach soon filtered through.[37] Halfway through the debates, the anniversary of the 1957 declaration was commented on by editorials in Moscow and Peking, which still showed a marked difference of emphasis,[38] on the primacy of revolutionary struggle in the *People's Daily,* on the "general line" of peaceful co-existence in *Pravda;* while, at the same time, a Chinese delegate to a session of the Afro-Asian Solidarity Committee threw off all restraint and claimed publicly that there could be no peaceful co-existence in those countries before the liquidation of colonialism, as the oppressed peoples would never accept "co-existence between the rider and the horse."[39] But it seems clear that, as the Moscow conclave wore on, the Chinese were only able to retain the support of a few Asian parties that were traditionally dependent on them or largely recruited from the Chinese minorities, of some rather weak Latin American parties, and of the faithful Albanians long tied to them by common enmity against the Yugoslav "revisionists."

THE MOSCOW STATEMENT

The long document on the strategy of international communism that was agreed in the end thus marks a clear Soviet victory on almost all the points that had still been in dispute in the preceding three months. But the Soviet position as defended since the July session of the Central Committee of the CPSU already contained substantial concessions to the original Chinese criticism of Soviet policy.

The 1960 Moscow statement [40] starts from the Soviet analysis that Lenin's views are partly outdated because the present epoch is no longer primarily that of imperialism but of the growing preponderance of the "Socialist world system" over the forces of imperialism. On this basis, it accepts not only the possibility of ending war forever with the world-wide victory of socialism, but of "freeing mankind from the nightmare of another world war even now" – of "banishing world war from the life of society even while capitalism still exists in part of the world." The thesis of the Twenty-first Congress of the CPSU which the Chinese had fought to the last has thus been reluctantly accepted by them,[41] and so has the full description of the horrors of nuclear war. The statement also proclaims the possibility not of preventing all local wars, but of "effectively fighting the local wars unleashed by the imperialists" and extinguishing them, and stresses the unanimity of all Communists in their support for "peaceful co-existence" and negotiation as the only alternative to destructive war. Finally, it recognizes the "historic" importance that a fulfillment of the Soviet program for general and complete disarmament would have, and states that its achievement, though difficult, may be accomplished in stages, if the masses and the governments of the "Socialist camp" resolutely fight for it.

At the same time, "peaceful co-existence" is described as "a form of the class struggle" (not, as in some Soviet documents, as "the highest form," because in the Chinese party doctrine that rank remains reserved for revolutionary war). The hope of preserving peace is squarely based on the strength of the "Socialist camp," the revolutionary movements and their sympathizers: it is admitted that the latter may be found also in "certain strata of the bourgeoisie of the advanced countries" who realize the new relation of forces and the catastrophic consequences of a world war, but this appears as a marginal factor. Gone are Khrushchev's "realistic statesmen" and his successful good-will visits; the emphasis is on the fact that the aggressive, warlike nature of imperialism has not changed, and that "American imperialism" as such – not only, as stated in 1957, "the aggressive imperialist *circles* of the United States" – has become the "main center of world reaction, the international gendarme, the enemy of the peoples of the whole world."[42] While condemning "the American doctrine of the Cold War," the document thus defines co-existence in rigid Cold War terms.

The statement allots to the "peace campaign" pride of place as likely to unite the broadest possible fronts under Communist leadership, and rejects the "slander" that the Communists need war for extending their sway or believe in "exporting revolution." But it also calls for the most determined international support, both by the mass movement and by "the power of the Socialist world system," of revolutionary movements anywhere against "the imperialist export of counter-revolution." The formula that "the Socialist states . . . have become an international force exerting a powerful influence on world developments. Hence real possibilities have appeared to settle the major problems of our age in a new manner, in the interest of peace, democracy, and socialism . . ." assumes a special meaning in this context: for the first time since Stalin's victory over Trotsky, active support for international revolution is proclaimed as an obligation of the Soviet government and all other Communist governments. But the crucial question of whether that obligation includes the risk of war, of whether "peaceful co-existence" or "revolutionary solidarity" is to receive priority in case of conflict, is not settled explicitly – for the possibility of conflict between the two principles is not admitted.

On the question of violent or peaceful roads to power, the view of the Russians and of the 1957 declaration that both may be used according to circumstances is clearly upheld. Equally "broadminded" are the statement's new directives for the policy of the Communists in underdeveloped countries toward their "national bourgeoisie" – that is, toward the nationalist, neutralist, and non-Communist, though in fact hardly ever bourgeois, regimes that have emerged from the struggle for national independence. The Communists are advised to aim at "national democratic" regimes, defined by their willingness to support the Soviet bloc against the "imperialists," to create the preconditions of progressive internal development by land reform, and to grant full freedom for the activity of the Communist Party and of Communist-controlled "mass organizations." They are told that those sections of the "national bourgeoisie" that oppose land reform and suppress the Communists, having taken a reactionary turn at home, will sooner or later also side with imperialism abroad. But again, the crucial question of a nationalist dictatorship that is willing to take Soviet aid and to vote anti-Western in the U.N. but jails its own Communists is shirked; [43] nor is there any clear indication of who is to interpret the ambiguous directives in case of conflict.

THE PROBLEM OF IDEOLOGICAL AUTHORITY

Thus matters come back to the ultimate issue of ideological authority – of the right to interpret ambiguous principles in a changing situation. Here the Soviets score a clear but very limited victory: they emerge as the most successful, but not as the only orthodox interpreters of the true doctrine. The Soviet Union is hailed as the only country that, having completed "Socialist construction," is engaged in building the "higher stage" of communism; the Chinese communes are not even mentioned, and the Soviet argument that Communist abundance is not possible short of the highest level of technical productivity, including automation, is hammered home. The CPSU is unanimously declared to be "the universally recognized vanguard of the world Communist movement," and its superior experience in conquering power and transforming society is stated to have fundamental lessons for all parties; the decisions of its Twentieth Congress in particular are said to have opened a new era for the whole international movement. But that new era now turns out to be an era of polycentric autonomy – just as the bolder spirits thought at the time.

For under the 1960 statement, the spiritual authority of the CPSU is not incarnated in the shape that all doctrinaire authority, and certainly all authority in the Bolshevik tradition, requires by its nature – the shape of hierarchical discipline. It is not only that the statement repeats the ancient pious formula about the independence and equality of all Communist parties; it is that it fails to establish a visible, single center for their dependence. It provides for irregular conferences, whether world-wide or regional, for mutual co-ordination, and for bipartite consultations between any two parties in case of differences. This may have been intended to rule out the circulation of

Chinese attacks on CPSU policy to third parties before the matter had been raised in Moscow directly; but it would not, on the face of it, prevent them from broadening the discussion again the next time they failed to get satisfaction in their direct contact with the "vanguard of the world movement." [44] Clearly the primacy of that vanguard was no longer that of an infallible Pope: the rule of *Moscow locuta, causa finita* was valid no more. For the first time in its forty years of history, international communism entered a "conciliary" period.

AN INTERIM BALANCE SHEET

The 1960 phase of open ideological controversy between Moscow and Peking had thus ended. The Chinese had withdrawn their open challenge to the Marxist-Leninist orthodoxy of the Soviet Communists, but not before they had extracted from it as much advantage for their foreign policy as they could hope to gain without risking an open breach. The underlying differences of interest and viewpoint remained, though their public expression was now to be muted for some time. But the phase that thus closed had not only had a considerable immediate impact on Soviet foreign policy; it was bound to produce lasting changes in the constellation of factors shaping that policy, in Soviet-Chinese relations, and in relations within the Communist world movement.

A measure of the immediate effect was the uncertainty of direction shown by Soviet diplomacy from the wrecking of the summit conference in May to the end of 1960. Having set out to induce the U.S., by a mixture of pressure and courtship, to abandon some exposed positions and allies for the sake of a temporary understanding with their chief antagonist, the Kremlin did not indeed abandon that objective, but wavered visibly between it and the Chinese objective of isolating the U.S. as the one irreconcilable enemy. The oscillations were too fast, the conciliatory gestures too half-hearted, and the brinkmanship too risky to be explained merely as the conscious use of zig-zag tactics to "soften up" the opponent; even if the Soviets intended all the time to reserve the next serious offer of relaxation for the next American President, a cool calculation of diplomatic expediency would hardly have led them to commit themselves in the meantime to the point to which they went over, say, Laos or Cuba. By depriving them of the power automatically to subordinate all revolutionary movements everywhere to Soviet diplomatic needs, the Chinese had forced Stalin's successors to compete for authority over those movements by playing up to them; and this meant that, while failing to impose on the Kremlin a policy made in Peking, the Chinese forced it to deviate from its own concepts to a significant extent.

Nor did they lose this power of interference as a result of the Moscow conference. True, they had failed to establish a power of veto over Soviet diplomacy in general and Soviet-American contacts in particular, as would have been the case if the Chinese theses of an unconditional priority of revolution over peace and of the hopelessness of any serious disarmament agreement with the "imperialists" had been adopted. There was nothing in the Moscow statement that would make it *impossible* for the Soviets still to agree with the Western powers on a permanent ban on nuclear test explosions with proper guarantees of inspection, hence on an attempt to close the "nuclear club." But there was much in it that would enable the Chinese to make it more difficult, and generally to raise suspicion against any direct Russo-American talks, and nothing that specifically endorsed Khrushchev's methods of personal diplomacy, from his pursuit of summit meetings to his proposals for "reforming" the United Nations. In fact, if the text of the statement is viewed in the context of the events leading up to it, it suggests that the Soviet Communist Party had only been able to win on the controversial questions of principle by silently disavowing some of the more spectacular actions of its leader, and that the latter emerged from the fight with his personal prestige noticeably impaired.

The statement's approval of the "general line" of peaceful co-existence and of the aim to eliminate world war in our time permitted the Soviets to go on pursuing their strategy of using both negotiation and violence short of world war as means to gain their ends; but it was not enough to assure them of tactical freedom to decide, in the light of their own interests alone, when and how far to use one or the other. To regain that freedom of maneuver, the Soviets would either have needed a plain and brutal statement that local revolutions might in certain circumstances have to be subordinated to the interest of preserving world peace and thereby protecting the achievements of "Socialist construction" against a nuclear holocaust; or they would have required an equally plain recognition of their right to act as the only legitimate interpreters of revolutionary doctrine for the world movement, and to enforce the strategic and tactical consequences of their interpretation by means of centralized discipline. But either way of ensuring Soviet primacy, so natural in the Stalinist age when the Soviet Union alone was "the fatherland of all toilers," proved impossible in the post-Stalinist age of "the Socialist world system" proclaimed by Khrushchev himself.

On the one side, the doctrine that "the dictatorship of the proletariat has become an international factor," first announced in Russia by M. A. Suslov and now substantially incorporated in the statement, amounted to a partial repeal of Stalin's "socialism in one country": it did not, of course, deny what had been achieved under the latter slogan, but it restored, in the new world situation, the idea of a duty of the Communist powers to aid the progress of world revolution for which Trotsky had fought. Even if this principle of solidarity was not formulated as an absolute and unlimited obligation, it was enough to expose Soviet diplomacy to constant pressure to take bolder risks — pressure of the kind that the Chinese had mobilized effectively during 1960, and remained free to use again.

On the other hand, the statement's recognition of the Soviet Communist Party as the "vanguard" of the world movement fell far short of establishing a permanent and unchallengeable doctrinaire authority, let alone a single center endowed with disciplinary powers. It even fell far short of the position conceded to the Soviet Union and the Soviet Communist Party at the time of the 1957 Moscow declaration — on Mao Tse-tung's initiative. Then, the Soviet Union had been consistently described as being "at the head of the Socialist camp," and Mao had publicly gone out of his way to speak of the need for a single leader both among Communist states and parties, and to insist that only the Russians could fill both roles.

Now, the Chinese talked quite openly and naturally about the special responsibilities of "the two great Socialist powers," the Soviet Union and China; and in the declaration itself, the vanguard role of the Soviet party was balanced in part by the recognition of the "enormous influence" exerted by the Chinese revolution on the peoples of Asia, Africa, and Latin America by its encouraging example to all movements of national liberation. In 1957, the failure to found a new formal international organization had only increased the influence of the large international liaison machinery developed within the secretariat of the Central Committee of the CPSU, compared with which all bilateral and regional contacts were bound to be of subordinate importance. In 1960, the failure formally to establish a single center conferred legitimacy on the *de facto* existence of two centers in Moscow and Peking, both with world-wide links and without any agreed division of labor, which would continue to co-operate on the basis of the declaration but also to give different advice on the questions it had left open and to compete for influence. And if Moscow was still the stronger power and the older authority, Peking was closer in its type of revolutionary experience and the emotional roots of its anticolonialist ardor to those parts of the world where the chances of Communist revolution were most promising.

A "POLYCENTRIC" COMMUNISM

In a long-range view, the relative victory of the Soviets in the 1960 phase of the dispute thus appeared less important than the fact that this phase marked a new stage in their abdication of their former position of exclusive leadership. The reports that the Soviets themselves expressed during the Moscow conference a wish that they should no longer be described as being "at the head of the Socialist camp" sounded plausible: finding themselves unable any longer to exert effective control over the whole world movement, they may have preferred not to be held responsible for all its actions by their enemies. In a bloc containing two Great Powers, in an international movement based on two great revolutions, such a development was indeed to be expected as soon as important differences appeared between them. But while the two protagonists remained as determined to continue to co-operate as they were unable to settle their disagreements, the result would not be a two-headed movement with neatly separated geographic spheres of control, but a truly polycentric one: many Communist parties outside the Soviet bloc may in future be able to gain increased tactical independence, based on their freedom of taking aid and advice from both Moscow and Peking, simultaneously or alternately – with all the risks that implies for the future unity of their doctrine and strategy.

The victory of communism in China, and the subsequent growth of Communist China into a Great Power, thus appears in retrospect as the beginning of the end of the single-centered Communist movement that Lenin created, and the single-centered Soviet bloc that Stalin built. The process took a decisive step forward in 1956, when the Twentieth Congress of the CPSU recognized the existence of a "Socialist world system" and of different roads to power, and when the destruction of the Stalin cult inflicted an irreparable blow on the type of Soviet authority that had depended on the infallibility of the "father of nations." Mao's victory had killed the uniqueness of the Soviet Union; Khrushchev's speech buried the myth built around that uniqueness.

It was at that moment that the specter of "polycentric communism" first appeared. But when "de-Stalinization" was quickly followed by the crisis of Russia's East European empire, the façade of single-centered unity was restored in the following year with the help of China's prestige and Mao's authority. Now that China herself had brought back the specter she helped to exorcise three years before, the process was no longer reversible. This time, polycentric communism had come to stay.

POSTSCRIPT

The above was written before the publication of Khrushchev's report on the Moscow conference,[45] given on January 6, 1961, to the party organizations of the Higher Party school, the Academy of Social Sciences and the Institute of Marxism-Leninism. Compared to the text of the statement, the report is distinguished by two diplomatic omissions and two theoretical elaborations.

Khrushchev made no mention of the role of U.S. imperialism as the gendarme of world reaction, and so forth, which would have embarrassed him in resuming diplomatic approaches to the new American administration; reactions to President Kennedy's first statements in Moscow and Peking promptly confirmed that the original foreign policy difference between the two great Communist powers had remained intact after the formal burial of the ideological dispute that had arisen from it.

The report also failed to define the new concept of "national democracy," created to designate the desirable type of regime in the underdeveloped, ex-colonial countries, by the criteria of land reform and freedom of Communist organization given in the statement. In view of the diplomatic importance of Soviet relations not only with Nasser's U.A.R. but even with traditionalist autocracies like Morocco and Ethiopia, this seemed understandable.

But Khrushchev was more precise than the statement in his comment on "wars of national liberation." He went further than any previous Soviet participant in the debate in agreeing with the Chinese that such just wars were "inevitable" so long as imperialism and colonialism existed, and he was emphatic about the need for all Communists to give them their fullest support. But he solved the apparent contradiction with his preceding condemnation of "local wars" — which might lead to the disaster of nuclear world war — by arguing that these wars of liberation were in their origin not "wars between states," but popular insurrections, and that the support which the Communist powers must give them should consist not in taking the initiative to internationalize the conflict, but in preventing the intervention of the major imperialist powers by the threat of their own counter-intervention — as in Vietnam and in the Cuban revolution — and thus assuring the victory of "the people." This was the most explicit formulation yet of the Soviet practice of "all aid by threats and indirect support short of war" for revolutionary movements.

Finally, Khrushchev confirmed publicly that it was the Soviet delegation that had asked for the omission of the flattering formula placing the Soviet Union "at the head of the Socialist camp" and the CPSU "at the head of the Communist world movement," which Mao had bestowed on them at the 1957 conference; and he bluntly stated his reason that this would have been a source of difficulties rather than advantages, as they were not in fact any longer in a position to act as a single center giving directives. The polycentrism implicit in the statement was thus made explicit for the first time through the mouth of the highest authority of Soviet communism.

In the circumstances, Khrushchev's assurance that the

Communist parties would in future be able to "synchronize their watches" without the help of a statute regulating their relations, merely by the light of their common ideology, amounted to little more than the hope that Russia and China would continue to be able to compromise their differences in the light of their common interests. Even assuming that this would still be true for a long time, nothing then indicated that the achievement of compromise would in future be easier, or the effects on the world Communist movement less critical, than during the 1960 dispute.

8

1961: FROM DISPUTE TO SCHISM

In the history of the Russian revolution and of international communism, N. S. Khrushchev is emerging with increasing clarity as a figure of transition. He, more than anyone else, has helped to destroy the Stalinist forms of organization and thought that were no longer adequate to the changing character of Soviet society and the changing international situation. Applying a rare combination of realistic shrewdness and primitive faith, he has striven valiantly to replace outdated dogma with a new ideological synthesis – to combine, inside the Soviet Union, the development of a new incentive economy with the continued monopolistic rule of the party and, beyond her frontiers, the expansion of Russian power with the advance of independent revolutionary allies in a single bid for world hegemony. Yet he is now beginning to see this beatific vision disintegrate before his eyes and to discover that, while his work of destruction will last, his synthesis is proving much more fragile and short-lived than the dogma it was intended to replace.

The Twenty-second Congress of the CPSU marks the

moment of truth when this discovery forced itself on Stalin's successor. Already labeled the Congress of the "second de-Stalinization," it has been widely interpreted as a new stage in a development that began at the Twentieth Congress in 1956. Certainly the great themes of post-Stalinist renewal were common to both Congresses: the denunciation of the regime of mass terrorism and the pledge to avoid its return, the proclamation of the autonomy of national parties within the Communist world movement and of the equality of Communist governments within the "Socialist world system," and the vision of world-wide victory without world war. Yet while the Twentieth Congress saw the birth of the new synthesis, the Twenty-second saw the beginning of its breakup.

The foundation of Khrushchev's policy for international communism had been his belief that there could be no major contradiction between the interests of Russian power and the interests of revolutionary expansion by independent Communist states and movements. The collapse of this assumption became manifest at the Twenty-second Congress with the breakdown of the Soviet-Chinese compromise that had been negotiated after prolonged debate at the 1960 Communist world conference. In contrast to the Twentieth Congress – where the dramatic form Khrushchev chose for "de-Stalinization" (his notorious "secret speech") was mainly due to domestic resistance within the party and government leadership to his political innovations – the principal cause of the dramatic events at the Twenty-second Congress was international: it was the open Chinese challenge to the authority of Khrushchev and his team, expressed in persistent and even provocative backing for the defeated Stalinist remnants in the USSR and the Soviet bloc, that forced the Soviet leaders publicly to destroy the last shreds of the Stalin legend and to remove the body of their teacher from Lenin's side – going far beyond the formal ideological résumé of the process of "de-Stalinization" for which the CPSU and the Russian people had been prepared.

The prospect of open and insoluble ideological quarrel between the two principal Communist powers leaves the international Communist movement bewildered and divided, without a recognized organizational center or ideological authority. In the Babel that has replaced the traditional *unisono,* some of the leaders can be overheard repeating lines familiar from the ideological crisis of 1956–57 – the crisis that followed the first "de-Stalinization." But that first crisis was overcome with the help of Chinese support for Soviet leadership. The new crisis is likely to prove more lasting – not only because the same solution is no longer open, but because the developments that have led to the crisis have also proven that the assumptions underlying Khrushchev's version of "proletarian internationalism" were hopelessly wrong.

KHRUSHCHEV'S STARTING-POINT

To grasp the depth of the new crisis in relations between the Soviet Union and the international Communist movement, we have to go back to the original contrast between Khrushchev's concept of these relations and Stalin's. Stalin won and consolidated his position of total control over the Soviet Union by proclaiming the principle that the power interests of the Soviet state – of the building of "socialism in one country" – must be given clear preference over the interests of "world revolution" whenever the two were in conflict. Recognition of the possibility of such conflict, and of the need for a clear choice, was the core of his ideological difference with Trotsky, his first and most formidable rival. Haunted by his vision of "capitalist encirclement" of the isolated Soviet state, and confirmed in his view by the failure of any Communist party outside Russia to win power by its own strength in twenty years, Stalin forced his principle on the international Communist movement, using the international centralism of the "World Party" created by Lenin to make all Communist parties accept the complete subordination of their struggle to the interests of the "fatherland of all toilers." In the end such subordination became, in the Stalinist view, the very criterion of true "proletarian internationalism." The annexation of the Baltic states, Eastern Poland, and Bessarabia during World War II, and the later creation of a Communist-governed empire in Eastern Europe by Soviet bayonets, were regarded as proof that the expansion of Soviet power was the only realistic way to promote the advance of the Communist system. To the believers, Stalin's choice appeared justified by success to the point where the very need for choice had vanished—where the interests of world revolution were wholly comprised in the interests of the Soviet Union.

Yet even then, the first case of an independent Communist revolution, that of Yugoslavia, was beginning to create unforeseen problems, and the victory of communism in China foreshadowed much greater difficulties. Consistent to the end, Stalin had advised against the decisive steps toward the conquest of power in both countries, whether from doubts about the possibility of success or from anxiety about its consequences. Communist states that had arisen by independent revolutions clearly could not be run by remote control from Moscow in the same way that Soviet-created satellite states or powerless Communist parties could; the attempt to establish such control failed dismally in Yugoslavia and was not even undertaken in China. Yet Stalin remained unwilling to abandon in principle his Soviet-centered definition of "proletarian internationalism" and his claim to the primacy of Soviet state interests for the whole worldwide Communist movement. This inability to adjust his outlook to the new fact of a plurality of independent Communist states – expressed, for example, in the pathological hunt for "Titoist conspirators" throughout Eastern Europe – remained a major source of political rigidity and an element of Soviet political weakness right to his death.

Khrushchev, on the contrary, started from a recognition of the new situation and from the conviction that it could be turned into a decisive source of strength. China and even Yugoslavia proved that the age of Soviet isolation and of "capitalist encirclement" was over. The old imperialist order had been weakened beyond the possibility of another long-term stabilization; it could no longer resist the revolutionary movements of the colonial peoples; and in a world in revolutionary flux, new independent Communist victories were possible, if only the USSR would use its own increased strength to aid and encourage them instead of anxiously seeking to control and restrain them. By recognizing the actual independence and equality of China and Yugoslavia, and by giving the fictitious independence of the satellite governments and parties some element of substance in the form of increased domestic autonomy, he hoped to strengthen greatly both the cohesion of the "Socialist camp" and its attraction for outsiders — while at the same time preserving the Soviet Union's leadership on the basis of its historic prestige and greater power. By proclaiming the right and duty of all Communist parties to find their own roads to victory according to national conditions, he wished to improve their chances to ride the crest of the new revolutionary wave. The "rebirth of Leninism" expressed above all Khrushchev's confident expectation that, after thirty years of a steady build-up of Soviet strength and a steady accumulation of "imperialist contradictions," the time had come at last when Soviet power and world revolution could advance in step — without a major conflict of interests and hence without subordination of the one to the other — to bring about a Communist-dominated world.

That had been the vision underlying Khrushchev's visit to Peking in the fall of 1954, when he negotiated a revision of Stalin's unequal treaty of alliance with Mao, as well as his journey to Belgrade in the spring of 1955, when he tried to win back Tito to the bloc by the disavowal of Stalin's policies and the recognition of "different roads to socialism." It was made explicit in Khrushchev's public report to the Twentieth Congress, when he advanced his concept of the "Socialist world system" as a commonwealth of equals, with scope for a diversity of institutional means in the pursuit of common aims on the basis of common principles. The position of the Soviet Union "at the head of the camp" was not even explicitly mentioned on this occasion, not because it had been abandoned but because it was taken as assured by the Soviet party's uncontested ideological authority and its unique role as the historically first and most powerful member of the system. The belief that the Soviet position no longer required enforcement through organizational means was further underlined two months later when the Cominform, once a key instrument of Stalinist discipline in the international Communist movement, was dissolved.

OVERCOMING THE FIRST CRISIS

In its essentials, this Khrushchevian vision was maintained even after the October crisis of 1956 had shaken the East European satellite empire to the point where its cohesion could be restored only by force, and had led to renewed discussion of inter-party relations throughout the international Communist movement. The October events were not, in fact, a necessary consequence of Khrushchev's belief in a harmonious alliance of independent revolutionary powers, or even of his loosening of the Soviet grip on the satellite empire. They occurred rather because this loosening coincided with a triple crisis of authority caused by the disclosure and disavowal of Stalin's crimes, by the involvement of many East European Communist leaders in the "anti-Titoist" phase of those crimes, and by uncertainty about the ultimate outcome of the succession struggle in the Soviet Union. This crisis of authority led to bitter and prolonged struggles within the leadership of a number of East European Communist parties – struggles in which the Yugoslavs intervened to some extent – and created the uncertainty at the top, without which an atmosphere of public criticism and finally of mass opposition to the regime could not have developed in Poland and Hungary.

The manner in which the Soviet leaders coped with the crisis was still characteristically Khrushchevian and non-Stalinist in that it allowed a considerable diversity of solutions and did not seek to restore the former type of detailed administrative control from Moscow. In Poland, the Soviets reluctantly accepted a change in leadership that went beyond their wishes and made considerable concessions to the desire of the new team to demonstrate its "equality" and internal autonomy; they insisted only on maintaining the Communist Party dictatorship and receiving new guarantees for continued unity in foreign policy. In Albania, as we now know, they accepted with equal reluctance the continued rule of the Stalinist team of Enver Hoxha, after backstairs promptings had failed to bring about a broadening of the leadership or a posthumous rehabilitation of Hoxha's executed "Titoist" opponent, Koci Xoxe.[1] Only in Hungary, where the "reformers" failed to gain control of the party in time to prevent a popular rising, and where the Nagy government thrown up by this rising proved willing to abandon the party dictatorship and the Soviet alliance, did the Soviets use armed force to retain the country within their empire — and even here they imposed a new leadership headed by "moderate reformers" and allowed it some degree of autonomy in domestic policy.

Nevertheless, the October events had posed new questions of principle for which different answers were put forward by various Communist parties; thus the Soviet leaders were confronted for the first time with the problem of how to define and preserve the necessary minimum of international unity in the new conditions. If the Budapest uprising had begun as a genuine workers' movement against a degenerate bureaucratic regime, and had only later fallen into the hands of "counter-revolutionary leaders — as not only the Yugoslavs but the Polish and Italian Communists at first maintained [2] — then a Communist Party dictatorship could no longer be regarded as the necessary form of the "dictatorship of the proletariat." If the Yugoslav Communists had the right to keep their "non-aligned" position in foreign policy, then Imre Nagy should also have had the right to take Hungary out of the Warsaw pact. If the new autonomy meant that there was no longer any "leading party," any single center for the Communist world movement, as Togliatti had claimed after the Twentieth Congress,[3] then no doctrinal judgment binding on all true Communists could be pronounced by any authority short of a unanimous world conference; if organized relations among autonomous Communist parties were to be confined to bilateral contacts, as the Poles suggested,[4] even that solution would be barred.

At the Moscow international conference of November 1957, the Soviet and Chinese Communist leaders, acting in concert,[5] succeeded in meeting these issues by defining the minimum requirements of international Communist unity without revoking the fundamental innovations of the Twentieth Congress. The admissibility of different roads to Communist power and of institutional diversity in its use was maintained; but the need for a common foreign policy of all "Socialist states" was sharply stressed, and ideological principles were formulated that would continue to distinguish all true Communists from "revisionist" traitors. To ensure unity in the interpretation of these principles as well as in the decision of foreign policy, the continued need for Soviet leadership both in the "Socialist camp" and in the world Communist movement was made explicit;[6] and while no new formal international organization was set up, an extended international liaison machinery of the CPSU and a Soviet-edited international journal were allowed to take its place, and the need to hold further international conferences from time to time was recognized.

This solution proved ultimately acceptable (despite strong Polish and Italian misgivings) to all but the Yugoslavs and some small "revisionist" minorities in the West. The crisis had apparently been overcome without a renunciation of Khrushchev's new faith in the harmony of the interests of the Soviet empire and of the world revolution; Soviet leadership had been restored without a return to the Stalinist subordination of world communism to Soviet interests, or to Stalinist methods of enforcing it.

In retrospect, it is clear that the basic reason for this temporary success was the actual harmony of Communist power interests within the Soviet empire. However different the national conditions and inner-party histories of the satellite states, their leaders – whether old "Stalinists" or "national Communist" reformers – felt ultimately dependent on Soviet backing for maintaining control over their own people, a feeling that was strengthened by the shock of the Hungarian uprising. Their desire for national autonomy was always limited by this consideration and, within this limit, could be satisfied by the Khrushchev type of Soviet leadership. The Yugoslav leaders, who had gained power on their own and maintained it for years in the face of Soviet hostility, were once again the only exception. The crisis could be solved with comparative ease because it had been caused by the temporary shock of "de-Stalinization," not by the nature of the new policy that had taken the place of the Stalinist synthesis, and because it had broken out in an area where the basic assumptions underlying the new policy were not put to the test, except in the marginal case of Yugoslavia.

MAO, THE KINGMAKER

The real major test could only be supplied by Soviet relations with Communist China. True, it was of symptomatic significance that Khrushchev's policy had failed to win back the one independent Communist state in Europe — that Tito remained unwilling to join the Warsaw pact in return for his "rehabilitation" as a good Marxist-Leninist and for a guarantee that he could retain the peculiar institutions he had developed in the meantime. But that failure could be explained by the prolonged dependence on Western aid into which the Yugoslav regime had been driven by Stalin's intolerance, and by the consequent weakening of its international revolutionary zeal. At any rate, Khrushchev felt able to regard Tito's obdurate nonalignment as no more than a minor irritant which could not possibly make him revise his basic outlook: even after the Yugoslavs in the spring of 1958 adopted a "revisionist" party program justifying their refusal to identify the Soviet bloc with the cause of socialism, Khrushchev had them expelled from the fraternal community of Communist parties once again, but carefully refrained from repeating Stalin's attempt to bring them to heel by economic, military, and political pressure. On the contrary, after a short period of vigorous ideological denunciation, he settled down to treat Yugoslavia as a reasonably friendly neutral state, and was rewarded by finding that the Yugoslavs this time made no sustained attempt to propagate their heresies within his East European empire.

The Chinese attitude, clearly, was of infinitely greater importance for future relations between the Soviet empire and world communism; and here Khrushchev's new outlook at first seemed to yield ample dividends. In 1954–55, the Chinese had been brilliant partners and even pioneers in the effort to overcome the rigid attitude toward the ex-colonial, uncommitted countries that the "Socialist camp" had inherited from Stalin — at the Geneva conference on Indochina, at the signing of the "five principles of peaceful co-existence and non-interference" with India, and at Bandung. In 1956, though worried by the drastic form of Khrushchev's downgrading of Stalin, they had publicly welcomed the substance of the critique of Stalin's "Great Power chauvinism," [7] including his policies toward Yugoslavia — and this at a time when Molotov was still defending those policies inside the Soviet leadership. During the crisis later on in the year, they had actively intervened in the Soviet-Polish dispute in favor of a compromise combining increased national autonomy for Poland with explicit recognition of Soviet leadership,[8] while vigorously defending Soviet intervention in Hungary against all critics. Finally, during the Moscow conference of November 1957, Mao had reacted to the double shock of Hungary and of discovering the strength of his own domestic opposition in the "Hundred Flowers Campaign" by placing strong emphasis on fighting "revisionism" as "the principal danger"; but he had also personally taken the initiative to have the Soviet Union's position "at the head of the Socialist camp" embodied in the Moscow declaration,[9] at a moment when Khrushchev had clearly eliminated the "Stalinist" opposition and established himself as the uncontested Soviet leader.

It may be readily assumed that not even at that time was this Chinese zeal for re-establishing the Soviet Union's position of international leadership based on unqualified admiration for Khrushchev's genius as a statesman or ideological innovator, nor on an absence of differences of doctrine and political style: the whole independent historical development of the Chinese party under Mao precluded that. But the Chinese Communists were then vitally interested in maintaining the cohesion of the bloc while preserving their post-Stalin gains of independent and equal status as well as of direct influence on the bloc's European members, and universal recognition of the leading role of a CPSU headed by Khrushchev seemed the best way to achieve both objectives. Would not Stalin's benevolent but comparatively inexperienced successor, once restored with Chinese help to a position of international pre-eminence at a moment of crisis, have to lean heavily on the advice of the kingmaker in Peking? The expectation seemed plausible enough, so long as one assumed that no major conflict of interest could arise between the two main powers of the Communist world. The outcome of the 1957 Moscow conference — the "Maoist reconstruction of the center" under Soviet leadership — was possible only because at that moment both Khrushchev and Mao Tse-tung still held that assumption.

IN PLACE OF HARMONY

By the spring of 1958, it must have been clear to the Chinese Communist leaders that their expectation of continued major influence on the formation of Soviet policy had been unfounded, and that Chinese interests had a fairly low place on Khrushchev's list of priorities. The sharp left turn in domestic economic policy taken by the second session of the Eighth Congress of the CPC — the "Great Leap Forward" and the first pilot schemes for the creation of the "people's communes" — is inexplicable without a sharp disappointment of Chinese hopes for massive new Soviet capital aid; and the same disappointment probably played its part in the Chinese pressure for treating the Yugoslavs once again as enemies: Why should people who took money from the American imperialists continue to receive Soviet credits as well? The summer brought the tentative Soviet acceptance of a summit conference on the Middle Eastern crisis "within the framework of the Security Council," with scant regard for Peking's political prestige, and (after the withdrawal of that acceptance) Khrushchev's visit to Peking and the joint communiqué promising "all-round consultation"; yet, while full Soviet political support was given to Peking during the subsequent bombardment of Quemoy, the military support appears to have been unsatisfactory at the crucial point. Most important of all, this was the year during which the Soviets first agreed to expert discussions on the possibility of an inspected ban on nuclear tests, and then, pending political three-power negotiations on the subject, to a moratorium on such tests. As they also consistently refused to supply their Chinese allies with ready-made nuclear arms, a successful test ban agreement could even then be seen as an attempt to exclude China permanently from the circle of nuclear powers.

The ground for the later Chinese charges of an opportunistic neglect of international revolutionary solidarity by the Soviet leaders must have been laid by these successive disappointments. As in Tito's case in 1948, though there had been long-standing ideological differences due to diversities of historical development, the conflict was not "about ideology": it was a clear conflict of national interest which took ideological forms. Finding that the Soviets consistently failed to give Chinese economic, political, and military objectives the same high priority as did the Chinese themselves, Mao naturally came to doubt the fitness of Khrushchev and his team for the role of international leadership for which he had cast them. As has frequently been pointed out, the claim in the

Chinese Central Committee's resolution on the "people's communes" that these revolutionary innovations constituted a direct short cut to the "higher stage" of communism amounted to an ideological preparation for challenging the right of the Russians – still halting at the "lower stage" of socialism – to lead the world Communist movement.[10]

The Soviet response showed instant awareness of the danger and a determination to forestall it: Moscow promptly described the new Soviet seven-year plan as a program for laying the foundations of communism and called an extra-ordinary party congress to adopt it; on the other hand, Soviet theoretical journals vigorously attacked as "utopian" any attempt to reach the "higher stage" before a high level of technical productivity had been achieved and the conditions for material abundance created. By December 1958, under the dual impact of Soviet criticism and the severe practical difficulties of the communes, the Chinese withdrew this first ideological challenge.[11] As the Twenty-first Congress of the CPSU opened in February 1959, a truce had clearly been called; Chou En-lai explicitly recognized that Russia alone had entered the road to the "higher stage," and a new Soviet-Chinese economic agreement was signed.

The truce was broken in the fall of the same year, once again for a non-ideological reason: Khrushchev's visit to the United States and his preparations for a summit conference revived intense Chinese fears of a possible Soviet-American agreement at Peking's expense – above all, presumably, in the form of a serious attempt to close the "nuclear club." [12] The new disagreement was soon reflected in the failure to issue a communiqué on the Khrushchev-Mao talks held in Peking on the Soviet Premier's return trip from the United States; in Khrushchev's subsequent public reference to the "Trotskyite adventurism" of a policy of "neither peace nor war"; in a series of warnings against illusions about the nature of American imperialism published in the Chinese press during the winter and repeated by the Chinese observer at a meeting of the Warsaw pact in February 1960: and in Khrushchev's ostentatious detachment from Chinese claims against India and Indonesia during his winter visit to both countries. This time, the Chinese did not stop at ideological preparations for challenging the "leading role" of the Soviets. They raised the charge of Soviet "opportunism" at a number of leadership meetings of international "front organizations," thus openly seeking to recruit allies in other Communist parties. Finally, on the occasion of the ninetieth anniversary of Lenin's birth in April, they published in a series of articles what amounted to the ideological platform for their attack.[13]

With that, the existence of a Russo-Chinese "ideological dispute" on the principal issues of international Communist strategy became public knowledge. Its course from April to the conference of the eighty-one Communist parties which met in Moscow in November, and to the compromise declaration published by it in December 1960, may be assumed here as generally known.[14] While that declaration on balance favored the Soviet viewpoint on the immediate matters in dispute, its most important aspect was that it *was* a compromise, and openly viewed as a starting-point for further compromises. Moscow's monopoly of ideological authority had been the implicit precondition for the unity of action of independent Communist powers and autonomous movements as conceived by Khrushchev at the time of the Twentieth Congress. It had been made explicit following the crisis in Eastern

Europe at the 1957 Moscow conference. Now it was explicitly renounced by Khrushchev himself; he reported that the Soviet delegation had asked that the formula referring to the CPSU as the "leading party" of the world movement be dropped from the 1960 declaration, because it had in fact become impossible to lead all Communist parties from a single center.[15] But without such a center, unity in both the world movement and the "Socialist camp" could henceforth be preserved only by a process of continuous adjustment leading to ever new compromises — as in any alliance of non-ideological governments or parties.

The harmony of interests between independent Communist powers and movements had supposedly been guaranteed by a common ideology, interpreted by a generally recognized authority. The actual conflicts of interest, leading to conflicting interpretations of the ideology, had destroyed that authority. There remained, of course, major common interests regarded by all sides as overriding the internecine conflicts, and it remained true that these common interests were rooted in the common ideological opposition of all Communist parties and governments to the non-Communist world. But it was the paradox of the new situation that this common "ideological" interest could now only be made to prevail over the differing national interests if the latter were adjusted in a non-ideological, pragmatic way, and not embittered by a continued struggle for ideological leadership.

ALBANIA AND THE FAILURE OF COMPROMISE

Yet when the 1960 Moscow compromise was concluded, the Chinese Communists were already determined to view it as a mere stepping-stone in a long-term struggle to win for themselves the international "leading role" that the Russians had just given up. The proof of this, and the root cause of the breakdown of the compromise, was that they persisted in supporting Khrushchev's "Stalinist" opponents within the Russians' European empire, with whom they had concluded a tactical alliance during the previous phase of open conflict. In the Chinese leaders' eyes such "factionalism" may have found part of its justification in the fact that Khrushchev himself had tried to encourage a "right-wing opposition" in the Chinese party — and that at the time of the 1959 truce.[16]

We have seen that, far from being genuine "Stalinists" in their outlook, the Chinese Communists had in effect supported Khrushchev during the critical period of 1956–57. Even the new "leftist" ideas which they developed during the first phase of Sino-Soviet tension in 1958 — ideas of "uninterrupted revolution" at home and unlimited support for revolutionary movements abroad — were "Trotskyite" rather than "Stalinist" in inspiration. Nevertheless, the common antagonism to Khrushchev on the part of the Chinese Communists and the defeated Russian "Stalinists" may have suggested a *rapprochement* between them even then. Both distrusted Khrushchev's personal diplomacy in general and his eagerness for top-level contacts with the Americans in particular. Both reproached him for his "softness" toward the Yugoslav heretics and for his costly foreign aid policy benefiting "bourgeois nationalist" rulers of uncommitted, ex-colonial countries. Finally, both believed that the road to the "higher stage" of communism lay through increasing the importance of payments in kind — as envisaged, in different ways, in Stalin's last pamphlet *Economic Problems of Socialism in the*

USSR and in the Chinese communes – whereas Khrushchev was seeking to put both agricultural deliveries and *kolkhoz* wages on a cash basis in order to subject costs and returns to "the yardstick of the ruble."

It is noteworthy that the same period (September-December 1958) that witnessed the Soviet ideological campaign against the "utopian" Chinese claims for the communes also saw a sharp revival of attacks on the "anti-party group," beginning with the disclosure of Bulganin's role in it and ending with obvious preparations for the expulsion of its members from the CPSU. (It was at the plenum of December 1958, the first Central Committee plenum for which minutes were published, that Khrushchev said that "the tongue rebels against calling these people comrades.") Conversely, when the Soviet truce with the Chinese was sealed at the Twenty-first CPSU Congress in February 1959, the prepared attacks from the floor on the "anti-party group" were not followed up by Khrushchev, and there was even talk at that time of sending Molotov as ambassador to The Hague – possibly in the expectation that he would first recant his errors. All this seems to suggest that Khrushchev at least suspected a link between the Chinese and the Russian "Stalinists" even then.

What must remain conjecture for the 1958 phase of the dispute may be regarded as definitely established for the 1960 phase. At the Twenty-second Congress, Central Committee secretary Ilychev disclosed that in April 1960 Molotov had submitted his first ideological statement since his 1957 defeat; it had arrived in the form of an article sent to *Kommunist* on the occasion of the ninetieth anniversary of Lenin's birth – the date when the public Chinese attack started.[17] Other speakers at the

Congress described the content of Molotov's position in terms closely paralleling the Chinese views.[18] Such harmony in both time and content could hardly have been accidental; nor can it have been accidental that within a few weeks after these moves Molotov was recalled from Ulan Bator, President Voroshilov (the last undisclosed member of the former "Stalinist" majority in the party Presidium) was prevailed upon to retire for reasons of health,[19] and *Pravda* published Tvardovsky's anti-Stalinist poem.[20]

About the same time, the Chinese also picked up the support of the Albanian "Stalinist" leaders, who had already enthusiastically joined in Peking's violent anti-Yugoslav campaign in 1958 and had only reluctantly been persuaded by Khrushchev to tone it down during the 1959 lull.[21] Up till then, Enver Hoxha and Mehmet Shehu had steadfastly refused to "de-Stalinize" their own regime but had never openly opposed Khrushchev. After the Chinese attacks, they refused to join in the proposal, made by Bulgaria and Rumania on Soviet instructions, for an atom-free zone in the Balkans, and they vigorously sided with the Chinese against Khrushchev at the Bucharest and Moscow conferences in 1960. Here, too, Khrushchev reacted quickly. By August 1960, two months after the Bucharest clash, pro-Soviet elements in the Albanian Central Committee apparently tried to rally opposition to Hoxha in preparation for the forthcoming Albanian party congress. They were promptly purged, however, and the congress was postponed till February 1961, while a number of pro-Soviet officials were arrested as "plotters."[22]

Now it seems clear that by the time of the Moscow conference Khrushchev was prepared to accept a prolonged period of "divergent unity"[23] with the Chinese – that he considered the preservation of the alliance and of a broad outward unity of world communism worth the price of putting up with recurrent disagreements on diplomatic tactics and continued competition for influence among some peripheral Communist parties. Unless he had made that judgment, he would not have accepted a compromise renouncing the Soviet claim to a monopoly of ideological leadership. But he could make that judgment only because he was confident that his own policy, based on the superior power of the Soviet Union and its East European empire, would on the whole continue to prevail in such an inter-Communist tug-of-war; and this presupposed that the substantial achievement of the 1957 settlement — the consolidation of his own power in the Soviet Union and of Soviet control in Eastern Europe — remained intact. Renunciation of sole leadership of the world Communist movement and acceptance of Chinese competition within it were possible for the sake of unity; renunciation of sole control over his own empire was out of the question.

Hence Khrushchev followed up the Moscow compromise by quiet steps to break the Albanian opposition, only to find that the Chinese continued to back Hoxha in his defiance. When the Soviets refused to grant Albania new aid agreements, the Chinese offered Tirana substantial new credits on the eve of the Albanian party congress, which endorsed Hoxha's policies. When the Albanian show-trial of pro-Soviet officials, on charges of plotting with Yugoslavia, Greece, and the United States to overthrow the Albanian regime, was answered in the summer of 1961 by the withdrawal of Soviet submarines and of Soviet and East European technicians from Albania, Chinese technicians moved into the breach.[24] Because they were consciously embarking on a long-term struggle for world Communist leadership, the Chinese Communists were not prepared to abandon their first small ally in Europe—nor do they seem to have discontinued their co-operation with Molotov, whose criticism of the draft CPSU program in a letter sent from his Vienna sinecure to the Central Committee, as summarized by *Pravda* editor Satyukov at the Twenty-second Congress, appeared to parallel closely the Chinese arguments.[25] Yet, for Khrushchev, Chinese willingness to respect his power within the USSR and the Soviet empire proper must have been the minimum test of the value of the 1960 compromise.

AFTER THE TWENTY-SECOND CONGRESS

I believe that the breakdown of the compromise at the Twenty-second Congress must be understood in that light. It is misleading to say that the attacks on Molotov and Hoxha in Khrushchev's opening report [26] were merely diplomatically veiled attacks on the Chinese. Khrushchev was really announcing his determination to liquidate the remnants of "Stalinist" opposition within the Soviet empire and was, by implication, warning the Chinese that he would do so whether they approved his action or not. Chou En-lai, by publicly criticizing the attack on Albania [27] and by laying a wreath at Stalin's tomb,[28] issued a counter-warning that China would refuse to sanction the expulsion of Albania from the Communist camp and was ready even to go to the defense of Stalin in order to challenge the legitimacy of Khrushchev's leadership of the Soviet Union. The compromise broke down because Khrushchev had to insist that ideological competition within the international Communist movement stop at the borders of the Soviet Union's own power sphere, and because the Chinese refused to respect these limits.

These events contained an element of mutual surprise. The Chinese seem to have expected that Khrushchev, for the sake of unity, would not dare bring the Albanian quarrel into the open; hence Chou's premature departure when Khrushchev did the contrary. The Soviets seem to have expected that the Chinese, for the sake of unity, would not dare go publicly to the defense of the Albanians and even of Stalin; hence the Soviet leadership's need, in the later stages of the Congress, to go far beyond Khrushchev's opening reports in the endeavor to destroy the Stalin image. But once faced with the prospect of open conflict, neither side retreated.

The Chinese Communists subsequently reprinted Hoxha's all-out attacks on the "anti-Marxist revisionism" of "Khrushchev and his group" along with the Soviet attacks on Hoxha, and Peking kept insisting at every opportunity on Albania's continued membership in the "Socialist camp" and the Communist world movement. More than that, Mao himself signed the messages conveying the CPC's congratulations to the Albanian party under Hoxha's leadership on its "correct policy" and particularly on its intransigent struggle against "revisionism" and for world Communist unity.[29] Meanwhile, the Soviets, having lined up the support of a safe majority of Communist parties for political condemnation of the Albanians, but having failed to win over a substantial minority, broke off diplomatic relations with Tirana without awaiting the formal verdict of any international Communist conference, induced most of the East European states to take corresponding measures, and stopped inviting the Albanians to the meetings of the Council for Mutual Economic Aid.[30] Again, the Chinese countered by refusing to send an observer to the CMEA meeting, by continuing demonstratively friendly exchanges with Albania after the Soviet break, and by causing the North Korean and North Vietnamese Communists to send clearly friendly and fraternal – if less demonstrative – New Year messages to the Albanian leaders as well.[31]

The resulting situation was unprecedented. As no international Communist conference has spoken, the Albanians must still be regarded even by the Russians as members of the international Communist movement; indeed, Albanian delegates took part in the Congress of the World Federation of Trade Unions in December 1961 and in the World Peace Congress of summer 1962 in Moscow itself, in spite of the rupture of Soviet-Albanian diplomatic relations![32] Again, at the Stockholm session of the World Peace Council in December 1961, an Albanian delegation actively co-operated with the Chinese, and that session showed by its debates and even by an open vote that the 1960 compromise had broken down as completely on general policy as on the form of unity, with the issue of priority for "peaceful co-existence" or for "wars of liberation" once again the center of dispute.[33] Thus, the world Communist movement, while openly divided politically, is not yet formally split in the organizational sense. Yet, at the same time, state relations between the Russians and their East European followers on one side and Albania on the other are already broken!

The date and conditions for another international Communist conference have been repeatedly discussed since that time, both in correspondence between the parties concerned and in public. In the spring of 1962, the Chinese Communists officially proposed to the Russians, following suggestions by several other parties, to call such a conference and the Soviets agreed to call one after proper preparation; [34] these confidential exchanges then formed the background to a lull in public Sino-Soviet polemics. Yet the crucial fact remains that Khrushchev has taken open governmental action without awaiting an international judgment. When both Tirana and Peking defied the public attack to which the Soviet leader had committed the prestige of his party and his government, he evidently came to view a demonstrative reassertion of Soviet imperial discipline as a matter of the utmost urgency — too urgent to await action by an international conference. Such a conference might have to be deferred while Moscow was working on the waverers; it might drag on owing to Chinese obstruction or to the desire of other parties to avoid a clear-cut stand; and its outcome might depend on Russian determination to force a majority vote and Chinese willingness to submit to it. So Khrushchev preferred to take unilateral state action and thus confront an eventual international conference with a *fait accompli.*

This means that Khrushchev, like Stalin, has been forced to make a hard choice between Soviet imperial interests and the unity of the world Communist movement — and that he has made the same choice as Stalin did. But for Khrushchev the choice was more drastic. For while Stalin was able to have Yugoslavia excommunicated by the Cominform before he took public state action against her, Khrushchev no longer had any such ready machinery of excommunication at his disposal. He had renounced that machinery in pursuit of his belief in the co-operation of equal and independent Communist powers and movements, and in the harmony of interests or at least the comparative ease of compromise between the Soviet empire and the forces of international revolution. He has been forced back to the "Stalinist" use of state power in inter-Communist relations because that belief, which was to distinguish his world role from Stalin's, has failed.

THE PROSPECT OF SCHISM

By the time of the 1960 Moscow compromise, it was already clear that there was no road back to the centralized World Party created by Lenin. There is none now. Independent Communist powers do exist; and experience has proved that independent Communist powers cannot be subordinated to the ideological authority and organizational discipline of a single center.

The alternative attempted by the 1960 conference was to preserve an alliance of autonomous parties held together by a common faith. It was implicitly admitted that differences about the interpretation of that faith in the light of different national interests might arise from time to time, but it was hoped that the common basis of ideology and interest would be strong enough for compromises to be reached again and again in a process of steady adjustment.

This "conciliar" model of world communism has broken down because of the inherent difficulties of compromise by pragmatic adjustment among totalitarian ideological parties and states. At least one of the two major state parties has refused to renounce the right to carry "ideological struggle" into the territory of the other. Yet without some mutual respect of parochial authority – or of the principle *"cuius regio, eius religio"* – ideologically independent state parties can hardly live together in a common ecumenic organization. The Italian Communist leaders have been quite right in arguing that open "comradely" debate of inter-party differences in a spirit of mutual understanding and respect is the only way to preserve some measure of Communist world unity in the present situation.[35] But they have only been able to suggest such an un-Leninist solution because they are constantly exposed to the anti-ideological influence of an atmosphere of "bourgeois liberalism."

The remaining alternative is schism, that is, permanent factional struggle, with each Communist party forced to take sides, whether formal mutual excommunication takes place or not. The Chinese Communists would probably like to preserve mutual recognition of some ultimate community of faith as a formal basis on which all-inclusive meetings could take place from time to time — just as common congresses of the Russian Social Democrats took place long after Bolsheviks and Mensheviks had established separate factional organizations.[36] Like their predecessors, these meetings would be forums for recurrent wrangles about the recognition of mandates (for, say, the Albanians or Yugoslavs) and recurrent contests for the votes of factionally uncommitted parties (such as Cuba). Such an arrangement would enable Mao to keep the Soviets ideologically bound to the alliance while he continued the struggle for leadership. Yet why the Russians should be willing to maintain such a fiction of unity without a minimum of submission to "majority rule" — a relation that would be as remote from democracy as from centralism — remains an unanswered question.

The effects of the schism on the chances of individual Communist parties are likely to differ widely. A few strongly entrenched and confident leaders may use the opportunity to acquire real political independence, shake off the identification with any foreign state, and actually improve their chances of gaining power, while remaining "national Communist" totalitarians. Other parties, whose leadership has proved divided in the past, may be paralyzed or split by the new factional struggle and find their attraction altogether destroyed. Probably the majority will at first side with Russia from automatic habit, but will face a gradual decline in their following as it becomes more and more evident that their position represents merely submission to a foreign power and no longer solidarity with a world-wide movement.

But the most profound repercussions may well be those on the Soviet Communist Party itself. Twice within five years, it has had to revise its image of its own international role. In 1956, Khrushchev ordered the party to abandon the Stalinist concept that the progress of world revolution was wholly dependent on Soviet strength. Now it will have to unlearn the Khrushchevian belief that the progress of world revolution would invariably increase that strength. Khrushchev was right in facing the fact that independent revolutions may occur outside Soviet control; Stalin was right in thinking that such revolutions may not necessarily be to the advantage of the Soviet Union. But if the progress of revolution and the expansion of Soviet power are distinct and sometimes mutually contradictory processes, it follows that the Soviet Union has as little chance to win world hegemony as any other power. This is not going to be the Russian Century after all.

No doubt, it will take time for these ideological implications of the schism to be generally realized by the Soviet Communists. But as the ultimate irrelevance of world revolution to the greatness of Russia comes to be understood, the disillusionment of the believers among them is bound to be profound. It is not easy to see how either the aggressive *élan* of Khrushchev's foreign policy or the zest of his campaign for a "Leninist" ideological revival at home can recover from this blow. Yet the self-confidence of the more pragmatic element among Russia's administrators, technicians, and scientists will not be impaired by the discomfiture of the ideologues. The Congress of the "second de-Stalinization" has also sown the seeds, then, of a future "de-Khrushchevization"; in the next crisis of succession, reassertion of the primacy of an ideological party may no longer be the safest road to victory.

EPILOGUE: ON THE STAGES OF INTERNATIONAL COMMUNISM

The death of Stalin in 1953 foreshadowed the abandonment of a historically unique enterprise – the attempt to transfer the centralism of a ruling totalitarian party to an international movement. The rise of Khrushchev to leadership of the Soviet empire was linked with the endeavor to replace the outlived model of a totalitarian World Party by a more flexible, but still single-centered, form of international co-operation, under which organizationally autonomous Communist parties and governments would nevertheless voluntarily submit to the ideological authority of the "leading party." By the end of 1960, the CPSU reacted to Chinese attacks on its policy by renouncing this "leading role" in the hope that it would thus escape the need for defending itself in recurrent ideological argument, yet maintain international unity on the basis of pragmatic compromise. Since then, Chinese insistence on unremitting ideological struggle has foiled that hope, and produced factional schism instead of pragmatic unity.

Today we are entitled to look back on the four main stages of the Communist world movement as on a finished period of history. The creation of the centralistic World Party was preceded by a loose alliance of rather heterogeneous revolutionary groups, developing from the "Zimmerwald Left" during the First World War and formalized under Bolshevik leadership by the foundation of the Communist International in 1919. The centralistic stage was by far the longest: it started well before Stalin's reign with the Second World Congress of the Comintern in 1920 and long outlived the formal dissolution of that body in 1943. The third stage opened with Khrushchev's first moves to establish his new type of international leadership in 1954; it was fully developed by 1957, but had become untenable by 1960. The final stage – the attempt at maintaining unity by compromise – can hardly be said to have worked at all.

In retrospect, one is struck both by the strangeness, not to say absurdity, of the concept of international centralism underlying more than thirty years of the Comintern's activity under Lenin and Stalin, and by the quick disintegration of the more "sensible" alternatives developed after Stalin's demise. The centralist structure of a totalitarian party serves to make it a fit instrument for the revolutionary conquest and preservation of total power, and the centralism of the Communist World Party was originally intended to serve this very purpose. Yet revolutionary parties have to win power within existing states by exploiting conditions of national crisis with the utmost flexibility and ruthlessness; they are bound to be inhibited if subjected to the instructions of an outside body tied to a foreign government, and in fact not a single Communist party was victorious for twenty years after the World

Party had been formed. Conversely, once one or more non-Russian Communist parties succeeded — whatever the exceptional conditions — in conquering power by their own efforts without receiving it from Russian hands, the eclipse of international centralism became merely a matter of time.

It may be argued, of course, that Stalin soon ceased to believe in the possibility, and even the desirability, of independent Communist revolutions, and that he increasingly used the centralist discipline of the World Party to turn its sections into mere tools of Soviet imperial interests. But while it is true that the centralism of the Comintern was more suitable for such employment than for its original purpose, such a view leaves us with two basic questions. One is why non-Russian revolutionaries should ever have accepted the concept of the centralist World Party under Soviet leadership with such blind faith as to allow their groups to be transformed into derivative totalitarian parties that could be used at will as tools of Russian foreign policy. The other is why a few of these derivative totalitarian parties nevertheless succeeded at a late stage in emancipating themselves from total dependence on Soviet instructions, so that they were able to work out a revolutionary strategy of their own and pursue it to the victorious conquest of power. The first question raises the problem of how the Communist World Party could ever arise; the second amounts to asking how, once its rigid discipline had been established, it could ever decay — how the fatal pluralism of independent Communist states could ever develop within such a system.

Finally, the ideological disintegration of world communism also raises the question of why it has proved impossible to maintain a single doctrinal authority for a movement ruling a plurality of independent states — why the unity of doctrine could not survive the diffusion of power. The answer must be sought in the "Caesaro-papist" nature of modern totalitarianism, with its inseparable unity between ideology and state power: here lies the fundamental difference between the structure of international communism and that of the Catholic Church. A spiritual movement may preserve its world-wide doctrinaire unity so long as — for all its determination to influence the conduct of peoples and governments in this world — it refrains from seeking to exert political power directly. But in a movement constructed on the Byzantine model, where loyalty to the faith and obedience to the state coincide, ideological fragmentation is bound to follow the growth of political pluralism.

LENIN AND THE CREATION OF THE "WORLD PARTY"

Totalitarian parties are not born full-grown. Lenin created his Bolshevik Party only by a long and difficult struggle to transform the ideas and organization of the Russian revolutionary Social Democrats so as to forge an effective instrument for the conquest of power. Loose, dispersed, democratic circles expressing the political needs and forms of action of the awakening Russian working class had to be turned into a disciplined party ready to tap all sources of discontent, to combine the use of legal propaganda and illegal preparations for armed insurrection, and to follow the leader in meeting each new situation by sudden tactical changes. A Marxist belief in the necessary victory of the working class, which would find in each country its appropriate road to emancipation by trial and error, had to be replaced by the conviction that the revolutionary overthrow of Tsarist despotism depended entirely on the "correct" strategy for rallying all revolutionary classes under the leadership of "the party," and that this strategy could only be worked out by the "right" leader combining profound scientific insight with tireless revolutionary zeal. Lenin did not set out to create a democratic party expressing the development of the working class, but rather a "Jacobin" party "linked" to the working class and using it to overthrow Tsarism; and what he in fact created was an instrument of power that did not depend on any one class but could use and abuse all classes at need.

No corresponding party existed outside Russia when the Bolsheviks seized power. None of the minority groups of revolutionary Marxists or syndicalists who became Lenin's allies during and immediately after World War I had similar ideas. On the contrary, German Spartacists and Dutch Tribunists, British shop stewards, French syndicalists, and American "Wobblies" (members of the IWW) all agreed that strict democracy in working-class organizations was the only road to revolutionary action: for they all believed that the workers would inevitably be revolutionized by their experience, and that reformism could be imposed on them only by the bureaucratic tricks of parliamentarians and trade union officials. The outlook of all these groups was thus much closer to that of Trotsky and of the revolutionary wing of the Mensheviks than to Lenin's concept; and Rosa Luxemburg, who was not only the foremost theoretician of the German Spartacists but had for many years participated in the factional struggles of the Russian underground as a leading member of one of the Polish Socialist groups, was fully aware of these affinities.[1] Hence these revolutionary minority groups rallied to the support of the Bolshevik Party after the latter's seizure of power in November 1917 mainly because of the Bolsheviks' claim to represent the rule of the Soviets and above all because of their determination to end the war, rather than from any sympathy for Bolshevik ideas of party centralism and party dictatorship.[2]

Nor had Lenin tried to convert them to those ideas even when he had most opportunity to do so — during the wartime co-operation of the revolutionary internationalists in the "Zimmerwald Left"; for at the time, Lenin himself did not believe that those ideas were applicable to the broad working-class movements of Western and Central Europe. Until the very eve of World War I, he had accepted the revolutionary declamations of the European Social Democrats at face value; then, shocked by the support most of the parties gave to national defense and by the resultant collapse of the International, he had tried to explain it as the "betrayal" of a few leaders, backed by a thin upper stratum of "working-class aristocrats" who had been bribed with a share of the spoils of imperialism. He thus agreed with the European revolutionary minorities that the bulk of the working class in their countries was "really" revolutionary and that it was only the machinations of reformist bureaucrats that prevented them temporarily from expressing their true attitude in action. His logical conclusion was that a clean break with the reformist leaders was needed both nationally and internationally — that the revolutionaries must organize in separate parties and set up a new Communist International in order to unfold the true banner of revolutionary Marxism and rally the majority of the workers to their side.

But it did not then occur to Lenin that the new Communist parties of Europe, working in quite different conditions, should be organized on the Bolshevik model; nor did he or any of his associates advance that demand when the Communist International was actually founded in the capital of the new Soviet state in March 1919. All that was then asked from its future members was that they support the new Russia, adopt a program of "proletarian dictatorship" exercised through Soviets, and make a clean break with the "reformists"; the expectation of an immediate, rapid advance of proletarian revolutions over most of industrial Europe precluded by itself any claim to lasting Russian leadership, or any thought of the need for laborious, preliminary transformation of existing revolutionary parties and groups.

Yet only a year later, the international outlook of Lenin and his team had changed completely. By then, the Bolshevik regime had emerged victorious from the most critical phase of the Civil War, and its prestige among the war-weary European workers stood high. But instead of the expected rapid spread of proletarian revolutions, the Bolsheviks' allies had suffered a number of bloody defeats, notably in Germany and Hungary, and the old order showed signs of consolidating itself.

In the spring of 1920, Lenin for the first time called on foreign Communists to study the tactics of the Bolshevik struggle for power as a model for their own action; [3] in the summer, at the Second World Congress of the Comintern, he took the decisive step of trying to impose the Bolshevik organizational model as well. The Red Army was then pursuing its offensive in Poland in the hope of giving a new impetus to Communist revolutions in Europe; and left-wing admiration for Soviet Russia caused a number of European Socialist leaders to apply for the admission of their parties to the Comintern, on condition of retaining full autonomy in their own affairs, as a means of avoiding a split. The Bolsheviks saw this as an attempt on the part of the reformist leaders to use the prestige of communism as a fig leaf while carrying on their policies of "betrayal" — and that at the very moment when true revolutionary action was more needed, and apparently more promising, than ever before. They reacted by making the Congress adopt twenty-one doctrinal and organizational conditions as the *sine qua non* for any party's admission to the Comintern.

The immediate, tactical purpose of the conditions was to deter the "reformist leaders" and to force the "waverers" to break with them; but this in itself implied that the revolutionary purity of each party and of the Comintern as a whole could be assured by organizational devices — a thoroughly Bolshevik idea. In detail, the conditions followed the Bolshevik model of "democratic centralism," with its strict subordination of the actions of party members in parliament, trade unions, and all other organizations to the Central Committee, and with the explicit obligation also for legally operating parties to maintain an underground apparatus for the preparation of armed risings. But the idea of organizational discipline as a guarantee against opportunism presupposes that the leadership — and ultimately one leader — possesses the "correct" scientific understanding of the road to victory; and that understanding, in the Bolshevik view, was fully developed only in the Bolshevik leaders themselves who had proved it by winning and holding power. Faced with the unforeseen problem of making sure that the international alliance of true revolutionaries would retain its ideological purity yet gain in effectiveness, the Bolsheviks automatically fell back on the familiar organizational devices of their own party structure.

In form, Lenin and his associates did not demand the subordination of all Communist parties to Russian leadership — only to the democratic decisions of a World Congress and to the executive committee elected by it; by statute, the ruling Russian party was just as much subject to this international discipline as its weaker brethren, and despite its overwhelming strength it held no majority in the Congress and the ECCI. But in practice, the placing of the Comintern's headquarters on the territory of the only Communist-ruled country, the staffing of the secretariat with Russians and exiles living in Russia, the dependence on Soviet financial and technical support for underground contacts with countries where the parties were banned, did combine with the explicit ideological recognition of the Bolshevik model to make Soviet influence irresistible in this framework. The statute created the structure of a centralized World Party; the ideology combined with the facts of power to ensure that it would be Russian-directed.

The transformation of the non-Russian revolutionary parties into "parties of the new type" thus proceeded under an impulse from outside; they were turned into *derivative totalitarian parties.* Moreover, this was done not by a leader of the stature of Lenin, who had other work to do, but by the people whom the ruling Bolsheviks could spare for this work and by their exile associates. At first, many leaders of the old revolutionary groups tried to resist this process by defending the tradition of inner-party democracy and arguing that only an autonomous national leadership could win the confidence of the working class and develop a strategy in accordance with national conditions. But in country after country, the *apparatchiki* of the Comintern and their local stooges, though often inferior in knowledge of the national situation and the traditions of the movement concerned, as well as in character and general ability, defeated the home-grown revolutionary leaders with comparative ease.[4] The reason seems to have been that almost all these leaders, impressed by the success of the Bolshevik revolution and by the failure of their own movement to equal it, had at least temporarily revised their own beliefs and adopted Leninist ideas as embodied in the twenty-one conditions. They had abdicated their own authority in favor of the Soviet myth, and now had no means to resist the authorized manipulators of that myth.

Moreover, the fact that the split in the working-class movement had now become permanent and that professed revolutionary parties continued to exist separately in what was often clearly a non-revolutionary situation meant that some of these parties had to rely increasingly on attracting a new type of follower, with few roots in the pre-1914 movement and little respect for the old revolutionary leaders, but with strong emotional ties to "Moscow" — a type far less self-reliant than the old revolutionary cadres and far more dependent on external sources of hope. In short, the political survival of the Communist parties in non-revolutionary conditions had become dependent on Moscow's moral even more than on its material support; hence leaders who defied the voice of Moscow found themselves in conflict both with the vested interest of their own party machine and with the emotional loyalties of their rank and file, and could easily be isolated and forced to submit, or expelled.

As the efficacy of the Comintern machine in imposing

the new type of control on its member parties was closely linked to the recession of the revolutionary wave, it came to bear little relation to Lenin's original purpose of making these parties fit for revolutionary action; and Lenin did indeed express doubts whether the process was not going too far for the future of the international revolution. At the Fourth World Congress of the Comintern in 1922, the last one he attended, he raised the "un-Leninist" query whether the resolution on organizational questions was not "too Russian," in the sense of being based on conditions alien to the foreign Communists and therefore unlikely to be fruitful for their practice.[5] Lenin was also worried at this time by the unintended consequences of the regime he had created in Russia itself – such as the growing power of the bureaucracy and the declining chances of its popular control. Yet, as with the Soviet regime, his doubts were also powerless to reverse the trend in the Comintern – the momentum of the new machine had already become too strong.

STALIN AND THE PRIMACY OF SOVIET INTERESTS

Stalin, in turn, was as little plagued by such doubts in the international as in the national field: the logic of totalitarianism, which had confronted Lenin with the unwelcome results of his actions, presented Stalin only with the welcome means of his ascent to power. By the time of Lenin's death, after the final flare-up in Germany in 1923, the European postwar crisis with its potential for revolutionary change had definitely ended, and Stalin recognized this fact in announcing the "relative stabilization of capitalism" and proclaiming the possibility of "building socialism in one country." He could therefore have neglected the Comintern for the time being – but for two circumstances. One was the fiction that made the Russian Bolsheviks formally subordinate to the World Party (which they in fact controlled); the other was the knowledge of the foreign governments with whom the USSR was now trying to establish normal relations that the Soviet leaders had the power to issue instructions to the Communist parties of their countries.

The formal subordination of the CPSU to the Comintern gave each of the contenders in the struggle for Lenin's succession a powerful interest in securing control of the Comintern and its affiliated parties for his own faction. As Zinoviev had headed the new International from its foundation and Trotsky enjoyed great authority in the international Communist movement, Stalin started with a serious handicap; to insure himself against the use of this potential instrument of moral pressure by his domestic rivals, he had to purge both the top personnel of the Comintern and the leadership of many affiliated parties of their supporters. As he had done before at home, Stalin first removed the followers of Trotsky with the help of Zinoviev; then, to get rid of Zinoviev and his associates, he inaugurated an international "right turn" with the help of Bukharin; and a few years later he instigated an international "left turn" to disembarrass himself of Bukharin and his international friends. The means used for this international extension of the inner-Russian power struggle were the same old Bolshevik methods that the *apparatchiki* of the Comintern had begun using against independent-minded foreign Communists in Lenin's lifetime; these methods were now justified as necessary to assure the "Bolshevization" of the non-Russian Communist parties. By the end of the 1920's this "Bolshevization by purge" had succeeded throughout the world in installing as party leaders "obedient blockheads" who would follow Stalin's every command without a murmur; to guard against any unexpected insubordination, Stalin's men moreover prevented the formation of homogeneous leading teams and kept alternate leaders in reserve within each party.

When Stalin first carried his domestic struggle for power into the Comintern, he may not have been as firmly convinced as in later times that no independent revolutionary victories by foreign Communist parties were to be expected or even to be desired. But he clearly did not regard the chance of such victories as topical,[6] and he had no compunction about using these obedient tools "in the meantime" for the benefit of such Soviet foreign policy objectives as the normalization of relations with the "capitalist" powers and the promotion of conflicts among them. He soon found that to make Soviet friendship for any particular non-Communist government credible, the policy of the local Communists had to be adjusted accordingly, and he proceeded to do so without hesitation.

It is sufficient to recall in this connection Soviet instructions to the Chinese Communists in the middle 1920's, when the latter were made to join the Kuomintang as a logical counterpart to Stalin's support for Sun Yat-sen and Chiang Kai-shek, and when during the northward offensive of the Chinese Nationalist armies they were instructed to avoid measures of land distribution that might endanger the unity of the national revolutionary forces, because Stalin regarded a united, nationalist China as the best chance of containing Japanese and British power on the Asian mainland. Despite the spectacular failure of this policy in the spring of 1927, when Chiang suppressed the Communists and ruined Stalin's plan for the Chinese revolution, many of its features were repeated in the middle 1930's, when Stalin not only urged an anti-Japanese "United Front" of Chinese Communists and Nationalists, but inaugurated the "Popular Front" policy in Western Europe in order to buttress his diplomacy of collective security against Nazi aggression: then, too, the Communists in France and above all in Spain were instructed to put the alliance with the democratic section of the bourgeoisie against the "Fascist powers" ahead of all thought of social revolution. Finally, after Hitler's attack on the Soviet Union, the Communists of all the Allied Nations were bidden to give unconditional support to their governments, while seeking to occupy key positions in the state machines of the free countries and in the resistance movements of the occupied countries – a policy that reached its logical culmination in the 1943 decision to "dissolve" the Comintern officially while maintaining its machinery in secret.[7]

Far from expressing a renunciation of Soviet control over the Communist parties of the world, the "dissolution" of 1943 may thus be said to have marked one of the high points of their subordination to Soviet interests.[8] By then experience had long proved the congenital inability of these foreign-directed, derivative totalitarian parties to win power by their own efforts. It was not only that at some critical moments in their history some of the more important parties had been directly prevented from making a bid for power by specific Soviet orders issued for reasons of foreign policy, but that by virtue of their dependence on an outside center they were permanently deprived of the main advantage enjoyed by an independent, home-grown totalitarian party over its democratic competitors — the single-minded concentration on the conquest of power.

In a grave social crisis, democratic parties are frequently handicapped by the fact that they are tied to specific interests, traditions, and methods — they cannot suddenly leap over their own shadow. A totalitarian party, which does not represent a particular section of society but a vision of its total transformation, is enabled by its centralist organization and by its belief in the overriding importance of the conquest of state power to exploit the crisis with ruthless opportunism, provided its leader is adequate to the task. In a home-grown totalitarian party, the leader is also the creator of the party: by forging his instrument he has already proved his ability as a technician of power and has established his authority in the process, and he will let nothing stand in the way of his ambition. But in the derivative totalitarian parties created by the Comintern, the leaders are as much creatures of a foreign will as are their organizations; they have been trained to act like subordinates who look for instructions before every decision; they have not established their authority in a struggle to get to the top but have received it ready-made from outside as a reward for faithful service, and they feel that it may be taken from them at any moment. Such a party is hampered in exploiting a crisis by the common knowledge of its dependence on outside orders and also by the fact that its drive to power is liable at any moment to be diverted by such orders — that its leaders have to look over their shoulder all the time instead of looking only to their goal. In the end, subordination to the interests of a foreign state must prove an even greater handicap than any tie to domestic sectional interests.

Because their will to power is conditional on foreign permission, such parties have never won power by their own efforts — they can only receive it from the conquering armies of their sponsoring country, as did the Communist parties of the Baltic states and of Eastern Europe during and after World War II. But this limitation, which might have worried Lenin, had long been consciously accepted by Stalin in his doctrine that the interests of world revolution were wholly comprised within the interests of the Soviet Union, and that any good Communist must willingly put the Soviet Union first. If the centralist World Party was a poor instrument for promoting independent revolutions, it was a useful weapon in the armory of Soviet power politics.

MAO AND TITO: THE TURN TO EMANCIPATION

Yet even while Stalin's centralized control of the World Party and its subordination to Soviet interests seemed perfect, the germs of independence and pluralism were at work within the supposedly monolithic structure. When the Yugoslav Communists got power during the Second World War and the Chinese Communists soon afterward, they did not receive it from the hands of the Soviet army. But these two seeming exceptions to the rule that derivative totalitarian parties are unable to win power by themselves did in fact confirm the rule — for both Tito and Mao Tse-tung gained victory by defying Stalin's "advice" at the most critical moment.

In the Yugoslav case that moment occurred in November 1943, when Tito's partisans formally "deposed" the Yugoslav exile government in London with which Stalin had urged them to co-operate and set up a "National Committee" as a virtual counter-government in the Bosnian mountains — a decision described at the time by the Comintern veteran Manuilski, on Stalin's authority, as "a stab in the back of the Soviet Union." [9] In the Chinese case, Mao appears to have defied Soviet pressure to negotiate an all-Chinese coalition government with Chiang and the integration of his armed forces into a single all-Chinese army after the end of the Japanese war in August 1945; [10] Mao's final decision to pass from partisan warfare to an all-out, southward offensive in the summer of 1948 may also have been taken against Soviet advice. [11]

None of the later crises leading to the present pluralistic decay of the former World Party could have occurred without the independent conquest of power by these two Communist parties. Yet neither victory would have been possible without acts of defiance against the Soviet leadership — acts that stand in stark contradiction to the customary posture of derivative parties led by obedient agents and dependent on an outside center. In other words, the germs of independence must have been present, at least in those two parties, *before* the final acts of defiance. In both cases, independent-minded leaders with a will to power must somehow have succeeded during the preceding years in building their own teams and emancipating themselves and their parties from total ideological and organizational dependence on the Comintern. If so, they must have worked by methods entirely different from those that had been attempted, with uniformly disastrous results, by the early Communist opposition groups: open appeals for party democracy and national autonomy were out of the question; in fact, they must have applied the utmost conspiratorial caution in order to avoid any open conflict with Moscow until their position was strong enough. Though such "emancipation by conspiracy" cannot, in its nature, be directly documented,

I believe that some of its main stages may be indirectly traced in both cases.

The Chinese Communists, whose final victory occurred after that of the Yugoslavs, were in fact ahead of them in this internal emancipation. Here we may start from a well-established fact – that Mao Tse-tung was the first, and for many years the only, Communist party leader who achieved his position without investiture by Moscow. He was elected party chairman during the Tsun-yi conference in January 1935 at a stage on the "long march" when even radio contact with Moscow was interrupted; [12] and he defeated his opponents at that time because his strategy of partisan warfare based on rural "Soviet areas" – tolerated at first by the preceding party leaders and by Moscow as a mere sideline to underground activity in the urban centers – had proved incomparably more successful than the latter, so much so that the areas under his control had eventually become the only remaining refuge for the Central Committee as well. Mao had thus become party leader with an independent strategic concept of his own. As to the crucial question of why Stalin subsequently confirmed the independent choice – apparently only after prolonged hesitation [13] – the most plausible answer seems to be that Moscow was then interested in using the limited but real strength of the Chinese Communist partisans to urge on the Nationalist government a truce in the civil war and a common front against Japan; that Mao proved both willing to accept this policy and able to carry it out successfully; and that Stalin's favorite, Wang Ming, could not have ousted him without destroying the effectiveness of his force. In the end, Stalin must have felt that Mao's value as an ally outweighed his failings as a subordinate.

Once confirmed in office and successful in pursuing

the immediate tactical task, Mao proceeded with further steps of emancipation — still avoiding any open conflict with Moscow. In 1939, he developed his original strategic concept of the "New Democracy," arguing that the four-class alliance envisaged by Lenin and Stalin for the first stage of the anti-imperialist and anti-feudal revolution in colonial and semi-colonial countries was indeed necessary, but that it must be formed from the start under the leadership of the Communist Party.[14] In 1941–42, he began to subject his entire party organization to a thorough ideological re-education — the "rectification of thought," intended to make them proudly conscious that the CPC had its own peculiar style of inner-party life (with special emphasis on the constant remolding of the consciousness, that is, "brain washing"), which was clearly superior to the crude methods of Stalin's blood purges.[15] It was the moral and political unity thus forged by years of common danger and hardship, by improbable successes, and by deliberate training in a new spirit, that enabled Mao to defy Stalin's advice after 1945; and once the plan for a Chiang-Mao coalition had been foiled — by Chiang's intransigence no less than by Mao's — the solid unity of Mao's team and the need for a counterweight to the "American party" in China forced Stalin to go on supporting him, even though with marked reserve.

In contrast to Mao, Tito was invested with the leadership of the Yugoslav party by Stalin, but in most peculiar circumstances. The decision was taken in Moscow in late 1937, at the height of the blood purge, and after some wavering whether it would not be wiser to dissolve the Yugoslav party altogether as too hopelessly disrupted by "enemy agents" — a fate that was soon to befall the Polish party. Of the top Yugoslav leaders then available in Moscow, Tito alone seems to have got out alive – and with full powers to reorganize the Yugoslav underground party from top to bottom. Not surprisingly, Tito has never revealed how he succeeded in obtaining that decision.[16] What seems clear, however, is that he used his powers to build up an unusually homogeneous leadership loyal to him personally (the Croat leader Andrija Hebrang seems to have been the only watchdog kept in reserve by Moscow from the start) and to make the organization as far as possible financially self-supporting.[17] It also appears that he envisaged at an early stage the possibility of Nazi occupation and partisan warfare as his chance: there is evidence, both in his wartime conduct and in his final report on the partisan campaign given to the Fifth Yugoslav Party Congress immediately after his excommunication in 1948, that he had carefully studied Mao's partisan tactics even before the war, though these were not then generally accepted as a model in the Comintern.[18]

With Tito, too, defiance of Moscow, when it finally came in 1943 over the issue of relations with the exile government, occurred at a time when he had become too important as an ally for open attack; and when the British and U.S. governments continued to supply Tito despite his open proclamation of his aims, the Soviets had to swallow their resentment at his insubordination and to take a meager share in aiding him as well.[19] Under cover of the wartime alliance, the transition from secret to open emancipation had been accomplished.

We can now see in what special conditions the emancipation of derivative totalitarian parties from Soviet control has been possible. First, unlike the luckless Communist opposition leaders of the 1920's, who were democratic revolutionaries unused to totalitarian methods, the new rebels against Moscow are authentic totalitarians, skilled in the arts of dissembling their thoughts and picking their cadres, and ruthless in the pursuit of national power. Second, both Mao and Tito have had the chance to build up homogeneous leading staffs in underground movements, where detailed observation was almost impossible for Moscow, and to strengthen the loyalty and cohesion of their teams in a prolonged struggle amidst great danger and hardship. Third, both impressed their followers by their strategic originality and by the successes due to it. Fourth, both took the risk of openly defying Moscow's orders only when their armies already represented a force of military value to Russia, so that an open attempt to use Soviet authority to disrupt them would have damaged the Russians themselves. Even given all these conditions, the successful emancipation of these two parties must have been immensely difficult – hardly less difficult, in fact, than the original creation of the first totalitarian party by Lenin. Yet once these two had succeeded, the monolithic shell of the World Party was cracked, and further rifts were bound to appear.

FROM STALIN TO KHRUSHCHEV: THE ROAD OF DECAY

The turning-point toward the pluralistic decay of the World Party was thus reached in Stalin's lifetime with the victories of the Yugoslav and Chinese Communists, achieved against his expectations and in defiance of his advice. With the emergence of the first independent Communist states outside Russia, further enforcement of centralistic discipline on a world scale became impossible, regardless of the intentions of the Communist leaders, Mao and Tito, who had emancipated their parties from

Soviet control before they achieved power, were now bound to see the interests of world communism as much from the viewpoints of their respective states as Stalin saw them from the viewpoint of the Soviet Union. Common principles would henceforth be interpreted in the light of different state interests.

Stalin was not prepared to admit this. True, when the Cominform was created in 1947 to co-ordinate the policies of the ruling Communist parties of Eastern Europe and the leading West European Communist parties in the struggle against the Marshall Plan, it was officially stated to be an organ for mutual consultation and exchange of experiences only. Moreover, it was located in Belgrade as a tribute to the achievement of the Yugoslav Communists, and the latter were even allowed to present their own militant strategy as a model for the less successful brethren.[20] But in practice Moscow insisted on retaining rigid control of the machinery and publications of the Cominform and sought to infiltrate its agents into the Yugoslav party and state machine, while the Yugoslavs began to compete with the Soviet influence in the Balkan satellites. When the resulting friction led, early in 1948, to acute conflicts concerning the plans for a Communist Balkan Federation and the prospects of the Greek civil war,[21] Stalin determined to break the independence of the Yugoslav Communists by excommunication, followed by economic and military pressure; but he succeeded only in breaking the façade of a united World Party.

With Communist China, Stalin applied far more caution than with little Yugoslavia: he does not seem to have attempted infiltration on any serious scale, nor to have tried to interfere in China's internal affairs. Mao's claim that Chinese strategy should become the model for the conquest of power in colonial and semi-colonial countries was at first supported in the Soviet and Cominform press,[22] and a regional bureau for the Communist-directed trade union movements of Asia and Australia was established in Peking. Yet there is no evidence that Stalin ever delegated to the Chinese Communists organizational authority over the Communist parties in that region, and even in state relations he could not bring himself fully to accept their independence and equality: at his insistence, they not only had to recognize formally the "leading role" of the Soviet Union and the CPSU but also, after prolonged negotiations, had to grant the Russians military and economic privileges on Chinese territory under the 1950 treaty of alliance. Soviet persistence in the obsolete claim to leadership of a single-centered World Party, a persistence that in the Yugoslav case had destroyed the very façade of unity, thus led in the Chinese case to preservation of the mere façade – at the price of hidden tensions.

Stalin's heirs seem to have realized from the start that this claim had become untenable in its old form, and Khrushchev in particular soon developed the concept that Soviet political leadership of the forces of international communism could no longer be based on their subjection to the organizational discipline of a World Party, but only on the ideological authority of the CPSU over parties that were in principle recognized as independent equals. This new concept was to apply both to parties that had in fact won power on their own (in the meantime, the Vietnamese Communists of Ho Chi-minh had joined the Yugoslav and Chinese in this category) and to others aspiring to do so. The concept was embodied in the 1954 revision of the Sino-Russian treaty, formulated on a basis of equality; in the 1955 attempt to persuade the Yugoslavs to rejoin the Soviet bloc as independent partners; in the

1956 statement, made in Khrushchev's report to the Twentieth CPSU Congress, that each Communist party must find its own road to power according to national conditions; and also in the dissolution of the Cominform that followed two months later. It was not, however, intended to apply to those East European Communist parties that had received power from the hands of the Soviet army and were therefore subject not merely to international discipline but to imperial domination: here Khrushchev was willing to loosen and modernize the form but not to renounce the substance of Soviet control.

Yet, in fact, this control was threatened almost at once by the crisis of Soviet authority in Eastern Europe caused by Khrushchev's denunciation of Stalin's crimes, including the persecution of East European "Titoists." The conflicts caused among the leading groups of the satellite parties by these disclosures led not only to the Hungarian popular revolt and its suppression, but also to the unique attempt of the Polish Communists to achieve emancipation from satellite status by a change of leadership, carried out in defiance of Russia and with broad popular support. This attempt was partly successful: though unable to gain real independence, the Polish Communists won a higher degree of domestic autonomy than Khrushchev had originally been willing to grant them, and similar autonomy henceforth had to be conceded to the other satellite parties as well. The indispensable measure of imperial control was safely assured again only when the Moscow Declaration of November 1957, forced upon the reluctant Poles by the joint pressure of the Soviet and Chinese Communist parties, defined the limits of the new autonomy by laying down a set of common ideological principles binding on all ruling Communist parties and, above all, by establishing the right of the CPSU, as the leading party to interpret these principles and determine a common foreign policy.

Khrushchev's attempt to replace the centralistic discipline of the former World Party by the ideological authority of Moscow over an alliance of formally equal and independent parties was bound to meet its crucial test, however, not inside the region where this authority could always be supplemented at need by imperial pressure, but outside it. Khrushchev's concept was based on the illusion that effective political unity among independent Communist governments and parties could be maintained by the mere ideological authority of the center, even though that center was no longer the only center of Communist power; and that illusion could last only so long as no other Communist power had serious reasons, in the light of different state interests, to prefer an interpretation of the common doctrine that differed from Moscow's. As soon as major differences of interest emerged between the Soviet Union and China, as they did in 1958 and more persistently since the winter of 1959–60, different interpretations of the doctrine were bound to lead to a challenge of Moscow's ideological authority; and in the absence of the former means for enforcing a binding decision by centralistic discipline, such a challenge could only lead either to an agreement to tolerate different points of view and reach adjustments by recurrent compromises, or to a permanent factional struggle for ideological leadership. By the time of the 1960 world conference of Communist parties in Moscow, it had become obvious that the doctrinal unity of international communism could no more survive the pluralism of Communist powers than could the centralist structure of the World Party; henceforth, the choice lay between pragmatic unity based on compromise and ideological struggle leading to schism.

Moscow's explicit renunciation of the "leading role" marked both its recognition of that fact and its preference for the pragmatic solution.

That preference had its solid reason in Moscow's superior power. China, the weaker and dependent ally, might hope to exert pressure on Russia's policy by submitting it to constant ideological scrutiny in the forum of international communism; hence, China's interest was to insist that there could be only one "correct" interpretation of Communist doctrine, and that it must be found by unending world-wide (though preferably esoteric) debate. Though Peking's followers might be a small minority at first, the common framework and the ideal of doctrinal unity must be preserved in order that the factional argument might continue and the "temporary" minority eventually emerge as a majority strong enough to impose its views on the mighty Soviet Union itself.[23] Conversely, once it was obvious that the Chinese minority could not be forced into submission, it was Russia's interest to foil the Chinese pressure by admitting that some differences of interpretation were inevitable in the present stage of historical development and thus making the ideological debate appear comparatively pointless. For in any adjustment of differences by pragmatic compromise, the superior weight of Soviet power was bound to ensure that Moscow's point of view would prevail with only minor concessions. In advocating unity based on toleration of a natural measure of disagreement, Moscow sought to silence ideological criticism and to gain a free hand for its foreign policy. In advocating unity based on correct principles, Peking sought to fetter Moscow's freedom of action and to reserve the right of recurrent ideological attack.

That the 1960 Moscow declaration had failed to settle

the issue became obvious in the course of the following year over the case of Albania. The Russians were prepared to tolerate (and largely ignore) Chinese disagreement, but not an ideological rebellion within their imperial sphere; the Chinese, on the other hand, could not abandon their first declared factional ally without ruining their prospects in the long-term ideological struggle they envisaged. Since the clash over Albania at the Twenty-second CPSU Congress, all efforts at reconciliation have broken down because both sides have become increasingly aware that their respective concepts of unity are themselves irreconcilable. By breaking relations with Albania but pursuing a policy of demonstrative *rapprochement* with Yugoslavia, the Russians have shown that they will accept co-operation based on imperfect ideological agreement, provided it goes with ideological non-aggression.[24] The Chinese, on the contrary, continue to stand for perfect doctrinal unity, to be achieved by unrestrained ideological criticism.

The result is that, as between the two principal antagonists, neither kind of unity can any longer be achieved. The Russians have taken their freedom of action in foreign policy, but so have the Chinese, and effective consultation between them has been reduced to zero, as the behavior of both powers in the Sino-Indian conflict and the Cuban crisis of the fall of 1962 showed clearly. The Chinese have taken full freedom of criticism in attacking Soviet "appeasement" in Cuba, but so have the Russians and their supporters in openly criticizing China at the series of European party congresses at the end of 1962. Subsequently, proposals for another world conference and a truce in public polemics were verbally supported by both sides, but qualified by each with conditions unacceptable to the other; even when both agreed to gratify the numerous appeals from "neutral" Communist parties for reconciliation by attempting a bilateral discussion, everything proceeded as if both Moscow and Peking had long resigned themselves to the inevitability of schism and each was only maneuvering to saddle the other with responsibility for it.

On the very eve of the bilateral meeting, the Chinese Communists confirmed this analysis by publishing (on June 14, 1963) their "Proposal for the General Line of the International Communist Movement," which extended the differences to an all-out attack on the 1961 program of the CPSU in a deliberate appeal to "Stalinist" traditions. The Central Committee of the CPSU reacted by authorizing an uncompromising rejection of the Chinese viewpoint, which after the failure of the talks was formulated in an open letter to all party units; at the same time it approved the policy that led to the agreement on a partial ban of nuclear tests with the United States and Britain. The breakdown of the Russo-Chinese talks and the signing of the test ban on July 25, denounced by Peking as a "betrayal," have marked the end of the period of tactical maneuvering and the admission of an open political break, characterized by a flood of "disclosures" from both sides about the earlier history of the conflict and by undisguised preparations for a formal split of the international Communist movement.[25]

THE PROSPECTS FOR "WORLD COMMUNISM"

In trying to envisage the likely effect of the schism on future relations among Communist governments and parties, we may start from the Chinese concept of these relations because it is comparatively well defined. In essence, it has not changed since the 1957 Moscow conference. In the Chinese view, the Communist parties cannot be run from a single center as a World Party, and should be fully autonomous in their organization; but they must be run on common ideological principles, and this requires recognition of the doctrinal authority of a leading party. Similarly, the Communist governments are sovereign and equal, but they need a common foreign policy, which must be laid down, after due consultation, by the government of the leading power. Yet while the Chinese Communists insisted in 1957 that this leading role could only be played by the CPSU and the Soviet government, they now consider that Khrushchev and his associates have proved unworthy of such leadership. In organizing the struggle against Soviet "revisionism," the Chinese have in fact, without so far formally announcing it, assumed the "leading role" themselves — at least for all those willing to adopt their factional platform.

We are thus observing the formation of a new Chinese-led international grouping comprising at least two other Communist governments (those of North Korea and Albania) and probably three (North Vietnam), a number of Asian Communist parties, important party minorities elsewhere in Asia and in Latin America, and preparatory contacts in a large number of other Communist parties and national revolutionary organizations. On the basis of their ideological statements, the Indonesian and Japanese Communist parties (the latter after expelling a dissident minority) must definitely be counted as part of this grouping, while the Malayan, Thai, and one of the rival Burmese parties (the illegal BCP) are known to be traditionally dependent on China, and the Indian Communist Party has a well-defined pro-Chinese minority.[26] The Vietnamese leadership had been desperately anxious to avoid taking sides but has been increasingly forced to do so.[27] Fidel Castro's Cuban regime has long tried to reconcile commitment to a partisan strategy of Latin American revolution closely resembling the Chinese type[28] with support for Soviet foreign policy, necessitated by its dependence on Soviet aid;[29] on the test ban, Castro has refrained from criticizing the Russians, but has refused to sign it himself, thus preserving an "intermediate" position and the political backing of both Moscow and Peking. The situation among the Latin American Communists seems generally in flux, with most of the older Communist leaders supporting Moscow but with the newer "Fidelist" groups admiring Peking and beginning to influence the party cadres as well.[30] Similarly, while the Arab Communist parties and the few Communists in tropical Africa are generally Moscow-oriented, the Afro-Asian "Solidarity Conferences" have reflected considerable Chinese influence among the extremist groups of revolutionary nationalists in this region; but here the Chinese have suffered defeat on the test ban issue.[31]

We know next to nothing about the organizational form of the ties between Peking and the various pro-Chinese parties and groups; yet this in itself suggests that the Chinese Communists, in harmony with their professed principles, have not generally attempted to intervene directly in the organizational setup of these groups. In the case of ruling parties or of such a strong party as the Indonesian, such attempts would obviously be condemned to failure. In fact, though the Chinese group, with its doctrinaire cohesion, is closer to the Comintern tradition than the Communist world movement was in the last years before the schism, it clearly carries within itself the germ of further pluralistic decay; there is no guarantee that Hoxha or Kim Il-sung, let alone Castro, Ho Chi-minh, or a victorious Aidit, will agree in the future with the Chinese version of Communist doctrine just because they do so now.

In the relations of the CPSU with its supporting parties and governments, the effect of the schism appears to be that the latter are with increasing clarity grouped in two layers: an inner ring of parties that rule states under Moscow's imperial control, that is, the member parties of Comecon; and an outer ring comprising the non-ruling pro-Soviet parties, but now also the Yugoslavs and potentially – if they should stay within the fold – the Cubans. Within the inner ring, where recognition of Soviet leadership in foreign policy has always been assured by the imperial power, there has lately been strong pressure to reduce the autonomy of the member states in the economic field as well, in favor of joint planning under Soviet direction. Far from relying on turning the termination of Moscow's doctrinal monopoly to their advantage, the satellites are afraid that the removal of the potential Chinese counterweight from inner-bloc affairs may increase Russia's effective power over them. The Rumanian leaders' delay in rallying to the Soviet position was directly linked to their determination to win their economic dispute with the Comecon *before* the completion of the Sino-Soviet break. Similarly, parties as firmly opposed to the Chinese outlook as the Polish and Hungarian Communists have been seeking to prevent a formal break of party ties in the interest of their own autonomy. But in the outer ring, where the facts of imperial power are not directly operative, the weakening of Soviet doctrinal authority and

Moscow's turn to a more pragmatic and tolerant concept of unity are likely to promote the development of a looser structure, with greater autonomy and variety than international communism has known at any time since 1920.

The key to this development may be found in the resumption of fraternal relations between the Soviet and Yugoslav Communist parties and in the arguments used by the Soviets to defend the *rapprochement* against Chinese criticism. The Russians may somewhat exaggerate (just as Tito somewhat understates) the extent to which the Yugoslavs have actually changed their point of view, but they do not deny that differences of doctrine still exist; their crucial point is that the large measure of practical support given by Yugoslavia to Soviet foreign policy, combined with the cessation of ideological attacks, are sufficient to make the resumption of party relations possible and useful. But this means that fraternal relations among Communist parties need not, in the present Soviet view, be based on identity of doctrine, or even on the pretense of such identity – only on agreement on some vital points of doctrine, combined with practical solidarity and absence of polemics. Of course, the Russians have not abandoned the claim that their own version of Marxism-Leninism, being based on the longest and widest experience, is true and will prevail in the end; but by admitting that different interpretations are historically inevitable even among sincere and authentic revolutionaries, once the latter head independent Communist parties and governments, they seek to free this claim of its divisive tendency. Such a point of view is more akin to that taken at the foundation of the Comintern than to the policy adopted by its Second Congress.

For the pro-Soviet Communist party leaders outside the

bloc, this attitude offers greatly increased freedom of "revisionist" experimentation in adapting the doctrine to their own problems. If only they will continue to support the Soviet Union and refrain from criticizing its rulers, emancipation in everything else is now theirs for the asking; except for their attitude to Soviet policies, how independent they will be now seems entirely a matter of their own ambition and ability. The new policy of the Italian Communists on West European integration,[32] or the attitude of the Indian Communists on national defense, already show the possibilities of the new situation, while the French Communist leadership remains typical of those who have grown so used to moving along well-worn dogmatic grooves that they are frightened rather than exhilarated by the chance to think for themselves.

Yet against the background of schism among the Communist powers and pragmatic tolerance within the Soviet camp, the one remaining fetter must appear all the more irksome: for if the Soviet Union is neither the recognized leader of all Communists nor the fountainhead of the only true doctrine, why should it continue to be treated as the "fatherland of all toilers," immune from criticism and deserving unconditional support? It was the myth of the unique achievement of the Bolsheviks that once made the creation of a Moscow-centered World Party possible; with the myth dissipated, it will be increasingly difficult to argue that the member parties of a loose international alliance should remain loyal to all of Moscow's policies — that, in the telling words of the Chinese, they should "obey every movement of someone's baton." [33] As the parties now backing Moscow in Western Europe and North America, in the Arab world and tropical Africa, and partly still in Asia and Latin America, learn to judge issues in terms of their own drive to power and acquire confidence in their own judgment, the tie to Moscow is bound to wear increasingly thin.

Finally, the conflict is likely to have a quite specific effect in tropical Africa, where hardly any Communist parties exist as yet. Historically, all Communist parties outside the Soviet Union, if not directly founded on Soviet initiative, have arisen through the ideological and organizational transformation of local groups of revolutionary Socialists under the influence of the Soviet model and of Soviet emissaries. A number of African states today clearly have the raw material for a similar transformation — parties or trade union groups headed by intellectuals with a Marxist education and a mixture of nationalist and social-revolutionary ideas. Their "Bolshevization," however, may prove far more difficult now that a unique, universally recognized model is lacking. The leaders of these "Afro-Marxist" groups are interested in the Communist model above all because of its effectiveness in securing unity of doctrine and of will; if it becomes instead a channel for importing foreign ideological and political splits, they may well prefer to go ahead in consolidating their own role with a home-made, eclectic ideology, as the Yugoslavs have been quietly advising them to do for some time. The anti-Communist turn of Sékou Touré, the Afro-Marxist ruler of Guinea, and the fact that he demanded the recall of the Soviet ambassador but made no complaint against the behavior of the Chinese (who are at least equally entrenched) may prove symptomatic of the way in which African leaders may use the new schism to preserve their own ideological and practical independence.

There remains the question whether even the basic totalitarian structure of the individual parties, once imposed on them from the outside by Moscow's authority, will stay immune from the consequences of polycentric decay. Here we must distinguish between the short-run effects of the factional struggle between Moscow's and Peking's supporters and the long-run effects of the search for an independent, national road to power. The factional struggle may normally be expected to lead to an early expulsion of the minority by the majority, whichever side the latter is on; and such a split may seriously impair the strength and outward attraction of some of the Communist parties, but it will leave their totalitarian inner structure intact. Yet the long-run revival of independent political thought may have very different effects, particularly where it takes place in the environment of a modern, democratic society.

Most of the leaders of Communist parties operating in such conditions seem to lack the stature to retain their position without the crutches of Soviet authority, and they are for that very reason reluctant to experiment with new ideas; as the respect for these crutches declines, they will find themselves under increasing criticism, with the influence of their parties reduced by recurrent crises—as we may already observe in the case of the Dutch and Scandinavian parties. But where the leaders are able and ambitious and the search for new policies correspondingly keen, as in Italy, the loosening of the dogmatic strait-jacket is bound to raise the question whether the party's tie to Russia and its undemocratic structure are not the two main causes of its isolation from the mainstream of the country's development, which is now flowing in the direction of democratic reform, and hence the main obstacles to its political effectiveness.[34] As Italy's revolutionary potential diminishes, so will the prospects for a totalitarian revolutionary party there; correspondingly the pressures for changing the character of the PCI and opening it widely to democratic currents will increase.

If I may venture a more general forecast at this early stage, I should say that those Communist parties that can only exist as derivative totalitarian parties will gradually wither away with the decline of Soviet authority; that parties rooted in the revolutionary tensions of their own country, but of a past or passing period, may suffer a democratic transformation, possibly culminating in a fusion with neighboring parties; and that only Communist parties in countries with a genuine potential for totalitarian revolution, or in the regions bordering the Communist empires, will survive as effective anti-democratic forces — the former in an increasingly independent, the latter in a continuing dependent position. The potentially independent totalitarian parties of the future are, of course, concentrated in the underdeveloped regions where today Chinese ideological influence is greatest. But the founder members of the Comintern, the Communist parties of industrial Europe that came into being through the transformation, under Bolshevik influence, of small democratic revolutionary groups, may yet end by reverting either to sectarian insignificance or to democratic independence.

NOTES

CHAPTER 1

1. Tito's official account of his wartime strategy in his *Political Report of the Central Committee of the CPY*, delivered at the Fifth Congress of the CPY, Belgrade, 1948, largely follows the pattern of Chinese partisan warfare as first described in Edgar Snow, *Red Star over China*, London, 1957, in Mao's own words. A later Yugoslav polemic against the Greek Communists (Svetozar Vukmanovic, *Ueber die Volksrevolution in Griechenland*, Belgrade, 1950) explains the victory of the Yugoslav partisans and the defeat of their Greek comrades specifically by the fact that the former had followed the Chinese model while the latter had not.
2. Compare the speeches of the Yugoslav delegates, Edvard Kardelj and Milovan Djilas, at the foundation meeting of the Cominform, in *For a Lasting Peace, For a People's Democracy*, November 10, 1947 (now also in Eugenio Reale, *Nascita del Cominform*, Rome, 1958); further, the account of the Soviet-Yugoslav disagreements on the project of a Balkan Federation and the prospects of the Greek civil war immediately preceding the break, in Vladimir Dedijer, *Tito Speaks*, London, 1953, and Milovan Djilas, *Conversations with Stalin*, London, 1962.
3. See, for example, Milovan Djilas's pamphlet, *Lenin ueber die Beziehungen zwischen sozialistischen Staaten*, Belgrade, 1950.
4. Since the above was written, the discussions in the Soviet Central Committee provoked by Khrushchev's Yugoslav policy in 1955 have become known in detail by the account of a former senior official of the Polish CP, Seweryn Bialer. According to this account, based on the minutes of a plenary session held in July 1955, Molotov had approved the normalization of state relations but had from the start opposed Khrushchev's bid for a resumption of party

relations with the Yugoslavs, on the grounds that toleration of their ideological deviations might encourage similar heresies in the satellite countries and in Poland particularly. See Bialer, "I Chose Truth," in *News from Behind the Iron Curtain,* New York, October 1956.

5. As I learned later from participants in the relevant discussions of the Yugoslav Central Committee, Khrushchev proposed in the preparatory correspondence that each side should assume part of the responsibility for the 1948 break but put the blame on a scapegoat: the Yugoslavs should blame their onetime ideological deviations on Djilas (who had been stripped of all party offices in early 1954 because of his attack on the one-party system); while the Soviets would declare Beria responsible for all their slanders of the Yugoslav regime and their persecution of "Titoists" throughout Eastern Europe. The Yugoslav Central Committee unanimously rejected this proposal on a motion of Tito's. This information shows that Isaac Deutscher's report that Djilas had been purged *in order* to pave the way for a reconciliation with the Soviets, published in 1955 without a source, reflected contemporary Soviet wishes rather than Yugoslav reality.
6. Edvard Kardelj, *La Democratie socialiste dans la pratique Yugoslave,* Brussels, 1955.
7. *Pravda,* May 27, 1955.
8. *Borba,* Belgrade, May 28, 1955.
9. Ibid. June 2, 1955.
10. Ibid. and *Izvestia,* June 3, 1955.
11. *Pravda,* July 16, 1955.
12. *Kommunist,* Belgrade, No. 6–7, July 1955.
13. *Borba,* July 28, 1955.
14. See, for example, the article "On the Road to Building Socialism" by the Rumanian chief planner M. Constantinescu in *For a Lasting Peace . . . ,* September 9, 1955. For later information on the beginning of the Soviet turn toward a planned division of labor within the bloc, see Fritz Schenk and Richard Lowenthal, "Khrushchev's Changing Empire," *Observer,* London, November 9, 16, and 23, 1958; and "Politics and Planning in the Soviet Empire," *New Leader,* February 5, 12, and 19, 1959.

CHAPTER 2

1. In the official report rendered in the name of the Central Committee by N. S. Khrushchev on February 14, 1956, and in the contribu-

tions made to its discussion by D. T. Shepilov, M. A. Suslov, and particularly A. I. Mikoyan on February 15 and 16.

2. For Spain, see David T. Cattell, *Communism and the Spanish Civil War*, Berkeley, 1955; for France, the growing moderation of Communist "United Front" and "Popular Front" programs between 1934 and 1936, as reflected in *Cahiers du Bolchevisme*, Paris.
3. English text in Leo Gruliow (ed.), *Current Soviet Policies*, New York, 1953.
4. For the Czech example see the speech of A. I. Mikoyan; for the Baltic, that of the Estonian First Secretary, I. G. Kebin, at the Twentieth Congress. The leader of the East German "Socialist Unity Party," Walter Ulbricht, on returning from the Congress also described the creation of the East German regime as an example of the "peaceful road" (*Neues Deutschland*, March 4, 1956).
5. See Togliatti's interview with *Nuovi Argumenti*, June 16, and his report to the Central Committee of the CPI, *Unita*, June 26, 1956. English texts are in *The Anti-Stalin Campaign and International Communism*, edited by the Russian Institute, Columbia University, New York, 1956.
6. See the theses on tactics in *Thesen und Resolutionen des IV. Weltkongresses der Kommunistischen Internationale*, Hamburg, 1923. Radek had first proposed Communist participation in a "workers' government" in *Rote Fahne*, Berlin, November 16, 1921, and was one of its principal advocates at the Fourth World Congress; see Jane Degras (ed.), *The Communist International 1919–1943, Documents*, Vol. I, London, 1956, p. 416.
7. See the theses on tactics of the Fifth World Congress of the Comintern, reinterpreting the "workers' and peasants' government" as "synonymous" with the dictatorship of the proletariat, and the account of the debate preceding their adoption in Degras, op. cit. Vol. II, London, 1960, p. 142 ff.
8. For the latest state of research on this attempt see Conrad Brandt, *Stalin's Failure in China*, Cambridge, Mass., 1958. Compare also Harold R. Isaacs, *The Tragedy of the Chinese Revolution*, London, 1938, and M. N. Roy, *Revolution and Counter-revolution in China*, Calcutta, 1948.
9. For Lenin's view see his "Preliminary Draft of Theses on the National and Colonial Questions," presented to the Second World Congress of the Comintern in July 1920, and his "Commission Report" on these questions to the same Congress in Lenin, *Selected Works*, Vol. X, London, 1938, pp. 231–44.
10. For a description of the effect produced on Stalin by the German events of June 30, 1934, see the testimony of W. G. Krivitsky, *In Stalin's Secret Service*, New York, 1939.

11. The original concept of the "Popular Front" governments still allowed for the possibility of using them as a transition to a Communist seizure of power, like the concept of "workers' government" in 1922 and that of "people's democratic government" in 1946; see the decisions of the Seventh World Congress, 1935. But deliberate confinement to the "capitalist framework" took place when such governments became a practical possibility in France and Spain in 1936 – see note 2 above.
12. For the 1946 concept of the "legal road" to "people's democracy" in Western Europe, see, in particular, Maurice Thorez's interview with *The Times* (London, November 18, 1946), reprinted in *Cahiers du Communisme*, Paris, November 1946. The seriousness of the hopes based by the Italian Communist leaders on this concept, at least until the elections of April 1948, was brought home to me when I learned from a personal communication that the 1950 breakaway of the former partisan leaders Magnani and Cucchi was in part an indirect consequence of the disappointment of these hopes: they broke when they understood that the party was no longer expecting to win power on its own.
13. In his address to the Sixth Congress of the East German "Socialist Unity Party" in early 1963, Khrushchev called the British Communist leaders as witnesses that Stalin himself had inspired their 1946 platform of the "peaceful road" (*Neues Deutschland*, January 17, 1963). See also Stalin's 1945 musings about the possibility of "socialism under the English monarchy" in Djilas, *Conversations with Stalin*, New York, 1962.
14. See, for example, the resolution of the CPGB executive of May 13, 1956, and the *Outlines of a Programmatic Declaration of the CPI*, adopted by its Central Committee in late September 1956.
15. See Mao's 1927 "Report of an Investigation into the Peasant Movement in Hunan," *Selected Works*, Vol. I, London, 1954, and its interpretation in Benjamin I. Schwartz, *Chinese Communism and the Rise of Mao*, Cambridge, Mass., 1952, pp. 72–9. For a dissenting view see K. A. Wittfogel, "'The Legend of 'Maoism,'" *China Quarterly*, No. 2, April-June 1960, pp. 18–21.
16. See, in particular, Edgar Snow, *Red Star over China*, London, 1937, and Mao's 1935 lectures on "Strategic Problems of China's Revolutionary War," *Selected Works*, Vol. I, London, 1954.
17. As well as the cited works of Benjamin Schwartz and Edgar Snow, see also Robert C. North, *Moscow and the Chinese Communists*, Stanford, 1953; Charles B. McLane, *Soviet Policy and the Chinese Communists, 1931–1946*, New York, 1958; and the party's official history as sketched in the pamphlet by Hu Chiao-mu, *Thirty Years of the Communist Party of China*, Peking, 1951.

18. See the Chinese Politburo statement "On the Historic Experience of the Dictatorship of the Proletariat," *People's Daily*, Peking, April 5, 1956, with its critique of the application to China of Stalin's formula about "isolating the center." Even the Chinese Communists' 1963 defense of Stalin against Khrushchev admits that "of the erroneous 'left' and 'right' opportunist lines which emerged in the Chinese CP at one time or another, some arose under the influence of certain mistakes of Stalin. . . ." *People's Daily*, September 13, 1963.
19. See Josip Broz-Tito, *Political Report of the Central Committee of the CPY to the Fifth Congress*, Belgrade, 1948. This account of Tito's partisan strategy is substantially confirmed by the reports of Allied liaison officers, for example, Fitzroy Maclean, *Disputed Barricade*, London, 1957.
20. Svetozar Vukmanovic, *Ueber die Volksrevolution in Griechenland*, Belgrade, 1950.
21. With the proclamation of Mao's slogan of "New Democracy" at the close of 1939, his program and practice in the areas he controlled became more radical, and the pretense of confining action to the "national" and "democratic" stage of the revolution and seeking continued co-operation with the Chungking government largely nominal; see Mao's "The Chinese Revolution and the Chinese Communist Party" and his "On New Democracy" in *Selected Works*, Vol. III, London, 1954; and the works by North and McLane cited in note 17 above.
22. For a fuller discussion see the final chapter of this book.
23. The reference is to Liu's report at the Peking regional conference of Asian and Australian trade unions affiliated to the WFTU, delivered on November 16, 1949, and reprinted in *For a Lasting Peace, For a People's Democracy*, December 30, 1949, and in *Pravda*, January 4, 1950.

CHAPTER 3

1. In Stalin's speech to the Central Committee of the CPSU in March 1937, published in English as *Mastering Bolshevism*, New York, 1937.
2. See Khrushchev's "Secret Speech" at the Twentieth Congress of the CPSU, as published in English in the selection of documents issued by the Russian Institute of Columbia University, *The Anti-Stalin Campaign and International Communism*, New York, 1956.
3. See Togliatti's interview with *Nuovi Argumenti* and his report to

the Central Committee of the CPI in the same collection, as quoted in note 5 in the preceding chapter of this book; see also the article of the Polish party secretary, Jerzy Morawski, *Trybuna Ludu*, February 27, 1956, in English in the parallel collection, *National Communism and Popular Revolt in Eastern Europe*, published by Columbia University's Program on East Central Europe, New York, 1956.

4. For the stages of this development see the English publication of the memoranda of Imre Nagy, *On Communism: In Defence of the New Course*, London, 1957.
5. These ideas were first systematically developed by Edvard Kardelj in his Oslo lecture in late 1954; first printed in *Borba*, January 1, 1955; and reissued as a pamphlet, *La Democratie socialiste dans la pratique Yougoslave*, Brussels, 1955.
6. See the memoranda quoted in note 4 above.
7. From the wealth of literature on Hungary, for the intellectual prehistory particularly, see the "White Book," *The Hungarian Revolution*, edited by Melvin J. Lasky for the Congress for Cultural Freedom, London, 1957; and T. Aczel and T. Meray, *The Revolt of the Mind*, New York, 1959. For the corresponding phase in Poland see *National Communism and Popular Revolt* . . . , pp. 40 ff., 49 ff.
8. See the resolution of the Central Committee of the CPSU of June 30, 1956, *Pravda*, July 2, 1956; in English in *The Anti-Stalin Campaign* . . . (see note 2 above).
9. For the decision rehabilitating the Polish party, see *Pravda*, February 21, 1956; in English in *National Communism and Popular Revolt* . . . , p. 37 ff.
10. See the proclamation of Polish Minister President J. Cyrankiewicz of June 29, and the *Pravda* commentary of July 1, 1956, in *National Communism and Popular Revolt* . . . , pp. 131 ff., 136 ff.
11. The Chinese backing for Polish automony, rumored in Poland at once, is now confirmed by the Chinese article "The Origin and Development of the Differences Between the Leadership of the CPSU and Ourselves" (by the editorial departments of the *People's Daily* and *Red Flag*), NCNA, September 6, 1963.
12. For the basic documents of the Polish October, see *National Communism and Popular Revolt* . . . , pp. 196–261.
13. See the communiqué of November 18, 1956, ibid. p. 306 ff.
14. For Tito's attempt to influence Hungarian internal developments via the Soviets see his speech at Pula after the crushing of the revolution, *Borba*, November 16, 1956; for the "neutral belt" concept see Imre Nagy, *On Communism* . . . , and Chapter 4.

15. The text of this circular has not been published, but the Yugoslavs appear to have learned of it at once. Reports of its contents were soon leaked to the Western press and confirmed by *Borba*, October 12, 1956.
16. For the conversations between Tito, Khrushchev, and Geroe, see the Pula speech cited in note 14; for the implementation of the promises by Geroe, see *National Communism and Popular Revolt* . . . , pp. 385–90.
17. For a description of these events, see the *Report of the U.N. Special Committee on Hungary*, 1957; Lasky, *The Hungarian Revolution*, London, 1957; and *National Communism and Popular Revolt* . . . , Chapters VI–IX.
18. In the two documents cited in note 3 above.
19. Ibid.
20. See note 8 above.
21. See *Paese Sera*, July 3, 1956; in English in *The Anti-Stalin Campaign* . . . , pp. 317–18.
22. *Mondo Operaio*, June 24, 1956; shortened English text in *The Anti-Stalin Campaign* . . . , p. 181 ff.
23. Some of these reports by Communist eye-witnesses are quoted in Lasky, *The Hungarian Revolution*.
24. The meeting of Soviet, Czechoslovakian, Bulgarian, Rumanian, and Hungarian party leaders took place January 1–4, 1957. Communiqué in *Pravda*, January 6, 1957.
25. For a fully documented analysis of this discussion see Zb. Brzezinski, *The Soviet Bloc*, Cambridge, Mass., 1960, Chapters 12 and 13.
26. Rosa Luxemburg, *Die russische Revolution*, Berlin, 1922. English edition with an introduction by Bertram D. Wolfe, *The Russian Revolution and Leninism or Marxism*, Ann Arbor, 1961.
27. *Po Prostu*, No. 7, 1957.
28. In a series of articles published in *Borba* during December 1953 and January 1954. Now in English in M. Djilas, *Anatomy of a Moral*, New York, 1959.
29. Speech to the Federal Assembly of December 7, 1956, printed in *International Affairs*, Belgrade, December 16, 1956.
30. In the *New Leader*, New York, December 19, 1956, and in his book *The New Class*, New York, 1957, which had actually been completed before the article.
31. See Carola Stern, *Portrait einer bolschewistischen Partei*, Cologne, 1957, p. 214 ff.
32. For a fuller discussion of the strong and weak points of the Communist model of development, see my "The Points of the Compass,"

Encounter, September 1960, and "Communism and Nationalism," *Problems of Communism*, November–December 1962.

33. See Chapter 5.
34. "On the Historic Experience of the Dictatorship of the Proletariat," *People's Daily*, April 5, 1956.
35. See note 11 above.
36. See the speeches made by Chou En-lai in Warsaw and Moscow during January 1957, and the account in Zb. Brzezinski, *The Soviet Bloc*, Chapter 12.
37. "More on the Historic Experience of the Dictatorship of the Proletariat," *People's Daily*, December 29, 1956.
38. Even during their bitter 1963 campaign against Khrushchev, in which they blamed the Soviet leaders for "chauvinism" toward the Polish Communists and for "capitulationist" tendencies in the Hungarian crisis, the Chinese did not claim that it was Khrushchev who wanted to capitulate. See the article of September 6, 1963, quoted in note 11 above.
39. The speech, made on February 27, 1957, was published by NCNA only on June 18; its official text is considerably "watered down" compared with unofficial versions that had leaked out before; see the *New York Times*, June 13, 1957.
40. See "Mao Tse-tung and the Rectification Campaign," *The World Today*, August 1957.
41. See the account of the ninth plenum of the Central Committee of the PPR, held in May 1957, with Gomulka's report and his reply to the debate, in *Nowe Drogi*, No. 6, 1957.
42. See the communiqué of the meeting between Khrushchev and Tito in Rumania, *Pravda*, August 4, 1957, and Khrushchev's later account of it (which Tito has never contested), ibid. July 12, 1958.
43. An English text of the Moscow declaration (originally published in *Pravda*, November 22, 1957) is in Hudson, Lowenthal, and McFarquhar, *The Sino-Soviet Dispute*, London and New York, 1961. See *Pravda*, November 5, 1957, for Gomulka's contribution to the discussion; *Trybuna Ludu*, November 29, for his report on it to the Polish party; and *Neues Deutschland*, November 30, for a report of the East German delegate, F. Ebert.

CHAPTER 4

1. See *Pravda*, June 4 and July 12, 1958.
2. Ibid. June 4, 1958.
3. See the summary of the minutes of the plenary session of the

Central Committee of the CPSU held in June 1955, given by former Polish Communist Party official Seweryn Bialer in *News from Behind the Iron Curtain,* October 1956.

4. The memoranda, smuggled out of Hungary after the defeat of the revolution and Nagy's arrest, are published in Imre Nagy, *On Communism: In Defence of the New Course,* London, 1957.
5. Ibid.
6. *Borba,* October 12, 1956, and note 15 to the preceding chapter.
7. Begovic's letter of October 14, quoted in the articles he published after the revolution in *Borba,* November 17–19, 1956, contained this statement: "People refuse to live in the old way, nor can the leadership govern in the old way. Conditions for an uprising have been created. Who will lead it when the working class is disoriented and the Party lags behind events and has lost authority over the masses?" [See tracts from the articles in Melvin J. Lasky (ed.), *The Hungarian Revolution,* London, 1957, pp. 39–41.] This largely refutes Tito's subsequent claim (in his Pula speech of November 11) that when receiving Geroe at Belgrade, the Yugoslav leaders "did not know" that "matters had already gone pretty far," so that "Geroe's coming to Yugoslavia and our joint declaration could no longer help."
8. Kadar had led the Hungarian delegation to the Chinese party congress in September; it is not unlikely that he had received encouragement of his desire for greater autonomy and bolder reforms similar to that which the Polish delegates are known to have brought home, and that he told Tito about it.
9. See Tito's message of October 28, expressing confidence in Kadar and Nagy, in *Politika,* Belgrade, October 29, and the *Borba* editorial of November 1, welcoming the Soviet government's declaration of October 30 on relations between Socialist states and expressing hope for its positive effect on the Hungarian situation. English texts in *National Communism and Popular Revolt . . . ,* pp. 446–8, 495–6.
10. *Borba,* November 16, 1956; *National Communism and Popular Revolt . . . ,* pp. 516–41.
11. Note of July 21, 1958, *Népszabadság,* July 23, 1958.
12. Three years after this essay was written, the fact of the flying visit was confirmed by Enver Hoxha's publication of a hitherto secret letter from Khrushchev to Tito. (See Hoxha's speech on the twentieth anniversary of the foundation of the Albanian CP, *Zeri i Popullit,* November 8, 1961; extensive English excerpts in William E. Griffith, *Albania and the Sino-Soviet Rift,* Cambridge, Mass., 1963, Document 14, where the Khrushchev letter is quoted on p. 259.) Hoxha quotes Khrushchev as having written to Tito on November

9, 1956, between the crushing of the revolution and Tito's speech in Pula, the following statement: "We note with satisfaction that, since the Brioni talks, you have been in full agreement with our attitude toward Comrade Janos Kadar as a distinguished personality with revolutionary authority in Hungary, capable of heading a new revolutionary government in these difficult times and conditions. . . ." Since Khrushchev's last publicly known visit to Brioni took place before Tito had ever met Kadar, and while Khrushchev was still favoring Geroe and no need for a "new revolutionary government" had arisen, the reference here can only be to a visit made in the course of the revolution.

13. Reports of Tito's advance consent were so widespread among Yugoslav Communists that the Yugoslav leader even called on his audience to "rest assured that we have never advised them to go ahead and use the army." But after explaining why the second Soviet intervention, though bad in itself, was in his view the lesser evil and might become "a positive thing" if it helped to save Hungarian socialism, "provided that the Soviet troops withdraw the moment the situation in that country is settled and quiet," he added: "We said this to the Soviet comrades. We concealed nothing. The Soviet comrades stated that their troops would then leave." (*National Communism and Popular Revolt . . .*, pp. 529–30.) *Read in the* context of the other known facts, this amounts to confirmation that Tito at least promised in advance not to attack the second intervention, in return for Khrushchev's promise not to reinstate the Hungarian "Stalinists" and to withdraw Soviet troops from Hungary as soon as possible.
14. In the same speech cited in note 10 above.
15. December 7, 1956; text in *Review of International Affairs*, Belgrade, December 16, 1956.
16. For the Soviet reply to Tito's speech, see *Pravda*, November 23, 1956; for their reply to Kardelj, ibid. December 19, 1956.
17. Prague Radio, July 11, 1957.
18. Communiqué of August 4, 1957, in *Review of International Affairs*, Belgrade, September 1, 1957.
19. *Pravda*, July 12, 1958.
20. Communiqué in *Review of International Affairs*, September 16, 1957.
21. October 16, 1957.
22. October 19, 1957.
23. October 4–17, 1957.
24. See T. Meray, *Thirteen Days That Shook the Kremlin*, New York, 1959, pp. 260–61. Gomulka later disclosed that about the same time, two members of the Politburo of the Polish party had visited

Yugoslavia in order to urge major changes in the draft program and thus avoid the new break if possible. (Speech at the Russo-Polish friendship meeting in Moscow; text in *Pravda*, November 10, 1958.

25. See Chapter 6.
26. See the report in *The Manchester Guardian*, April 11, 1958.
27. Communiqué broadcast by Moscow and Budapest during the night of June 16–17, 1958.

CHAPTER 5

1. These claims were first announced to the outside world by Liu Shao-ch'i in his 1946 interview with Anna Louise Strong; see A. L. Strong, "The Thought of Mao Tse-tung," *Amerasia*, June 1947. Liu repeated them with increased authority immediately after the proclamation of the Chinese People's Republic in his report to the Peking conference of Asian and Australasian unions affiliated to the WFTU, held in November 1949; text in *For a Lasting Peace, For a People's Democracy*, December 30, 1949.
2. A fairly up-to-date view of the two rival systems may be obtained by reading the Chinese Communist Party's letter to the Soviet party of June 14, 1963, and the Soviet reply dated July 14, 1963. Both texts are printed in William E. Griffith, *The Sino-Soviet Rift*, Cambridge, Mass., 1964.
3. See Chapters 6 and 7; also R. Lowenthal, "Factors of Unity and Factors of Conflict," in the issue "Communist China and the Soviet Bloc" of the *Annals of the American Academy of Political and Social Science*, Vol. 349, September 1963.
4. The emphasis on the distinctive features of the "Maoist" strategy was first developed in Benjamin Schwartz, *Chinese Communism and the Rise of Mao*, Cambridge, Mass., 1951, and in Conrad Brandt, Benjamin Schwartz, and John K. Fairbank, *A Documentary History of Chinese Communism*, Cambridge, Mass., 1952. Professor Schwartz has modified his views in the light of new evidence and defended them in a number of later papers, notably "On the 'Originality' of Mao Tse-tung," *Foreign Affairs*, October 1955; "New Trends in Maoism," *Problems of Communism*, July–August 1957; "Mao Tse-tung and Communist Theory," *New Leader*, April 4, 1960; "The Legend of the 'Legend of Maoism,'" *China Quarterly*, No. 2, April–June 1960. The chief exponent of the emphasis on Mao's orthodoxy is Professor K. A. Wittfogel. See, in particular, his "The Influence of Leninism-Stalinism on China," *Annals of the American Academy of Political and Social Science*,

September 1951; "Lenin and Mao Tse-tung," *New Leader,* April 11, 1960; "The Legend of 'Maoism,'" *China Quarterly,* Nos. 1 and 2, January–March, April–June 1960. For the latest presentation and appraisal of relevant sources, see also Stuart R. Schram, *The Political Thought of Mao Tse-tung,* New York and London, 1963.

5. See Chapter 3.
6. See Chapter 6.
7. For the latest historical study of the period, see Conrad Brandt, *Stalin's Failure in China, 1924–27,* Cambridge, Mass., 1958.
8. See Mao's own account in Edgar Snow, *Red Star over China,* London, 1937.
9. For Mao's prolonged struggle to win control of his party see, besides the book by Schwartz cited in note 4, Robert C. North, *Moscow and the Chinese Communists,* Stanford, 1953.
10. The first Soviet publication to "recognize" Mao as party leader was the *Bolshaya Sovetskaya Entsikopediya* in 1938. The ambiguous publicity given to Mao's role in Soviet and Comintern organs up to then is analyzed in C. B. McLane, *Soviet Policy and the Chinese Communists,* New York, 1958, p. 34.
11. Professor Schwartz, in the latest of the articles cited in note 4, has expressed this in the formula that while Lenin's conception "opened the door to the Maoist development," Lenin, at the time of his death, "had not yet marched through all the doors which he had opened."
12. See Mao Tse-tung, "The Chinese Revolution and the Chinese Communist Party" and "On New Democracy" in *Selected Works,* Vol. III, London, 1954, in particular, pp. 96–7, 119–21. Because the Communists' claim of representing all the allied classes was implied rather than explicitly stated in these writings and made obvious only in their practice, its importance as a new departure was long overlooked. It was first pointed out, in connection with its "neo-Maoist" applications in other countries, by Bernard S. Morris and Morris Watnick, "Current Communist Strategy in Non-Industrialized Countries," *Problems of Communism,* September–October 1955, and further developed by John H. Kautsky, *Moscow and the Communist Party of India,* New York and London, 1956; see also John H. Kautsky, "From Marx to Mao," *Survey,* June–July, 1957.
13. Mao Tse-tung, *Selected Works,* Vol. III, London, 1954, p. 121.
14. See Mao Tse-tung's party directive, *Problems of Political Power in the Anti-Japanese Base Areas,* ibid. pp. 189–92.
15. See the resolution of the Central Committee of the CPC, "On the Formation of People's Communes in the Countryside," adopted August 29, 1958, *Peking Review,* September 16, 1958.

16. See the account of the origins of the communal "free supply system" given by NCNA, September 29, 1958.
17. For implied Soviet criticism of the utopian aspects of the "people's communes," see T. Khachaturian in *Voprosy Ekonomiki*, No. 8, 1958, and *Pravda*, September 26, 1958; see also Khrushchev's report to the Twenty-first Congress of the CPSU, *Pravda*, January 28, 1959.
18. See, for this point, R. Lowenthal, "Stalin and Ideology," *Survey*, July–September 1960.
19. The following remarks on this campaign are based on the extracts from party documents and comments contained in Brandt, Schwartz, and Fairbank, *A Documentary History of Chinese Communism*, Cambridge, Mass., 1952. I have not been able to use the fuller collection of Boyd Compton, *Mao's China: Party Reform Documents 1942–44*, Seattle, 1952.
20. Extract in *Documentary History*, p. 353 ff.
21. For Mao's principal contributions, see Documentary History, pp. 373–418.
22. As early as 1952 the late Franz Borkenau based a prediction that Stalin's death would be followed by an outbreak of Sino-Soviet ideological rivalry in part on the Cheng Feng documents: F. Borkenau, "Mao Tse-tung," *The Twentieth Century*, August 1952.
23. "More on the Historic Experience of the Dictatorship of the Proletariat," editorial of the *People's Daily* based on discussions of the Politburo of the CPC, NCNA, December 29, 1956.
24. Mao's speech, "On the Correct Handling of Contradictions among the People," delivered on February 27, 1957, was officially published almost four months later, apparently in a watered-down version: NCNA, June 18, 1957. For the more far-reaching extracts that had become known unofficially before, see the *New York Times*, June 13, 1957.
25. Since the summer of 1963, the Chinese Communists have, for tactical reasons, exaggerated their initial disagreement with Khrushchev's "de-Stalinization"; see, in particular, the joint editorial of *People's Daily* and *Red Flag*, "On the Question of Stalin," NCNA, September 13, 1963. Originally, while worried about the form of Khrushchev's attack, the Chinese welcomed at least part of its contents, in particular, the repudiation of Stalin's "Great Power chauvinism"; see the *People's Daily* editorial, "On the Historic Experience of the Dictatorship of the Proletariat," NCNA, April 5, 1956.
26. Liu's report was reprinted in the Cominform weekly, *For a Lasting Peace, For a People's Democracy*, December 30, 1949, and in *Pravda*, January 4, 1950.

27. See for this whole episode the analysis by John H. Kautsky, *Moscow and the Communist Party of India,* New York and London, 1956, Chapter 4.
28. See Khrushchev's report in the name of the Central Committee to the Twentieth Congress, *Pravda,* February 15, 1956.
29. See the document cited in note 23 above.
30. See Chapter 3.
31. See the account of Mao's role at the conference in the report of the East German delegate, F. Ebert, *Neues Deutschland,* November 30, 1957. The Chinese determination to avoid any public appearance of rivalry at the time is underlined by recent Chinese disclosures of partial Sino-Soviet disagreements that took place even at that conference and were then settled by compromise in camera: see the joint editorials of *People's Daily* and *Red Flag,* "The Origin and Development of the Differences Between the Leaders of the CPSU and Ourselves," NCNA, September 6, 1963, and "The Proletarian Revolution and Khrushchev's Revisionism," NCNA, March 30, 1964.
32. According to Peking Radio, August 18, 1958, the Wei-hsing (Sputnik) Commune was founded in April 1958. See its statutes in NCNA, September 5, 1958.
33. See also Chapter 6.
34. See note 15 above.
35. See note 17 above.
36. See Hoxha's speech on the ninth anniversary of the Chinese People's Republic glorifying the "people's communes," *Bakshimi,* October 2, 1958.
37. See Liliana Brisby, "Bulgaria: Leaping Forward Without Communes," *China Quarterly,* No. 3, 1960.
38. Resolution of the Central Committee of the CPC on problems of the "people's communes" of December 10, 1958, *Peking Review,* December 23, 1958.
39. See Chou En-lai's address to the Twenty-first Congress of the CPSU, *Pravda,* January 29, 1959.
40. TASS, February 7, 1959.

CHAPTER 6

1. Communiqué of August 3, *Pravda,* August 4, 1958.
2. "More on the Historic Experience of the Dictatorship of the Proletariat," *People's Daily,* Peking, December 29, 1956.
3. See the report on Mao's role at the Moscow conference of Novem-

ber 1957, by the East German delegate, F. Ebert, *Neues Deutschland,* November 30, 1957. Later disclosures that strategic differences between Mao and the Soviet leaders had emerged during that conference do not change the fact that he was then still hoping to convince them, and therefore seeking to strengthen rather than weaken their authority in the international movement.

4. See Chapter 4.
5. *Borba,* April 20, 1958.
6. See Gomulka's speech at the Soviet-Polish friendship meeting in Moscow, *Pravda,* November 10, 1958.
7. *Pravda,* April 23, 1958.
8. See the report from Warsaw, *New York Times,* April 25, and from Bonn, ibid. April 27, 1958.
9. See, for example, Chen Po-ta, "Yugoslav Revisionism Is a Product
10. In a report by the Lithuanian party secretary Snieckus to his Cen-
1, 1958.
10. In a report by the Lithuanian party secretary Snieckus to his Central Committee, *Sovyetskaya Litva,* May 17, 1958.
11. See the Hungarian "White Book" ("The Counterrevolutionary Conspiracy of Imre Nagy and His Accomplices," Budapest, 1958), as cited in Ferenc A. Vali, *Rift and Revolt in Hungary,* Cambridge, Mass., 1961.
12. *Pravda,* June 4, 1958.
13. See the official Chinese figures in *Economic Survey for Asia and the Far East,* Bangkok, 1958, p. 103, and the detailed analysis by Oleg Hoeffding, "Sino-Soviet Economic Relations in Recent Years," in Kurt London (ed.), *Unity and Contradiction,* New York, 1962.
14. See Khrushchev's speech at the Soviet-Polish friendship meeting in Moscow, *Pravda,* November 10, 1958.
15. *Die Welt,* Hamburg, May 12, 1958. A number of indications that the Chinese did not in fact count on Soviet nuclear aid at that time have been listed by Donald S. Zagoria, *The Sino-Soviet Conflict,* Princeton, 1962, pp. 189–94. This may have been connected with the Chinese rejection in the same year of what a later Chinese document has darkly described as "unreasonable demands designed to bring China under Soviet military control." See "The Origin and Development of the Differences Between the Leadership of the CPSU and Ourselves" (comment on the Open Letter of the Central Committee of the CPSU by the editorial departments of the *People's Daily* and *Red Flag*), NCNA, September 6, 1963.
16. Following the signing of the partial test ban agreement by the Soviet government in 1963, Peking disclosed that a Chinese request for a sample atom bomb and technical data for its production had been turned down by Moscow in June 1959, and claimed that this

constituted a breach of an agreement on defense technology concluded by the two Communist powers in October 1957. See the NCNA text of the Chinese government statement of August 15, 1963, and the article quoted in note 15 above.

17. See Herbert Ritvo, "Sino-Soviet Relations and the Summit," *Problems of Communism*, September–October 1958.
18. *Pravda*, August 4, 1958.
19. Facts that have come to light since the above was written suggest that even in the fall of 1958, Chinese influence on Soviet policy was more limited than the text assumes. The limitations of Soviet support for the Quemoy venture analyzed by Zagoria, op. cit. pp. 206–17, and, in particular, the apparent Soviet refusal to match the U.S. side-winder missiles given to Chiang's air force by the delivery of corresponding weapons to Peking, seem to have contributed decisively to the failure of that enterprise. Nevertheless I still incline to the view that the bombardment was started with Soviet approval, as a compromise between Soviet caution and more ambitious Chinese plans conceived at the height of the Middle Eastern crisis.
20. See Tito's attack in his Labin speech on "people who emphasize that 300 million of them would survive a war" (*Borba*, June 16, 1958). This is the earliest public reference to an alleged personal statement of Mao's apparently based on his speech at the November 1957 Moscow conference. According to an official Soviet account, Mao said there that half mankind might be destroyed in an atomic war, but imperialism would perish. See the TASS texts of the Soviet government statements of August 21 and September 21, 1963.
21. See note 3 above.
22. See the account of the origin of the "free supply system" in the "people's communes," NCNA, September 29, 1958; also A. Smerdov, "Birth of a People's Commune," in *Literaturnaya Gazeta*, Moscow, September 30, 1958.
23. See, for example, "Concerning the Creation of People's Communes in the Villages," *People's Daily*, September 10, and Soong Ching-ling, "The Socialist Camp in the Present World Situation," ibid. November 7, 1958.
24. See T. Khachaturov in *Voprosy Ekonomiki*, No. 8, 1958, and *Pravda*, September 26, 1958. The fact that far more direct criticism of the communes and the whole policy of the "Great Leap Forward" was voiced by N. S. Khrushchev personally to Mao Tse-tung, during his visit to Peking in early August 1958, has been disclosed only recently by the Soviet government in its declaration of September 21, 1963 (TASS, same date).
25. Ts. A. Stepanyan, "The October Revolution and the Process of

Communist Formation," *Voprosy Filosofii*, No. 10, 1958. Following the Chinese retreat of December 1958, and the partial withdrawal of Peking's controversial ideological claims, Stepanyan's theory was disavowed at the Twenty-first Congress of the CPSU by Khrushchev himself, in favor of the thesis that all member states of the bloc would make the transition to Communism "more or less simultaneously." (See Khrushchev's Congress report, *Pravda*, January 28, 1959.) As Donald Zagoria (op. cit. p. 131) has pointed out, P. Yudin, then Soviet ambassador to Peking, explained in effect, at the same Congress, that such "simultaneous transition" depended on close co-ordination of economic plans.

26. See Khrushchev's report to the plenary session of the Central Committee of the CPSU, *Pravda*, December 16, 1958.
27. NCNA, December 17, 1958.
28. Text in *Peking Review*, 23 XII, 1958.

CHAPTER 7

1. See Chapter 5 for a fuller treatment.
2. In a catalogue of their grievances published in 1963, the Chinese claimed that in 1958 the Soviets had put forward "unreasonable demands designed to bring China under Soviet military control" that were "rightly and firmly rejected by the Chinese government" — apparently referring to a reported proposal for a joint navel command for the Pacific by which the Soviets had hoped to restrain Chinese activities in the Taiwan straits; that during the Quemoy crisis of the same year, the Soviets had only gone on record backing Peking when they were sure that the danger of nuclear escalation was over; that in June 1959, the Soviets had refused a Chinese request for a sample atomic bomb and production designs, though in Peking's view an agreement on technological military aid, concluded in October 1957, obliged them to furnish them; and that in October 1959 Khrushchev had suggested to Mao that he should try to get the Americans out of Taiwan as Lenin had got the Japanese out of Siberia — by agreeing with them on setting up a buffer state. See the Chinese government statement of September 1, 1963, and the joint editorial of *People's Daily* and *Red Flag*, NCNA, September 6, 1963.
3. See A. M. Halpern, "Communist China and Peaceful Co-existence," *China Quarterly*, No. 3, July–September 1960, for a detailed study of Chinese arguments during this phase.
4. Moscow Radio, October 31, 1959.

5. For example, Yü Chao-li, "The Chinese People's Great Victory in the Fight against Imperialism," *Peking Review*, September 22, 1959 (from *Red Flag*, No. 18, 1959); *idem*, "Excellent Situation for the Struggle for Peace," *Peking Review*, January 5, 1960 (from *Red Flag*, No. 1, 1960).
6. Text of the declaration and of K'ang Sheng's speech in *China Quarterly*, No. 2, April–June 1960, pp. 75–89.
7. For example, at the Rome meeting of the Presidium of the World Peace Council and the sessions of the secretariat of the Afro-Asian Solidarity Committee held in Cairo in January 1960. Chinese contributions disappeared from *Problems of Peace and Socialism*, the Soviet-controlled international Communist monthly, from November 1959.
8. Editorial "Long Live Leninism" (now ascribed by the Soviets to Mao Tse-tung), *Peking Review*, April 26, 1960 (from *Red Flag*, No. 8, 1960); editorial, *People's Daily*, April 22, 1960; Lu Ting-yi, "Get United under Lenin's Revolutionary Banner," speech at Lenin commemoration meeting, NCNA same date; also the preparatory articles by Yü Chao-li, "On Imperialism as a Source of War in Modern Times" and "On the Way for All Peoples to Struggle for Peace," NCNA, March 30, 1960, from *Red Flag*, No. 7, 1960.
9. In 1963, it was disclosed by both sides that the text of the 1957 declaration was already a compromise between the Soviet stress on the "general line of peaceful co-existence" and the Chinese stress on the warlike tendencies of imperialism in general and U.S. imperialism in particular, and that Mao emphasized the possibility of a Socialist civilization surviving even a nuclear world war: see the joint editorial of *People's Daily and Red Flag* of September 6, quoted in note 2 above, and the slightly different versions of Mao's argument in the Chinese government statement, NCNA, September 1, 1963, and the Soviet government statement, TASS, September 21, 1963. None of these new materials, however, invalidates my statement that the Chinese agreed that nuclear war could be avoided and only opposed policies that, in their view, put the brake on revolutionary violence from excessive fear of nuclear escalation. As the Chinese documents indicate, the serious behind-the-scenes controversy at the 1957 conference was not on the question of war, but on the possibility of a "peaceful transition" to socialism *within* a given country.
10. Speech at Lenin commemoration meeting in Moscow, April 22, 1960, *Pravda*, April 23, 1960.
11. R. Lowenthal, "The Nature of Khrushchev's Power," *Problems of Communism*, July–August 1960.

12. See Khrushchev's speeches to the Supreme Soviet on May 5 and 7, and at the reception given by the Czechoslovak Embassy in Moscow on May 9, 1960.
13. NCNA, June 8, 1960.
14. Articles on the fortieth anniversary of Lenin's "Left-wing Communism, an Infantile Disorder" by D. Shevlyagin in *Sovyetskaya Rossiya,* June 10, and by "N. Matkovsky" in *Pravda,* June 12, 1960; *Pravda* editorial "Full Support" on the Soviet disarmament proposals, June 13, 1960.
15. Foa in *Avanti,* June 15; Novella in *Unita,* June 19, 1960.
16. NCNA, April 22, 1960.
17. "N. Matkovsky" on June 12.
18. June 20, 1960.
19. The Chinese Communists have since confirmed that on the opening day of the conference, June 21, the Soviets distributed or read to various party leaders present a document addressed to the Chinese party and containing a systematic criticism of its stand. They claim that the Soviets made this "surprise assault" and forced the adoption of a joint communiqué by the conference although they had agreed, during preliminary correspondence with the Chinese, that only an informal exchange of views should take place at the Bucharest meeting, with all decisions postponed pending a full world conference of Communist parties. See the Chinese article of September 6, 1963, quoted in note 2 above.
20. Speech at the Bucharest congress, TASS, June 21, 1960.
21. NCNA, June 22, 1960. For P'eng Chen's reply to Khrushchev's assault in the internal meeting, made after consultation with his Central Committee, see Appendix II to the Chinese article of September 6, 1963.
22. F. Konstantinov and Kh. Momdzhan, "Dialectics and the Present," *Kommunist,* No. 10, 1960; *Pravda* editorial, July 20; Togliatti's speech to the Italian Central Committee, *Pravda,* July 28; speech by M. A. Suslov, *Pravda,* July 30; Y. Frantsev, *Pravda,* August 7; B. Ponomarev, *Pravda,* August 12; T. Zhivkov in *World Marxist Review,* August 1960.
23. "Socialism and War," first published in *Borba,* August 12–20, 1960; English edition, London, 1961.
24. A. Arzumanyan and V. Koryonov, *Pravda,* September 2, 1960.
25. The last Chinese statement on these lines seems to have been the article on the tenth anniversary of the outbreak of the Korean War by Gen. Li Chih-min, *People's Daily,* June 25, 1960.
26. *People's Daily* editorial commenting on Bucharest communiqué, June 29; Liao Ch'eng-chih's speech to Bureau of World Peace Council in Stockholm, July 10; Ch'en Yi's speech in Peking, NCNA,

July 15; Li Fu-ch'un's speech to the Vietnamese party congress, NCNA, September 6, 1960.

27. The issue was publicly stressed by the Chinese only in the last weeks before the Moscow conference, notably in comments on the publication of the fourth volume of the works of Mao; see, for example, the *People's Daily* editorial, October 6, and, in particular, the *Red Flag* editorial, November 2. But as Peking has since disclosed, the Chinese had criticized the concept of the "peaceful road" in private discussions with the Soviet leaders soon after it had been first adopted by the Twentieth Congress of the CPSU in 1956, and had submitted a written outline stating their different views during the Moscow world conference of 1957. See also the Chinese article of September 6, 1963, quoted in note 2, particularly Appendix I.
28. A. Belyakov and F. Burlatsky in *Kommunist,* No. 13, 1960.
29. Since the above was written it has become clear that the issue of the "peaceful road" has had a broader and more serious significance in the development of the dispute than the author assumed in 1960. As indicated in the documents cited in note 27 above, the Chinese seem to have seriously feared that the proclamation of this possibility by the Twentieth Congress of the CPSU would lead to a reformist degeneration of the Western Communist parties; moreover, the extension of the "peaceful road" strategy to underdeveloped countries has proved a subject of serious controversy—and an effective lever for Chinese factional activity—not only in India, but also in Ceylon, and, above all, in a number of Latin American countries. In the light of what we know today, it is arguable that this issue may have been one of the factors, together with the destruction of the continuity of Soviet authority by Khrushchev's attack on Stalin, that started the Chinese Communist leaders wondering whether they would not have to present themselves as alternative leaders of the world Communist movement if the Soviets proved unfit for continued leadership. See the preface to the English edition of this book.
30. Y. Zhukov in *Pravda,* August 26, 1960.
31. S. Titarenko in *Sovyetskaya Latvya* and other papers, August 16, 1960.
32. Li Fu-ch'un in *Red Flag*, No. 16, 1960.
33. The Chinese article of September 6, 1963, disclosed that in July 1960, the Soviet government decided to recall all Soviet technicians working in China within a month, and charged that this was done in order to apply economic pressure to China. The Soviets have since confirmed that they took this step but tried to explain it as a result of the difficulties caused for these specialists by Chinese

disregard of their technical advice, Chinese attempts to incite them against their own government, and finally by Chinese police harassments: see M. A. Suslov's report to the Central Committee of the CPSU, rendered on February 14, 1964, *Pravda,* April 3, 1964.

34. The Chinese article of September 6, 1963, confirms that the Chinese full-length reply to the Soviet charges of June 21 was issued on September 10, 1960. According to reports that leaked through at the time from both pro-Soviet and pro-Chinese sources, this Chinese document already dated the origin of the differences back to the events of 1956, and was circulated to other Communist parties in preparation for the Moscow conference. See the reports of Edward Crankshaw in the London *Observer,* February 12 and 19, 1961, and in the Indian weekly, *Link,* October 16, 1960.
35. See the articles quoted in note 27 above; also Marshal Lo Jui-ching's article for the (North) *Korean People's Forces Journal* on the tenth anniversary of Chinese intervention in Korea, NCNA, October 25, 1960.
36. See P. J. Honey's analysis of the North Vietnamese party congress in *China Quarterly* No. 4, October–December 1960.
37. Fairly detailed pro-Soviet versions of the discussions have since been published by the Italian and French Communist parties: *Interventi della delegazione del P.C.I. alla Conferenza degli 81 partiti comunisti e operai,* Rome, January 15, 1962; *Problèmes du Mouvement Communiste International,* Paris, January 1963. For the Chinese version, see the Chinese article of September 6, 1963. Compare with these versions the "Preliminary Reconstruction" of the conference undertaken, in the light of all the documentation available at the time, by William E. Griffith, *China Quarterly,* No. 11, July–September 1962.
38. *People's Daily,* November 21; *Pravda,* November 23, 1960.
39. NCNA, November 21, 1960.
40. Text in *World Marxist Review,* December 1960; also in G. F. Hudson, R. Lowenthal, and R. McFarquhar, *The Sino-Soviet Dispute,* London and New York, 1961.
41. No use, however, was made of it in Chinese propaganda, and the origin of the text as a reluctantly accepted compromise has since been admitted by the Chinese Communists.
42. This formula, in turn, was not quoted in Khrushchev's report on the conference.
43. In practice, various nationalist regimes – particularly those of Egypt and of Arab North Africa – have since continued to enjoy Soviet diplomatic support, while being vigorously criticized for suppressing their Communists by Soviet-controlled organs of the Communist world movement, and at times even by *Pravda.*

44. All the reports cited in note 37 above agree that the Chinese succeeded in preventing any assertion of international discipline founded on majority decisions and any condemnation of "factionalism."
45. *Kommunist*, No. 1, 1961; *World Marxist Review*, No. 1, 1961.

CHAPTER 8

1. On those "backstairs promptings" see Enver Hoxha's speech on the occasion of the twentieth anniversary of the foundation of the Albanian CP, *Zeri i Popullit*, November 8, 1961. Full English excerpts in William E. Griffith, *Albania and the Sino-Soviet Rift*, Cambridge, Mass., 1963.
2. See Chapter 3.
3. See Zb. Brzezinski, *The Soviet Bloc*, Cambridge, Mass., 1960, p. 272 ff.
4. In September 1963, the Chinese Communists began to emphasize that their differences with the Soviet Communists had begun as far back as 1956, over the methods of "de-Stalinization" and the "peaceful road to socialism"; one document published by them (*People's Daily* and *Red Flag*, September 6, 1963) shows that serious discussions on the latter issue took place at the 1957 Moscow conference. This does not affect the statement in the text that at that conference, Chinese and Soviet Communists were acting in concert in restoring the doctrinaire and political unity of the Soviet bloc and the Communist world movement under Soviet leadership, for reasons and in ways discussed below.
5. English text of the declaration in G. F. Hudson, R. Lowenthal, and R. McFarquhar, *The Sino-Soviet Dispute*, London and New York, 1961.
6. "On Historic Experience of the Dictatorship of the Proletariat," *People's Daily*, Peking, April 5, 1956.
7. See Chapter 3.
8. See Mao's Moscow speech in *Pravda*, November 22, 1957, and Khrushchev's later statement that the original Soviet draft of the declaration did not contain this formula – *Pravda*, July 12, 1958.
9. See Chapters 5 and 6.
10. See the resolution of the Central Committee of the CPC December 10, 1958 on problems of the "people's communes," *Peking Review*, December 23, 1958.
11. See Chou En-lai's speech at the Twenty-first Congress of the CPSU, *Pravda*, January 29, 1959.

12. The Chinese have since charged that the Soviet government definitely refused to provide them with a sample atom bomb and designs for its manufacture in June 1959, that is, while Khrushchev's visit to the United States was being prepared. (*People's Daily* and *Red Flag*, September 6, 1963.)
13. See, above all, the *Red Flag* editorial "Long Live Leninism"; in English in *Peking Review*, No. 17, 1960, and also as a pamphlet.
14. See Chapter 7 and *The Sino-Soviet Dispute*, cited in note 5 above.
15. See Khrushchev's report on the conference in *World Marxist Review*, January 1961.
16. See David A. Charles, "The Dismissal of Marshal P'eng Teh-huai," *China Quarterly*, October–December 1961.
17. See Ilychev's speech of October 24, 1961, in the Congress minutes, *XXII. Syzed Kommunisticheskoy Partii Sovyetskogo Soyuza*, Moscow, 1962.
18. See the speech by Satyukov, the editor-in-chief of *Pravda*, of October 25, 1961, ibid.
19. Communiqué of the plenum of the Central Committee of the CPSU, *Pravda*, May 5, 1960.
20. *Pravda*, April 30, 1960.
21. For the whole development of relations between Hoxha and Khrushchev, see Hoxha's speech of November 8, 1961, as cited in note 1 above.
22. See, besides Hoxha's speech, the communiqué of the Albanian Central Committee in *Zeri i Popullit*, September 9, 1960, quoted in Griffith, *Albania and the Sino-Soviet Rift*, Cambridge, Mass., 1963, and the remarks by Mikoyan at the Twenty-second Congress of the CPSU, *Pravda*, October 22, 1961.
23. The term is Zbigniew Brzezinski's.
24. For this whole period compare Griffith, op. cit. Chapters 2 and 3, with the Albanian "act of accusation" against Khrushchev, as drawn up in *Zeri i Popullit*, March 25, 1962, and fully translated in Griffith's book. From this it appears that Soviet pressure on Albania, and Chinese aid to her, began soon after the Bucharest clash of June 1960, and not only after the Moscow compromise of December.
25. See note 18 above.
26. *Pravda*, October 18, 1961.
27. October 19, 1961; text in *Peking Review*, October 27, 1961.
28. On October 21.
29. *Peking Review*, December 1, 1961.
30. The break in Soviet-Albanian diplomatic relations was brought about by the Soviet "verbal notes" of November 25 and December 3,

1961, and completed by the decision to withdraw all diplomatic personnel taken by both sides on December 10; see the documentation issued respectively by the Albanian Telegraph Agency on December 10 and by TASS on December 11, 1961. For corresponding steps by the East German regime see *Neues Deutschland,* December 18. The Czechoslovak government withdrew its ambassador and expelled the Albanian ambassador, but left a chargé d'affaires in Tirana, who was also entrusted with looking after Soviet interests there: Prague Radio, December 12. The Council for Mutual Economic Aid met without Albanian representatives in Warsaw, December 12–15, 1961, and again in Moscow, June 6–7, 1962; on the second occasion, the Albanians protested publicly against the failure to invite them. The Chinese observers stayed away from both meetings.

31. See, for example, Chou En-lai's speech to the Albanian delegation at the signing of a new trade and co-operation agreement, NCNA, January 13, 1962; see also the messages of greetings to the Albanian party leaders issued by North Korea (over Radio Pyongyang, November 28) and by North Vietnam (over Radio Tirana, November 29, 1961 and January 5, 1962).

32. On Albanian participation in the Moscow WFTU Congress, December 4–15, 1961, see Griffith, op. cit. p. 122; on their participation in the Moscow World Peace Congress in July 1962, see *Pravda,* July 9, 1962.

33. See the full inside account of the Stockholm debates by the Italian delegate, Velio Spano, *Unita,* December 23, 1961; see also Griffith, op. cit. p. 129.

34. In an unpublished letter to the CPSU of April 7, 1962, the Chinese supported suggestions for a world conference put forward by the Communist parties of Indonesia, North Vietnam, Sweden, Great Britain, and New Zealand; they disclosed this a year later in the published letter to the CPSU of March 9, 1963. The Soviet agreement to the principle of a new conference and the Soviet view about its tasks were first expressed in an unpublished letter of May 31, 1962, and first publicly referred to in a Soviet letter to the CPC of February 21, 1963. Both published letters are in *Peking Review,* March 22, 1963; also in William E. Griffith, *The Sino-Soviet Rift,* Cambridge, Mass., 1964.

35. See the debate in the Italian Central Committee session of November 1961, and the subsequent communiqué of its secretariat printed in *Unita,* November 12 and 28, 1961; full English extracts in Alexander Dallin (ed.), *Diversity in International Communism: A Documentary Record, 1961–1963,* New York, 1963.

36. For the consciousness of this comparison, see, for example, Pien Chung-yin, "The Revolutionary Tradition of Political Parties of the Proletariat," *Red Flag,* May 16, 1962; for an indication that the Soviets might prefer a clean break to a permanent factional struggle, see P. Pospelov, "Lenin and the Prague Conference," *Pravda,* January 18, 1962. English texts of both in A. Dallin, op. cit.

EPILOGUE

1. See Rosa Luxemburg, "Organisatsionnye Veprosy Russkoi Sotsialdomokratii" (Organizational Problems of Russian Social Democracy), *Iskra,* No. 69, July 1904, now in English as "Leninism or Marxism" in *The Russian Revolution and Leninism or Marxism,* edited by Betram D. Wolfe, Ann Arbor, 1961. See now also G. Haupt, "Correspondance entre Lenine et Camille Huysmans, 1905–14," Part II, in *Cahiers du monde Russe et Sovietique,* Paris, January–February 1963, where further sources on the conflict between Lenin and Luxemburg are cited, and, in particular, the circular of October 1912 published as Annex IV to this paper.
2. See Rosa Luxemburg's posthumously published critique *The Russian Revolution,* in Bertram D. Wolfe's edition quoted above.
3. In his pamphlet "Left-wing Communism, an Infantile Disorder": *Selected Works,* Vol. X, London, 1938.
4. For a study of the model case of this process, see R. Lowenthal, "The Bolshevisation of the Spartacus League," in *St. Antony's Papers,"* No. 9, *International Communism,* London, 1960.
5. Lenin, *Selected Works,* Vol. X, London, 1938, p. 332.
6. See Stalin's speech of June 9, 1925, at the Sverdlov University, in which he discussed the problems of Soviet domestic policy on the assumption that no proletarian revolution in the West would occur "in the next ten to fifteen years," *Sochineniya,* VII, p. 156 ff.
7. For first-hand evidence, see Wolfgang Leonhard, *Child of the Revolution,* Chicago, 1957.
8. See, however, Milovan Djilas, *Conversations with Stalin,* London, 1962, p. 34, for the contrary impression that the Comintern officials' only job after 1943 was "to gather information about Communist parties and to give advice to the Soviet Government and Party." As will be suggested below, this impression was largely due to Stalin's reluctant acceptance of the effective emancipation of the Yugoslav party from his control. But the extent to which other Communist parties, too, were temporarily granted a higher measure of autonomy between 1943 and 1947 seems to require further investigation.

9. Quoted in Vladimir Dedijer, *Tito Speaks,* London, 1953, p. 207. See also the earlier radio exchanges between Tito and Moscow on relations with the exile government as reproduced in Dedijer's authorized biography and in M. Pijade, *La Fable de l'aide Sovietique a l'insurrection nationale Yougoslave,* Belgrade, 1950, and the statement in Djilas, op. cit. p. 14, that the Yugoslav leaders kept their preparations for the crucial proclamation secret from Moscow.
10. This was disclosed by Stalin in conversation with Yugoslav and Bulgarian Communist leaders in February 1958: see the accounts in Dedijer, op. cit. p. 331, and Djilas, op. cit. pp. 164–5.
11. Reports to that effect which reached the West at the time are quoted in C. P. Fitzgerald, *Revolution in China,* London, 1952, pp. 103–4, and mentioned as "probably well founded" by M. Beloff, *Soviet Policy in the Far East,* London, 1953, pp. 60–61.
12. This account, first given in Robert C. North, *Moscow and the Chinese Communists,* Stanford, 1953, pp. 165–67, and based both on official Chinese Communist versions and on an interview with the leading ex-Communist Chang Kuo-t'ao, seems now to be generally accepted.
13. No Soviet publication specifically mentioned Mao as party leader before 1938, though he was freely praised as head of the Chinese "Soviets." As late as December 1937, the previous leader, Wang Ming, returned from Moscow to China with special instructions from Stalin. For an account of this whole obscure transition period, see Charles B. McLane, *Soviet Policy and the Chinese Communists, 1931–1946,* New York, 1958.
14. See "The Chinese Revolution and the Chinese CP," December 1939; and "On New Democracy," January 1940; both in Mao Tse-tung, *Selected Works,* Vol. III, London, 1954.
15. See Mao's 1942 essays on the rectification of the party's style, in *Selected Works,* Vol. IV, London, 1956, and particularly Liu Shao-ch'i's 1941 essay "On the Inner-Party Struggle," with its warning that the "administrative methods" proper for police action against enemies should not be used in fighting erroneous views inside the party, in Brandt, Schwartz, and Fairbanks, *A Documentary History of Chinese Communism,* London, 1952, p. 353 ff.
16. Tito's first account of these events – in Dedijer, op. cit. p. 109 ff. – shows him profiting from the official charges of "anti-party-activity" against Gorkic, his factional enemy and predecessor as party leader – charges which have been retained in Yugoslav party publications even after the break with Moscow. A later interview, granted by Tito to *Kommunist, Belgrade,* April 16, 1959, confirms the statement first made by the Bulgarian Communist exile Karaivanov in *International Affairs,* Belgrade, May 16, 1952,

that Tito's decisive struggle for control of the CPY took place, *after* the fall of Gorkic, against one Petko Miletic; Miletic, with the backing of some Bulgarian members of the cadre department of Comintern, is said to have accused Tito of "Trotskyism," but in the end, the GPU arrested not Tito but Miletic, and deported him to Kolyma. The deadly accusation may have been based on the fact that Tito's Russian-born first wife had been arrested in early 1935 for secret participation in a Yugoslav "leftist" opposition group in Moscow; but she had joined that group while Tito was in a Yugoslav prison, and Tito, apparently accepting her arrest and subsequent death without protest, had convinced the GPU that he knew nothing of her guilty activities. (The sources are quoted in an article by the Yugoslav ex-Communist Ante Ciliga, who once belonged to the same opposition group in Moscow, in *Corrispondenza Socialista,* Rome, July 1961.) He must have appeared to them as the most loyal Stalinist in the Yugoslav party.

17. Dedijer, op. cit. pp. 111–12. At the Fifth Congress of the CPY in July 1948, A. Rankovic quoted from the May 1939 issue of *Proleter,* then the party's clandestine organ, a long list of former leading party militants expelled in Tito's prewar purge. The list is reproduced in the Ciliga article mentioned in note 16 above.
18. Tito's description of the organization and tactics of his partisans — in his *Political Report of the Central Committee of the CPY to the Fifth Congress,* Belgrade, 1948 — closely parallels Mao's description of the early years of his partisan army, as rendered in Edgar Snow, *Red Star over China,* London, 1937. From independent testimony on Yugoslav partisan warfare it seems clear that the parallel existed in fact, and was not only "put on" in retrospect. After the defeat of the Greek Communists in their second civil war, Svetozar Vukmanovic criticized their failure to learn from the Chinese partisans as the Yugoslavs had done, in *Ueber die Volksrevolution in Griechenland,* Belgrade, 1950.
19. The Soviet announcement of December 14, 1943, belatedly approving the formation of the Yugoslav "National Committee" and promising the dispatch of a Soviet military mission, explicitly refers to the fact that Tito's move had "already met with understanding in Britain and the U.S." See Dedijer, op. cit. pp. 207–8.
20. See the record of the foundation meeting in *For a Lasting Peace, For a People's Democracy,"* November 10, 1947, and the personal account of the Italian participant Eugenio Reale, *Nascita del Cominform,* Rome, 1958.
21. The parallel accounts of Dedijer, op. cit. Chapter 19, and Djilas, op. cit. pp. 154–68, indicate clearly that these issues were decisive for the break.

22. The report by Liu Shao-ch'i to the Peking conference of WFTU, held in November 1949, which explicitly made the claim, was reprinted in *For a Lasting Peace . . .*, December 30, 1949, and in *Pravda,* January 4, 1950. It was editorially supported in *For a Lasting Peace . . .*, January 27, 1950.
23. See the Peking *People's Daily,* December 15, 1962, on the concept of the "temporary minority," and the angry retort by *Pravda,* January 7, 1963.
24. This is most explicit in the defense of the *rapprochement* with Yugoslavia by *Pravda,* February 10, 1963, against the attack in *People's Daily,* January 27, 1963.
25. For the fullest documentation on Sino-Soviet exchanges between the Twenty-second Congress of the CPSU and the disclosures of the fall of 1963, see William E. Griffith, *The Sino-Soviet Rift,* Cambridge, Mass., 1964; see also A. Dallin (ed.), *Diversity in International Communism: A Documentary Record, 1961–1963,* New York, 1963 (particularly Chapters III, IX, and X).
26. For a careful survey of alignments in Asia, see R. A. Scalopino, "Moscow, Peking, and the Communist Parties of Asia," *Foreign Affairs,* New York, January 1963; for a more recent statement, see Francis Watson, "Communist Rivalries in Asia," *Survey,* London, October 1963; for documentation to the spring of 1962, see Dallin, op. cit. Chapters V and VII. For evidence that the Indonesian and Japanese parties, often described as "neutral" in the dispute, are favoring conciliation in form but siding with Peking in substance, see NCNA, February 10 and 14, 1963, and *Peking Review,* Nos. 23, 29, and 41, 1963, on Indonesia, and *Peking Review,* Nos. 27 and 32, 1963, on Japan.
27. See the shift from the "neutralist" statement of the Vietnamese Politburo, *Pravda,* February 12, 1963, to the "anti-revisionist" communiqué signed during Liu Shao-ch'i's visit to Hanoi in May, *Peking Review,* No. 21, 1963.
28. See, in particular, Castro's speech to the Havana "Congress of American Women," *Revolución,* January 16, 1963. For the independent origin of this strategy, see Ernst Halperin, "Castroism – Challenge to the Latin-American Communists," *Problems of Communism,* September–October 1963.
29. See the detailed study by Andres Suarez, "Castro between Moscow and Peking," *Problems of Communism,* September–October 1963.
30. See Daniel Tretiak, "Sino-Soviet Rivalry in Latin America," *Problems of Communism,* January–February 1963, and the Halperin article cited in note 28 above.
31. For Chinese exploitation of the Afro-Asian solidarity movement, see my chapter on China in Zb. Brzezinski (ed.), *Africa and the*

Communist World, Stanford, 1963, pp. 153–5, 174–8, 194–200. For the Chinese defeat on the test ban issue, see the resolution of the Nicosia meeting of the Executive Committee, *Pravda*, September 14, 1963.

32. See the Italian Communists' comment on the Moscow conference on contemporary capitalism, *Unita*, September 3–4, 1962; the theses presented to the CPI congress, ibid. September 13; the protest against the circular of WFTU secretary Louis Saillant, ibid. September 29; and the speeches made by the Italian representatives at the Leipzig WFTU conference in mid-December 1962.
33. *People's Daily*, February 27, 1963.
34. During the election campaign of spring 1963, the Italian Communists openly criticized the campaign then being conducted by Khrushchev and the leadership of the CPSU against Soviet artists and writers who asserted their claim to decide the subject and form of their creative work for themselves. They thus denied, if only for opportunistic reasons, both the infallibility of the Soviet leadership and the principle that literature and art must be subordinated to the needs of the party.